Should I Be Afraid?

JUDY HANNA

Should I Be Afraid?

A Survival Guide *for* Baby Boomers and Senior Citizens

CHALFANT ECKERT
PUBLISHING

Should I Be Afraid? A Survival Guide for Baby Boomers and Senior Citizens

Copyright © 2014 Judy Hanna. All Rights Reserved.

No rights claimed for public domain material, all rights reserved. No parts of this publication may be reproduced, stored in any retrieval system, or transmitted in any form or by any means, electronic, mechanical, recording, or otherwise, without the prior written permission of the author. Violations may be subject to civil or criminal penalties. If you have a need to reproduce this material, use it in a group educational or other settings, or wish to have the author speak to or assist your organization, please contact author at the address below.

Library of Congress Control Number: 2014952829

ISBN: 978-1-63308-110-9 (paperback journal edition)

Interior Design by R'tor John D. Maghuyop

1028 S Bishop Avenue, Dept. 178
Rolla, MO 65401

seniorsstandingstrong.com
judyhanna.com
eventcentral@valornet.com

Printed in the United States of America

This book is dedicated in loving memory to my Mother, Ruth Marie Alldredge Trice, a published writer and poet, a newspaper proofreader and writer of a newspaper column. Fitting for the dedication of this book, is one of her writings.

Owner's Manual for Senior Citizens

By Ruth M. Trice

Life does not begin at forty,
Bad eyesight does;
Get glasses;
Get over it.

Life does not begin at fifty,
The next half-century does;
Get a hobby;
Get ready for the long haul.

Life does not begin at sixty,
Retirement does;
Get a motor home;
Get away;
Get a new life.

Life doesn't begin at seventy,
Trips to the doctor do;
Be glad there are doctors;
Be glad there are pills;
Get down and praise the Almighty if
You're healthy.

Life doesn't begin at eighty;
Steady trips to the graveyard do;
Bury your friends;
Bury unrealistic ambitions;
Bury your hatreds, stresses, and bad
Habits;
You might make it to a hundred.

Life doesn't begin at ninety,
Nursing homes do;
Be alert, be foxy;
Keep notes so they'll think your memory
Is great;
Laugh when the bunch laughs, even
Though you didn't hear the joke;
Or if you heard it, didn't get it.

Sit with the great-grandchildren at
Family affairs;
They will be interested in hearing about
The good old days;
Your aging offspring won't be,
They will roll their eyes and say, "She's
Telling it again"

Life begins at a hundred,
Great honors will come your way;
Willard Scott will wish you a happy
Birthday on national TV;
Newspapers will print five-generation
Photos of you and your descendants;
Your wall will be full of trophies you've
Won for the "oldest person there"
Make 'em notice you until you die,
You're a treasure and deserve the
Treatment of royalty.

Never wallow in self-pity
Don't whine about unimportant things,
Be kind to your keepers, maybe they
Won't put you away before you're dead.

Bon voyage!

TABLE OF CONTENTS

Preface 13
Acknowledgements 17
Disclaimer 19
About The Author 21

PART I
ARE THEY PICKING US OFF ONE BY ONE?

The Journey 25
Chapter 1: Lost Dignity, Broken Trust 31
Chapter 2: Living Older and Praying For Quality Care 39
Chapter 3: Surge In Senior Population To Create Healthcare Crisis 41
Chapter 4: Bullying Of Seniors: An Embarrassing Societal Culture 47
Chapter 5: 78 Million Baby Boomers Will "All" Be Classified As Elderly In 17 Years 53
Chapter 6: The Tragedy of Abuse 57
Chapter 7: Not Analyzing Your Medications Can Cause Dangerous Consequences To Your Life 61
Chapter 8: Nine Out of Ten People Surveyed Did Not Know The Types of Abuse and Mistreatment Against Senior Citizens 65
Chapter 9: Nursing Homes–The Dreaded Life Sentence 71

PART II
ANGELS OF THE COURTS

Chapter 10: If Violators of Your Rights Won't Listen, Then, Hit Them in The Pocketbook 87

PART III
SECRETS THAT WILL HELP YOU MAKE GOOD CHOICES

Chapter 11: Independent Living: Not Always The Ticket To Freedom 97

Chapter 12: I Have A Right To Be Involved In My Hospital Care. Hospitals Pose Risks To Senior Patients 103

Chapter 13: Dangerous Antipsychotic Drugs DOPING SENIORS TO DEATH 109

PART IV
SECRETS ABOUT MEDICATIONS THAT LEAVE YOU VULNERABLE TO MISTREATMENT

Chapter 14: Diagnosed With Alzheimer's and Dementia When It May Be Medicines or Lack of Vitamin B-12 Causing Memory Problems? 127

PART V
ALL WE WANT IS YOUR MONEY THE ABUSE OF SCAMS

Chapter 15: Leave Us Alone, We Will No Longer Be Your Meal Ticket 135

Chapter 16: Famous Actor Abused 147

PART VI
STATE BY STATE MONITORING OF LIVING ACCOMODATIONS

Chapter 17: How Your State Monitors Assisted Living Facilities 153

PART VII
SUCCESSFUL LAWSUITS ON BEHALF OF SENIOR CITIZENS

Chapter 18: Lawsuits: Your Voice, Your Power 223

Chapter 19: Mistreatment of Senior Citizens is a Criminal Problem 233

Chapter 20: Days and Months Just for You 237

PART XII
LIVING HEALTHY – LIVING LONGER NUTRITION RESOURCES

Chapter 21: Your Aha Moments..243

Review: the deadly secrets revealed 261

A Senior Citizen's Prayer...266

Fastest Growing Population Demographic In America...267

Appendix I: Excerpts From U.S. Government Report – Senior Given Antipsychotic Drugs For "Complaining" (May 2011 Oei-07-08-00150) 273

Resources For Seniors 282

Appendix II: Review of Congressional Reports........................299

Where To Report Abuse In Your State 302

References..312

PREFACE

What does the future hold for you when you are sixty or older? Will you keep working or will you retire? Will you kick up your heels, travel, or just enjoy many wonders of the world not yet explored? What will you do if life throws you a curve ball? When the unexpected happens, have you ever asked yourself, "Should I be afraid?" Fear of the unknown is not unusual, but those who make the journey armed with truths and information can emerge as victors, not victims. Your future is like planning a road trip. You take out a map, activate the GPS, and plot your course. Your objective is to find the shortest, safest, and most efficient route to your destination.

Throughout history, generals have led soldiers through conflict with a strategic battle plan in hand, so if you are walking into a minefield where casualties are high, wouldn't you want a survival guide that sounds an alarm about critical areas you should avoid? The challenges faced by senior citizens and baby boomers have been experienced by so many others. It is smart to plot your course onto the senior care minefield with your eyes wide open and activate your survival plan.

For the one in four of over forty million senior citizens who fall prey to daily abusers, and the 78 million baby boomers entering the rank and file as seniors, information is power. The crimes against seniors are everybody's business, and you can prevent the tragedies by arming yourself with information and remaining proactive and vigilant.

SHOULD I BE AFRAID?: Deadly Secrets Revealed That Could Save Your Life is a survival guide for baby boomers and senior citizens. It exposes real-life accounts of the crimes that happen daily in life, family homes, hospitals, senior facilities, and assisted living residences, many of which are unnoticed, under reported, and under investigated. You will learn about the diverse categories of senior mistreatment, warning signs, little known facts, and available remedies on a state-by-state basis, as well as how to disarm and impede those who walk on your rights and the rights of others. Very few senior information outlets are serving up a raw dish of prevention for seniors and boomers before the crimes occur. *This book dares to expose the well-kept secrets that have been swept under the rug for years.*

Part II, *Angels of the Courts* will introduce a well-known litigation attorney, a pioneer in the fight for senior human rights, who has won more than $140 million dollars on behalf of violated seniors and their families. The monetary awards that he has recovered for victims of crime and negligence send a strong message that poor care and abuse will not be tolerated or go unnoticed.

You will read the late Mickey Rooney's personal story of financial abuse, and the message he stressed that "you need to tell everyone in your path what is happening to you." You will learn how the federal government and organizations are working hard to address the crisis. You will also find out about self-help resources that are available to everyone. You will read the stories of seniors now 90 years and older, who are doing everything from running multimillion dollar businesses to teaching yoga.

The social dynamics of mainstream contemporary culture marginalize millions of senior citizens sixty and older through negative stereotyping, abuse and disrespect. This condemnation manifests through subtle, veiled abuse fueled by the rampant dynamics of societal disrespect that has caused discrimination against seniors to reach epidemic proportions.

Hindsight is 20/20 with a clarity of understanding, and no person wants to believe that any ill will come their way, but obstacles, lack of financial resources, loss of cognitive function, lack of proximity to healthcare facilities and unforeseen circumstances, leave many seniors subject to substandard care. Interestingly, many boomers and seniors have said they don't know what is considered a violation of their rights. They didn't know that a senior falling while in the care of any facility is neglect or abuse, or that bedsores and dehydration are abuse or neglect. Some of those same seniors are walking through the mall with bruise marks on their arms after being hit by a drunken spouse, whose abuse is worse now than it was thirty years ago. You notice the senior who cringes in reaction to being slapped or shoved by an adult child, or when someone raises a hand. Others are on a one-way trip while doped on antipsychotic drugs.

Just to give you a sense of the magnitude of poor treatment of people age 60 and over: Over 80% of senior citizens are the target of some form of daily verbal abuse from society and 90% of senior citizens are targeted for varied types of scams. Advertising of senior products generally paints seniors as vulnerable and weak. Making fun of seniors comes in daily doses while one in five senior citizens living at home with relatives is verbally and physically abused, and sixty six percent of the abuse comes from family members or spouses. Healthcare professionals overmedicate seniors and one in three residential care facilities in the United States is reported for abuse. Fact is—the way seniors are treated by society in general is a national embarrassment.

Today, everyone knows about child abuse, the variables and Child Protective Services (CPS), and people are not shy about reporting anyone who is involved in abusing a child. In a well-informed future, all people will know that the same principles apply to senior abuse but the call to be made is to Adult Protective Services (APS) or 911.

The mission of this book is to provide a safety net through sharing facts and solutions. Mission accomplished will occur when the "would be abusers" are afraid of the consequences, are in prison, and stop what they are doing. Seniors are too special, too precious to suffer in ways that you and I can prevent. My mission is to help you do just that.

Dana Starr: *"Judy Hanna, that's so impressive and such a huge amount of work for such an important subject. I hope people will read it BEFORE they actually need the knowledge."*

Heather Payne: *"So proud of you for speaking out about the abuses. You gave me the strength I needed to stand up for my mother, and understand what was happening to her in a facility recently. This will definitely educate where it is much needed."*

April Gordon: *"They all deserve a voice. Amazing all the bad that goes on that we don't hear about."*

Ben Lipscomb: *"It's amazing to me that people can treat others so badly."*

ACKNOWLEDGEMENTS

This book, *Should I Be Afraid?*, took on a life of its own and I simply followed. Each person who helped along the way led me to another person, and I realized that one story could not be told without the next. I have always believed that "no" person achieves goals, and dreams alone but instead, through the help of kind souls who reach out beyond their busy lives to lend a hand. Profound gratitude and appreciation goes to those who contributed to this book through their expertise, personal experience, support, and understanding.

Attorney Steven M. Levin, co-founder and senior partner of Levin & Perconti, is a nationally known trial lawyer, who provided exceptional views into the depths of the courtroom. I am thankful for his time and effort provided through this process.

My warmth and gratitude goes out to those who shared their stories: Heather Dodson Payne, Dana Starr, DeeAnn Curry, Tao Porchon Lynch, Kathryn Wilson, Dorothy Runnels, Larry Milberger, Donnice Carruth, Thelma Hinson, Shannon Pettigrew, and Pat Martz Huntley.

Sincere appreciation goes to Cindy Bentle, Bob Reid, Bill and John Trice, and Sherman Lynn Trice. Kind thanks to Scott and Allison Mulkey, and to Dr. Kitty Bickford for providing a foundation and support above and beyond the call of duty.

DISCLAIMER

While the information contained in this book was prepared with best efforts and in good faith, the publisher and author make no representations or warranties with respect to the accuracy or completeness of the contents herein.

This work (in any electronic or digital form or in any other printed material form) is not intended for use as a source of legal, medical, or financial advice. If advice concerning legal, medical, financial, or any other professional advice is needed, the services of a qualified, properly licensed and competent professional should be sought.

The contents of this work reflect the views and opinions of the author. The author and publisher have made their best effort to produce a high quality, informative and helpful course on matters that affect baby boomers and senior citizens but they make no representation or warranties of any kind with regard to the completeness and accuracy of the contents of the material. Any slights of people and/or organizations are unintentional.

Neither the author nor the publisher accept any liability of any kind for any losses or damages caused or alleged to be caused, directly or indirectly, from using the information contained in this book. Every individual must make his or her own decisions. Although this book describes the experiences of senior citizens, outcomes, remedies, it in no way guarantees similar outcomes for others. Every effort has been made to ensure that this publication is free from errors and/or problems.

ABOUT THE AUTHOR

TWENTY-YEAR MEDIA CAREER AND HONORS

Judy Hanna's career as a television newswoman and daily newspaper publisher spans over twenty years. She has more than 4,000 published articles and television news clips to her credit. She has a strong, successful background in managing a multi million-dollar media business, human resource management, marketing, public relations, and multi-state promotion creation for maximum returns to consumers and clients. Hanna has received prestigious awards such as the Jacqueline Kennedy Onassis Jefferson Awards, Gubernatorial Awards for Outstanding State Woman in New Mexico, Secretary of State Award of Nobility, Martin Luther King, Jr. Public Service Awards, Congressional Award of Merit, Rotary International Paul Harris Award, Who's Who in American Women, and more than one hundred awards from non-profit organizations. She served on the Board of Directors of the New Mexico Press Association, Served as a Rotary Member, was on the National Enrichment Facility Regional committee for The Urenco Group, a nuclear fuel company operating several uranium enrichment plants in Germany, the Netherlands, United States, and United Kingdom.

HISTORY OF INVOLVEMENT WITH SENIOR CITIZENS

For many years, senior citizens and families have sought her guidance and expertise to shine a light on, and expose the widespread crimes committed against senior citizens at home, in hospitals, independent living facilities, assisted living homes, and in nursing homes. She has helped many people save their loved ones from the dangerous situations that threatened to harm them. As the reports across the nation have intensified regarding transgressions against seniors, Hanna's passion to help senior citizens led to the intensive research and development of *SHOULD I BE AFRAID?*

Hanna believes the moral test of a society is how those in the dawn of their lives (the children), and how those in the twilight of their lives (the senior citizens) are treated. Hanna has created many events and educational publications for seniors to bring positive activities to their lives. Hanna holds a Bachelor's Degree in Business Administration and a Master's Degree of Science in Education Administration, but above all, she holds a burning fire in her heart to help you understand that *you hold the power* to put a stop to this shameful epidemic in America – the disrespect toward senior citizens. She believes your freedom will be defined by positive activism to create societal change, regain respect from mainstream culture, and stand strong for your constitutional human rights.

PART I

ARE THEY PICKING US OFF ONE BY ONE?

THE JOURNEY

In a land, not so far away, etched within the fabric of what is known as cultural history, it was widely known and believed that there was great wisdom to be shared by elders…and all should respect and honor them. It was a time when the best part of life was the laughter and warmth of Gramma's Kingdom. She knew about everything…

Grandpas throughout the land had twinkles in their eyes… *always*…and the stories shared about life would live on forever within the minds of all people touched by Grandpas everywhere.

Grandpas would say, "Always take the high road; don't spend your life fighting windmills; save your energy for the big battles that may cross your path; and *always* remember that you *must* be a good and kind person." Children were raised from a young age to treat older people with genuine kindness, and *always* be respectful.

There was a time when no older person worried about going to a hospital or facility for care, because older folks had deep trust in those who cared for them, and they just knew they were in good hands.

But in the blink of an eye, something went terribly wrong… something that would change lives…forever…a Paradigm Shift.

It was a very sad day throughout the land.

People forgot to teach their children to honor and respect adults.

Someone stole money from older folks…and got away with it.

Someone locked their aging parents in a basement…and got away with it.

Someone shoved a senior citizen down…and got away with it.

Someone made fun of an older person and everyone laughed.

Few people in the land told anyone that someone was taking their money.

Few people told anyone that someone was hitting them over and over again.

Few people told anyone that someone was making fun of them.

Few people told anyone that someone caused them to be sick on purpose.

And few people told anyone they were locked in their room every day.

A wise old man wondered why his friends wouldn't tell anyone the secrets that were making them so sad.

The woman sitting next to him in church hid her bruises and cuts under a long skirt, and when the old man asked why she had a bruise on her lip, she told him, " I don't want to get anyone in trouble."

Across the land, things just got worse and there seemed to be no respect left.

Jokes began to surface for the world to see…most of those jokes are very hurtful, but alas, those in the land who make fun of older people seemed to get the same pleasure from it as the little mean kid who bullies other kids on the playground.

The people in the land wiped away their tears as they heard about the attitudes of so many that no longer cared.

One bully yelled, "CHEER UP, OLD AGE DOESN'T LAST THAT LONG…"

A little kid poked an older woman at a funeral and told her, "You're next!"…all because the little kid hated it when older people poked him at weddings and told him he was next.

This type of disrespect happens every day…somewhere in every town.

As time went on, the bad people in the land discovered that others didn't believe it when an older person said, "Someone tried to hurt me."

It was easy to tell others the older person had memory problems, and probably just got things mixed up. No one would question that, and few did.

It was easy to say an older person was sleepy. It made a perfect job of dangerously drugging a senior, and no one would notice…everyone would think all senior citizens are just sleepy.

No one wondered why the older people were sleepy. No one wondered why older people were having memory problems. No one looked at the medications they were taking. No one suspected there might be a vitamin deficiency causing problems. No one questioned the bruises and cuts, because someone said, "he just fell," and everyone believed it. When he died, no one asked questions.

No one could have predicted in this land that older people would be outcasts, and it would be okay to disrespect and mistreat them.

Word traveled from town to town that for the first time ever, seniors were not safe.

The ageing process for millions of people in the land were filled with fearful nightmares of horror, not knowing whom to trust. They knew they were not safe...they heard tales about friends who fell prey to thousands of villains who roamed the earth being mean to seniors. They prayed they would be the lucky ones and avoid the dangers, but with one in four seniors already being mistreated, the odds were not looking good for the people.

No longer could life be that magical fantasy tale of what it used to be. The truths outweighed the myths and these facts became reality in a shattered kingdom. These are the whispered facts we heard:

- Six million undetected and unpunished homicides annually of people 60 and older
- The government calls it an epidemic
- The treatment of senior citizens has become a national tragedy...an embarrassment
- Medical Examiners rarely perform autopsies on people over sixty. Deaths are simply written off as old age, heart attacks, or whatever is convenient.

No one questions when an old person dies...they say, "She lived a good, long life"...*BUT, WHAT IF SHE COULD HAVE LIVED FIVE MORE YEARS IF SOMEONE HADN'T CUT HER LIFE SHORT?* No one is asking that question in the land.

Many adult children in the land took away their parent's car keys after, let's say, a minor fender bender. Older folks didn't understand why they lost their keys when most of the wrecks in the land were caused by 16 – 19 year olds, and no one took away their keys. It seemed to the seniors that the only thing accomplished was taking away a little bit more of their independence, confidence, and security. They wondered, "Who gave our kids the right to suddenly think they are in charge of our lives?" A woman softly said, "They do this because we allow it."

Finally, one sunny day, some older folks began to talk and share their stories with each other. They cried, and cried, and hugged.

"What we need to do," one woman said, "is take our lives back. We have the power to be in control of our own destiny. We need to learn who is hurting us, how they do it, where it happens, and then, outsmart those who try to take our lives away."

The gathering and talks grew as the older people began to compile a check-list of dangers.

Hattie, a petite 84 year old took charge.

"Ok," she said, "we now know that more than 75% of the crimes against us happen in our own homes. We're afraid to say anything because we know there are worse places we could land, and frankly, we are comfortable despite the horrid treatment some of us get from our family members. We must, however understand that it is important to say something and regain our dignity."

She revealed the secrets. The group listened with great interest. Hattie said, "You need to know these secrets – they will help you avoid the dangers."

"If something happens and you *have* to go to the hospital, you NEED to know that some hospitals drug senior citizens with antipsychotic drugs. These drugs are used often as a chemical restraint to control you when they are short handed. These drugs can be especially dangerous for older folks, and some can even cause strokes. They destroy your spirit, and the side effects of hallucinations and changed behavior can be devastating and make you less able to communicate. Your friends need to know to look for these changes, and you need to demand that they do not give you these drugs."

Hattie continued, "The second secret is that you are overmedicated. Go look in your drug cabinet. Get on the computer and start checking to see how your drugs interact with each other. Go look at the side effects of every medication and make a chart. I promise that you will be shocked to see how much of what you are given can cause you to fall, cause memory loss, and dangerous interactions that absolutely do affect your health. Once you have done your research, get ahold of your doctor and tell him you want to try something different. If your doctor chews you out for telling him how to do his job …. FIRE HIM! Always remember, it is your right to choose, and it is your right to have a doctor who listens, cares, and allows you to be involved. You hired him, and you are paying him to do a job for you. You are in charge."

"You must tell someone if your adult children or spouse mistreats you. You need to know that your risk of premature death is increased by 300% if someone is abusing you mentally, physically, financially, or sexually."

"Did you know," Hattie said, "That you are being abused if you are being belittled, humiliated, yelled at, hit, or pushed? That it is abuse if someone is on your bank account and taking your money, if you are threatened, if your needs come last or are ignored, or if you are treated like a child in your own home?"

"You must put a stop to it. You are in charge, and your life depends on it. Get a roommate, move out, or lay down the law and refuse to be treated that way. Turn the abusers in to Adult Protective Services or report them to the law."

"Now, you all know," Hattie said "that we get depressed sometimes. We can't let that take a toll on us. Again, check your medications and if depression is one of the side effects, you may need a change. I found that vitamins, healthy shakes, and peppermints melted in hot tea help my attitude. Depression affects our health, and if we need to start juicing, let's do it. I have always believed that nutrition and exercise are the keys to staying out of the doctor's office, getting off meds, and living longer."

In some ways, that very day, that group started a movement toward changing the way they viewed taking charge of their own destinies.

People in the land began to hear stories of how senior citizens were educating themselves about the dangers they face, and instead of hoping someone else noticed the signs, they started their own revolt to save themselves! "Why wait until it is too late and wade into those tragic waters without being armed first!" they exclaimed.

Even sad tales can have happy endings because honorable people in the land, like you, can cause positive change for all people.

It all started with AGEISM, the illegal discrimination and stereotyping of people because of their ages. Seniors were asked to retire from jobs they loved; people made fun of seniors for hearing loss, memory loss, slow movement, and spread the myth of thinking that all seniors are sick and frail. Those acts fueled the universal acceptance of mistreatment of seniors.

The pain can all end with ACTIVISM, the act of changing societal attitudes and causing positive movement toward equal rights for senior citizens in all areas of life, health, activities, care, and outcomes. Will you stand up for your civil rights, turn over a new leaf, and say no to being treated like a second-class citizen?

Moral of this tale: Be involved in your destiny and care, let no one in the land disrespect you, and you will find greater peace and safety in your journey.

CHAPTER 1

LOST DIGNITY, BROKEN TRUST

NURSE GETS CHARLIE'S POISONED COFFEE IN HER FACE

The smell of fresh brewed coffee, a cup of hot tea, and the unmistakable scent of toast fill your home to signal the beginning of a new day. You step outside and snuggle into a comfortable patio chair to listen to the birds sing. You marvel at the blessings of God's flawless artwork in the sky and in the flowers. You can't imagine a more perfect existence.

But what if, in one split second, something happened – a stroke, a heart attack, a misstep that leaves you helpless, or with a broken hip or shattered bone? What if you suddenly lose a spouse and have to relocate? What if you move to a senior apartment complex that looks so perfect, and find out after a few weeks that predators are on the grounds threatening your safety and no one will do anything about it? What if your sanctuary of peace is replaced with the stark white walls of a hospital or care facility where your morning coffee is laced with poisonous drugs? What if the nurse or aide you hire to watch over you in your home has an agenda that is not in your best interest, and nobody believes you because, "the person hired seems so sweet and thoughtful."

You don't understand why you're suddenly sleepy, listless, and confused all day. Such things happen more often than you might imagine. It happens without your consent, without medical diagnosis, and without your knowledge.

It happened to Beth's grandfather, Charlie, in a hospital. That is, it happened to him until he figured out why he felt exhausted and sleepy after his morning coffee every day. He had enjoyed his morning coffee all of his adult life and knew it gave him his caffeine kick for the day. Something was wrong with how this coffee made him feel. Then, to his credit, he figured it out.

One day, in anger and frustration, he threw the coffee cup at the nurse and declared, "From now on I'll make my own damn coffee."

He recognized that what was happening to him was not normal, and he courageously stood up to those who were engaging in covertly drugging him. Those responsible for drugging this man, and millions of other senior citizens, are engaging in criminal behavior.

DATE RAPE DRUGS

Have you ever heard of so-called *date rape drugs*? You probably have since the subject has received a great deal of news coverage. These are drugs that are dropped into the drink of an unsuspecting person. That person then becomes unconscious and unable to defend herself. Later there is no memory of what happened during that period the drug was doing its deadly work.

Would you agree that this is a crime?

The truth is, there's no difference between the criminal act of spiking a drink of a young person, and spiking a drink of a senior citizen. The end result is the same: the purpose is to take advantage of, or render that person helpless.

THE STARK CONTRAST

There is a stark contrast, however. The investigation that follows the spiking of a senior's coffee with drugs is less likely to be pursued with the same degree of urgency that happens after the drugging of a teen's drink.

Why is this so? Because it has become a common practice in this country to disregard seniors' complaints. Instead, the blame is placed on a failing memory. Plus the fact is assumed that seniors will not be believed because they're perceived as "old." This then allows the criminals to continue their purposeful violation of seniors without much worry about being found out – or being prosecuted.

LOW EXPOSURE

In the past year, over 33,000 news articles have been aired or printed across America that told the sad stories of mistreatment and premature death of senior citizens age 60 and older.

On the surface, that may seem like a lot of news coverage. The truth is this is a small number of cases when you consider that *The National Center on Senior Abuse, Bureau of Justice* documents over *six million cases* per year. (You read that right – six million!)

The failure to preserve grandma's or grandpa's dignity, or the act of poisoning grandpa's coffee isn't very exciting news compared to shootings and tsunamis. With low exposure to the magnitude and daily frequency of crimes against seniors, the knowledge of this widespread condition is limited. For the most part, it's obscured from general public view.

Most people have no clue how often older citizens are being viciously hit in the face by caregivers, bitten by family members, struck by blunt objects, kicked, and yelled at by people they trust. You may actually see or read only five or six of these stories annually due to airing on local stations or in local newspapers to which you have no access. Unless the local stations or newspapers submit a particular news item to a nationwide news service, the articles are generally viewed only by a geographic area.

IT'S A CRIME

Care providers who have *always* used antipsychotic drugs to control seniors, and with no repercussions, may be shocked to learn that they could be sent to prison for these acts. Doping anyone with chemical restraints is a crime, no matter who is being drugged. A relatively healthy person of any age can be rendered helpless at the hands of these criminals. It is often the *purposeful* act of caregivers that cause the senior to become a vulnerable victim.

A director of nursing, hospital administrator, pharmacist, and staff physician at a nursing home in California got caught. This sordid team came face to face with prison sentences. Among the charges was a*ssault with a deadly weapon against senior patients*. That deadly weapon was the drug Risperdal. (More about these drugs later in the book.)

The Department of California Public Health sent an investigative team with a doctor, a nurse, and a doctor of pharmacology. They determined that twenty-two patients – including some who were suffering from Alzheimer's – were being given high doses of psychotropic medications. This medication was not for therapeutic purposes, but to simply control and quiet the residents for the convenience of the staff.

Several of these patients were alleged to have had medical complications as a result of being given these psychotropic medications. Complication included lethargy and the inability to eat or drink properly. It's believed that three patients died, and one patient suffered great bodily injury as a result.

The investigation was set in motion due to the action of an ombudsman who reported to the California Department of Public Health about a patient being held down and given an injection of psychotropic medication by force. It could safely be said that the recognition of, and action against, this type of criminal activity resulted in saving countless lives of seniors.

EMPOWERING PATIENTS, FAMILIES, AND OMBUDSMEN

The challenge then is to inform and empower patients, families, friends, and ombudsmen nationwide. They must be aware that it is their right and duty to recognize and report all hospitals, doctors, nurses, aides, individuals, and long-term assisted care facilities that engage in these violations of Civil Rights. The crimes are far reaching and include some things many may not be aware of, like allowing a patient to develop a bedsore or become dehydrated. It is neglect of patients when they fall in your care. Patients who are forced to sleep on urine soaked or soiled sheets, caregivers leaving uneaten trays of food for patients who can't feed themselves, and physical, mental, financial and sexual abuses are all against the law. These acts should be reported to the state's attorney general and Adult Protective Services Departments, or call 911. A crime has been committed.

SOMETIMES IT'S FAMILY

Can you imagine the terror a 70-year-old Kentucky woman must have felt while living with her daughter who isolated her from even the simple pleasures of life? She was pushed, kicked, and called names. Adult Protective Services investigated and found the 70-year-old locked in a basement. The daughter fed her food straight from a can, and made her watch while others ate.

APS helped the woman get an Emergency Protective Order (EPO) against this daughter, and helped her find an apartment in a retirement tower. APS opened an ongoing case to help her stabilize, and a local domestic violence shelter supplied her with a cellular phone for emergency use in case of a *violation of the EPO* (*Case Histories of Senior Abuse and Neglect*, www.chfs.ky.gov).

In Georgia, a woman and her boyfriend were sentenced in court for cruelty and exploitation of an older woman – the woman's own mother. Reports state that the mother had been deprived of food and water, and her medications had been withheld. Evidence showed that an air conditioning unit had been removed and windows were boarded up in the room where the woman spent most of her time. The report also indicated that the woman had been dragged around the house by one of the suspects. Additionally, there was evidence that her Social Security checks had been stolen.

The abused woman died, and the offenders will spend time in prison. In the majority of cases, however, it is not uncommon for charges to be dropped, reduced or removed from court dockets. First-degree senior abuse is a felony and many states have added additional years if the crime is perpetrated against a senior. (News media, 2/20/2014, WSAV TV, WTOC TV, NASGA)

GRANNY CAMS AND HIDDEN CAMERAS

What's causing a good portion of justice to be served? It is family members and friends who are on high alert and are placing cameras in their family homes, and in medical facilities. Those who are aware that one in three long-term care facilities in the U.S. have been written up for their horrible mistreatment and abuse of seniors are waking up and taking action.

After listening to the lies of care facilities staff, and witnessing lack of action regarding questions pertaining wrongdoing about patients, more and more family members are taking action. Some have disguised video cams so they can have a fly-on-the-wall view of how their loved ones are being treated. Those videos are capturing some chilling evidence that is being presented in court, and result in awarding guilty caregivers a ticket to prison. Some families say, "We are renting a high dollar room, paying people to take care of our loved ones, so watching over our senior family members in this manner is no different than renting a house, hiring a babysitter, and having a hidden camera in place to ensure that our kids are being treated right."

DOESN'T ANYBODY CARE?

Senior citizens say they don't understand why concerns for their safety and human rights are unimportant. In America when a child is drugged, abused or killed, families and authorities rally all resources to apprehend a perpetrator to hold accountable for the crime. News media focuses on the heart-wrenching details, and the general public is outraged.

Even animal cruelty gains higher societal concern than the despicable acts against senior citizens. Commercials flood television outlets with pictures of abused animals and homeless animals in shelters. The goal is to seek funding to fight against shelters that euthanize. Animal Rights groups are to be commended for their relentless efforts and effective campaigns that reach and inform all people. There is a profound absence of coordinated media campaigns that could empower everyone to take action to stop the criminal and social issues that spiral around seniors.

An older person dies every sixty seconds from chemical drug poisoning, beating, neglect, abuse, abandonment, and bullying, yet, there is little or no attention focused on the crimes, deaths or abuse unless there is a high profile lawsuit, an arrest, and media attention, or unless the complaints are reported to state and federal agencies.

There are plenty of seniors who are not frail and weak, but are simply people who trust easily and get hurt in the process. Isn't it time to wake up and smell the coffee? Otherwise, will it just be another day, different people, different place, but the same outcomes over and over for years to come?

The senior population has great power, the highest numbers of any demographic population. Seniors have the power to influence elections, put a stop to the ageism that plagues the nation, and to incarcerate every person that violates their rights.

Some have said, "I will be able to afford to go to a place where bad things don't happen to senior citizens, a senior country club of sorts." When it comes to *you* landing in any hospital, living village, or care facility, do you know what to expect? As with any business or organization, it is likely that one bad apple will eventually slip through the door, or even the unsavory senior neighbor that moves in could be a predator. If you look at the National Sex Offender Registry at www.watchdog.us you can click on a square in your area. You will see exactly what those individuals look like and where those offenders live or work near you. Wouldn't it be nice to have a Senior Citizen Abuser Registry with photos of your violators so you could choose not to live anywhere near them, but have the peace of mind of recognizing them should they surface in your area?

As long as the public turns a blind eye, it's true, every baby boomer and senior citizen will continue to be an *easy target*, but it doesn't have to be that way.

CHAPTER 2

LIVING OLDER AND PRAYING FOR QUALITY CARE

Regardless of age, you might say that *intrinsic* "old age" or being of "senior status" is a state of mind and body, based on activity level, lifestyle and the biological changes that occur as you age.

Today, worldwide, more than 340,000 senior citizens are 100 hundred years old – or older, and that number is expected to grow to 400,000 centenarians by 2050.

At age 100, Texas resident Thelma Hinson joins the elite group centenarians. With a keen memory and quick wit, she is active and mobile with a very dry sense of humor. Thelma enjoys quilting, working crossword puzzles, and reading, which she says, "Keeps my brain sharp." She is the only surviving member of her immediate family. She has outlived her parents, brother, sisters, husband, and three children. She has lost three grandchildren and one great-grandchild. Her strength and determination remain unmeasured. When asked if she was ready to die, she said, "I'm ready, but I don't want to go yet. I imagine I need to check on my husband and the kids though. They are probably causing mischief in Heaven." A cartoon she cut from a newspaper hung on her refrigerator for years showing an older person saying, "I'm getting so old my friends in Heaven will think I didn't make it."

With so many Americans living longer, traveling, engaging in senior citizen community activities, dancing, singing, and interacting in athletic events, you can understand other people commenting on a senior who gets ill saying, "Well, he's old and has lived a good life," rather than, "He just needs a shot of B-complex, and he'll be fine." (More on health and nutrition later in the book.) You see, for too long people have been of the mindset that all "old people" just die of old age. In reality, the statistical data supports a different story of how millions are sent to an early grave at the hands of fellow Americans. For those who end up in ill-equipped hospitals and medical facilities or nursing homes, the stories unfold for each individual based on the quality of care and compassion. The stories of millions of seniors will never be told as they take their fears and terrors to their graves where they finally find peace.

CHAPTER 3

SURGE IN SENIOR POPULATION TO CREATE HEALTHCARE CRISIS

Healthcare availability and insurance will be a defining factor in the overall mortality and morbidity for quality of life of senior citizens. With the predicted doubling of senior population growth, financial analysts project that healthcare spending in the U.S. will quickly exceed the $4 trillion mark in coming years.

- Healthcare spending in the United States in recent years includes $2.7 trillion spent on health care services and products, 61 percent of which purchased hospital care, physician and clinical services, and retail prescription drugs.
- Private health insurance paid for 33 percent, out-of-pocket sources for 11 percent, and other third party payers and programs for 7 percent.
- In 2011, the two largest government health care programs, Medicare and Medicaid, purchased $961.9 billion worth of health care goods and services. These purchases accounted for 36 percent of total health care spending.
- Finally, the Department of Defense and the Department of Veterans Affairs accounted for a combined 3.6 percent. (Hartman et al. 2013).

Health care spending in the United States jumped to $3.8 trillion in 2014 and is characterized as being the most costly per person as compared to all other countries. Despite this spending, the quality of health care overall is low by some measures.

The Health and Human Services Department expects that the health share of GDP will continue its historical upward trend, reaching 19.5% of GDP by 2017.

Of each dollar spent on health care in the United States, 31% goes to hospital care, 21% goes to physician/clinical services, 10% to pharmaceuticals, 4% to dental, 6% to nursing homes, 3% to home health care, 3% for other retail products, 3% for government public health activities, 7% to administrative costs, 7% to investment, and 6% to other professional services (physical therapists, optometrists, etc.).

The Commonwealth Fund, a private foundation, ranked the United States last in the quality of health care among similar countries, although costs in the U.S. were the highest.

Senior citizens face many challenges with skyrocketing healthcare costs, the drain on Medicare and Medicaid funds which are expected to be paid out in years to come, coupled with the prediction that 1 in 5 Americans will be elderly between 2030 and 2050. Lack of insurance or government funding is already getting senior citizens kicked out of skilled nursing facilities. As individuals reach their limits on long-term care coverage, facilities are telling residents to "pay up or get out."

Seniors are struggling with the day-to-day rigors of juggling finances to meet the high cost of medical care. For many, it signals financial ruin and the uncertainty of where they will end up in the failed system of care for seniors.

Lorraine Martz, 84, faces the struggles of financial strain and uncertainty. Pat Martz Huntley says her dad and stepmom have been fortunate to have enough to pay for necessary care, so far. But Lorraine's husband says the insurance doesn't cover what it should anymore, and with the additional medicine bills of late, the couple is facing possible bankruptcy. Pat says, "My dad was a senior vice president for a major insurance company…had much more coverage than the average couple. He can't understand what happened."

You can avoid financial surprises by knowing who will and who will not pay for your long-term care, so you don't land in a substandard facility.

MEDICARE

Seniors have said they thought Medicare would take care of their needs in the case of paying for long-term care. It is important to understand the different types of insurance that are available to older people. Many people believe that Medicare will cover long-term care needs. It will not.

Medicare is a federal health insurance program that helps defray many of the medical expenses of most Americans over the age of 65. Medicare has two parts:

(Part A) Hospital Insurance helps pay the cost of inpatient hospital care. The number of days in the hospital paid for by Medicare is governed by a system based upon patient diagnosis and medical necessity for hospital care. Once it is no longer medically necessary for the person to remain in the hospital, the physician will begin the discharge process. If the person or the family disagrees with this decision, they may appeal to the state's Peer Review Organization.

Medicare does not pay for custodial care or nursing home care. It will, however, cover up to 60 days in a nursing home as part of convalescence after hospitalization.

(Part B) Medical Insurance pays for many necessary doctors' services, outpatient services, and some other medical services. Enrollees pay a monthly premium.

MEDICAID

Medicaid is a joint federal-state health care program for people with low income. The program is administered by each state and the type of services covered differs. There are strict income requirements, so it is necessary for the person to "spend down" all income and assets to poverty levels before becoming eligible. Medicaid is the major payer of nursing home care.

However, the Medicaid requirement to "spend down" all income and assets created hardship for the spouse of a person needing care. Changes in the Medicaid rules now allow the spouse to keep a monthly income and some assets, including the primary residence. The amounts allowed change, so you must check for current levels.

MEDIGAP INSURANCE

Why buy other insurance? The purchase of additional insurance gives the policyholder access to a greater choice of facilities without having to tap into other financial resources. Medigap is the name given to privately-purchased supplemental health insurance. It is designed to help cover some of the gaps in Medicare coverage but does not cover long-term care. Before buying Medigap policies, individuals or their family members should review them carefully to be sure they provide the necessary protection and aren't duplicating other health insurance.

Long-Term Care insurance is a private insurance that is usually either an indemnity policy or part of an individual life insurance policy. An indemnity policy pays a set amount per day for nursing home or home health care. Under the life insurance policy, a certain percentage of the death benefit is paid for each month the policyholder requires long-term care. Policies are priced differently depending on the age of the policyholder, the deductible periods chosen, and indemnity value or duration of benefits.

FRAUDULANT BILLING OF YOUR ACCOUNT MAY BE YOUR FIRST PERSONAL INTRODUCTION TO ABUSE AND FRAUD COMMITTED AGAINST YOU

As the cost to taxpayers for government programs increases annually, so does abuse of the system for the wrong reasons. Billions of dollars are charged to senior citizen's accounts for services never rendered. Senior citizens can help to stop the flow of funds to unscrupulous providers by reviewing their bills or "explanation of benefits" to make sure they're not being billed for medications, services and procedures that never occurred during treatment. By reporting falsely stated services to Medicare, not only will providers and individuals be punished for committing the fraud, the reports will help the funds flow to people who rightfully need and receive the services. Healthcare fraud and abuse is a criminal activity that affects everyone, and is on the rise. In a pro forma House session, U.S. Representative John Carney introduced legislation to fight Medicare fraud, a problem that is conservatively estimated to cost taxpayers $50 billion annually or 10 percent of the total cost of Medicare.

Who is committing fraudulent Medicare billing practices at your expense and the expense of American Taxpayers?

Reports indicate unethical doctors, nurses, hospital personnel, and other professional care providers are primarily the ones who carry out this type of fraud.

Examples of healthcare fraud and abuse regarding your bills include:

- Not providing healthcare, but charging for it
- Overcharging or double-billing for medical care or services
- Getting kickbacks for referrals to other providers or for prescribing certain drugs
- Overmedicating and under medicating
- Recommending fraudulent remedies for illnesses or other medical conditions

WHAT CAN YOU DO TO STOP THIS ABUSE?

The minute you notice that care providers have placed fraudulent charges on your bill, REPORT ABUSES OF FRAUD AGAINST YOU TO:

1-800-MEDICARE

CHAPTER 4

BULLYING OF SENIORS: AN EMBARRASSING SOCIETAL CULTURE

A *notable outward* change in society today, *is* the attitude and perception of younger society toward the older population. The abuse of the older population in general, often begins with disrespect. This disrespect comes from children, teenagers, young adults, adults or individuals who lack the capacity of compassion, understanding, and human value. Young children aren't born as bullies. They mirror what they observe and hear regarding older folks. They interact with social media sites and advertisements that devalue old age. Below is just one of thousands of disrespectful photo quotes that surfaces often on social media public venues.

Youth role models, parents, peers, family members or friends may have been the instigators of disrespecting or bullying an older person. Call it a revolving door. In the workplace, some have said it's a sense of insecurity, stress and re-directed hostility that causes some bullies to pick on older workers either seeing them as a threat due to their work ethic or seeing them as too old to fight back verbally or physically. Call it a desperate need for power. Bullying can give a person a feeling of inflated importance in the eyes of their peers. Unfortunately, group mentality,

> **I promise to take care of you when you're old, but if you hit me with your cane, I'll wash your dentures in toilet water**

morals, values and behavior tend to fishtail into each other when it comes to bullying. Senior citizens say they fear reporting bullying in the workplace, "I have to work; I can't afford to lose my job, and I won't report it and risk the complaint reflecting on me as the problematic employee."

It's not just the younger generation to blame for bullying older folks. There have been reports of senior citizens bullying each other. Make no mistake, there are some seniors who are bitter, angry and disrespectful who perhaps have inflamed negative perception in certain circumstances, but regardless of what prompts a bullying situation, it is unacceptable and can be grounds for litigation, or incarceration.

Senior citizens explain that they commonly experience the impatience and rudeness of the younger generation in retail outlets, restaurants, grocery stores, and on the road. A teenager loudly whispered in a grocery store "I wish that old lady would hurry up and, get out of my way." Another yelled vulgarities at a senior citizen at the gas pump as he fumbled with his credit card and the prompts at the pump. In restaurants, servers have been overheard making fun of seniors who demand that their food as ordered and hot. Some servers have been overheard laughing about spitting in the food before it was delivered.

> **Old people always poke me at weddings and say, "you're next," so…I started poking them at funerals and saying, "you're next."**

Have you known someone who was asked to take a retirement package? Did the company see the person as someone who needed to be replaced with a younger worker? Did the employer think money could be saved by getting rid of someone who had risen to high pay over many years of service? It happens all too often that older workers find themselves pushed out of a job and into retirement. It's just another example of societal disrespect to discard older workers, and in some cases, it is outright age discrimination or Ageism at work.

Have you noticed that older people are often told that based on their age, surgery is risky? Even if you are healthy for your age, this happens. Do you think you would be placed at the top of a transplant list if you needed a new liver or kidney? The answer to that is, probably not. Most of these decisions are made by people in a society that may not value saving a person based on their age. What if the surgeries could actually add ten or fifteen years to your life? Your course of action could be to seek a second or third opinion in varied demographic areas. Your outcomes could dramatically change if your objective is to have the same treatment that is afforded to a thirty something. You do not have to settle for a life sentence where your health is concerned, if you are willing to take a risk and experience a second chance regardless of the outcome.

AN UNMONITORED BULLING PLAYGROUND WHERE YOU ARE DEVALUED

- Among those who devalue senior citizens are workers who are BULLYING and "taking care of senior citizens"

The fear factor for seniors about the younger generation is two-fold. First, if America's younger generation perceives "all old people" as a burden, a group to be discarded, scoffed at, and degraded, how are they going to treat this group in their jobs? The younger generation is a majority of the working class, those who are nurses, doctors, retirement village administrators and caretakers.

Second, if America's leaders, role models and families do not educate the younger generation and society in general that it is wrong to marginalize, devalue, and stereotype old age, seniors–the toll on senior citizens will continue to rise and they will continue to be poisoned and picked off one by one.

- The way your doctor treats you speaks volumes about whether or not you are devalued by your doctor

The doctor who immediately begins to talk to a Senior Citizen in his "yelling" voice is *assuming* that all seniors have hearing problems. Not only is this practice stereotyping, this practice is annoying to seniors who can hear a whisper or "inside voice" just fine. Another irritation point, seniors say, is the doctor who turns to the adult children in their presence to discuss their care. The senior wants to shake the doctor, and say, "I'm here, I'm your patient, talk to me!" This practice is demeaning, and devalues the self-worth of the older patient. A doctor recently said to a patient's daughter in the presence of the senior patient, "She has arthritis, she's just old and there's nothing I can do for her." The same doctor told another patient's daughter, "I wouldn't advise you to transfuse her again. She is going to die of something anyway like a catheter infection or pneumonia."

Patient families say they think their senior relatives are also devalued through insensitivity.

Through the sadness and tears of losing her dad, Dee Ann explains how a medical practice devalued her dad's last days. "My dad passed away last month. He was in the hospital 4 days after a light stroke at 89, and in a rehab place for a month. In rehab he wore a purple bracelet with DNR in bold black letters. This is an example of insensitivity. He was in his right mind, and I thought it was sad he had to look at his wrist and be reminded of his end of life choice. There should have been a more discrete way to code this. The location where he stayed was over crowded and understaffed. My brother and other family members were there daily. I don't know what would have happened had we not been very active on his daily care. He still fell 3 times. The alarm system was a joke.

There were some very kind helpful employees but the whole situation was the saddest part of my Hero's final days."

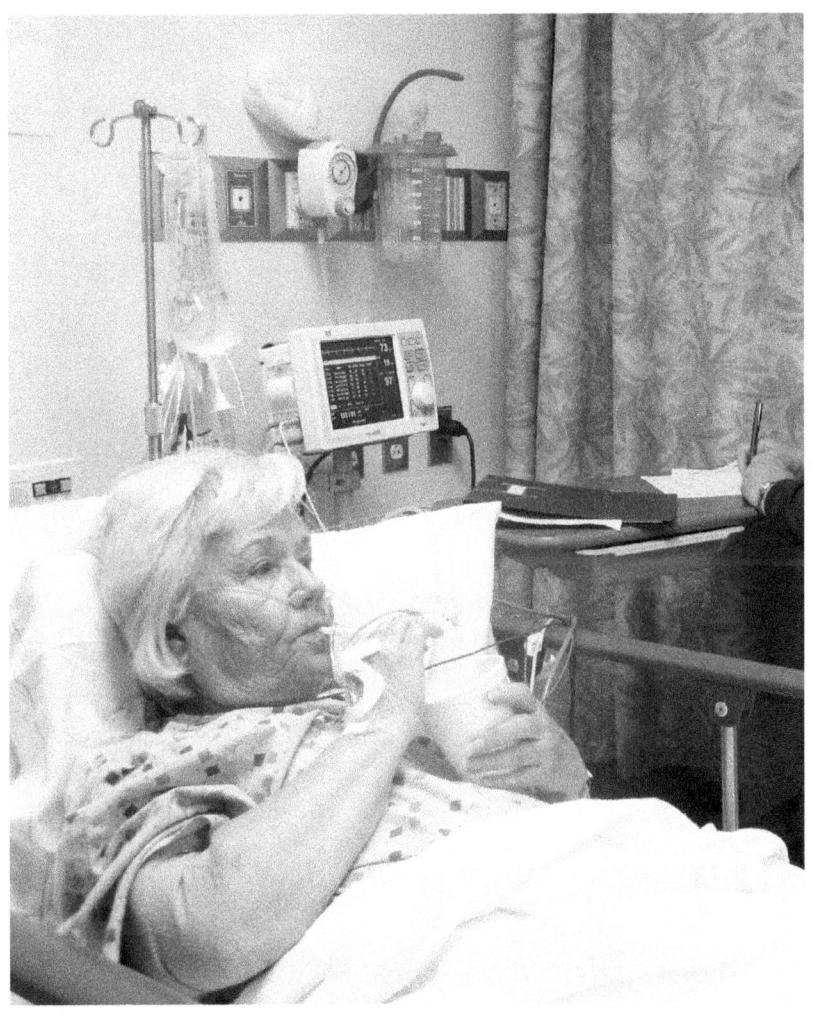

Every senior's wish is to be able to trust healthcare professionals and caregivers, and they expect to receive the same quality of care afforded to younger generations. They say, "I don't want to be discarded or prematurely exterminated due to advanced age because society thinks it is okay to treat us that way."

CHAPTER 5

78 MILLION BABY BOOMERS WILL "ALL" BE CLASSIFIED AS ELDERLY IN 17 YEARS

Since 2011, 14 million boomers are already classified as elderly today. Many boomers are proud to say, "I was a flower child of the '60s, had a VW van with flowers on it, and, peace and love was our motto." They also reflect on serving the country in the Vietnam War, watching the protests, experiencing psychedelic drugs, and dressing like hippies. They will tell you they were deeply defined personally by rock music of the era, the Beatles, the Rolling Stones, Mick Jagger, and Led Zeppelin, but if you ask them if they consider themselves to be elderly, most will retort, "No, I'm not elderly." However, according to government accounts of people at various ages, any way you cut it, boomers are counted as elderly at the age of 65. How will they react when they are treated with disrespect? Who will they depend on to make sure they are cared for? Will there be enough care providers to meet the increased demand for services?

Baby boomers are taking center stage as they enter the aging population, and headlines signal a trend that suggests survival pre-planning is needed. Here is a small sample of these headlines.

MEDIA HEADLINES

NBC: Aging baby boomers may find long-term care elusive
Bertha Coombs, Friday, 2 Aug 2013

CBS NEWS: *June 20, 2011*
BOOMERS: "Almost half of those surveyed at home said they couldn't name a single drug their parents took."

Washington Post: Huge shortage of caregivers looms for baby boomers, report says. By Tara Bahrampour, Published: August 25, 2013

HEALTH NEWS: Baby boomers ill equipped for senior care
June 17, 2011

Psychology Today: Baby Boomers Caring for Elderly Parents: Published on December 23, 2011 by Ann Bettencourt, Ph.D.
Managed Care Magazine: Unprepared for the Boomers

Can MCOs cope with conflicting demands for cost shifting, comprehensive care, and new services for an extremely influential demographic? By John Carroll, *Contributing Editor*

Senior Living News and Trends: Baby Boomers and Healthcare: What Are the Problems, and What Can Be Done? Suggestions for solving the healthcare troubles facing baby boomers: SATURDAY, NOV 26, 2011, About.com Senior Living

Salon: The dilemma of taking care of elderly parents: Aging boomers are agonizing over how to help Mom and Dad. I should know – my daughter is one of them: LILLIAN RUBIN

March 25, 2013 in Features, Health: Aging boomers be warned: Kids may be unable to care for you: Rebecca Nappi The Spokesman-Review

New America Media: From Trauma to Dancing—Senior care Will Challenge Boomer Generation

The two primary lines of defense for seniors and boomers in the healthcare system should include knowing your rights, and preparing a plan of action now.

Boomers are a resourceful generation, a generation that understands activism and the fight for equal human rights. They are already experiencing first-hand, the transgressions against their parents, and the cases in court whereby their parent's wishes are not being honored. They say, "Legal documents and directives are proving in many cases to–not be worth the paper they are written on."

LET THE REVOLUTION BEGIN

Needless to say, a revolution is not out of the question as seniors and boomers stand together to fight for rights, and fight against those who take advantage of trust. The key to your rights is directly affected by whether or not you let it happen. Saying nothing is a statement of acceptance for the way society discards and disrespects you.

CHAPTER 6

THE TRAGEDY OF ABUSE

ABUSE STARTED LONG AGO IN AMERICA

It is important to understand the history of abuse in America. High healthcare costs, lack of proper planning, and lack of public education regarding abuse are all contributing factors to what comes next. Healthcare decisions are typically made on the spur of the moment when unexpected situations happen. Those spur of the moment decisions, void of proper planning, knowledge, and research are one of the key reasons that more than twenty million Senior Citizens face some type of abuse every year. Your goal is to plan against the odds. What hospital will offer the best care in the case of an emergency? What if you need to locate a good rehabilitation unit? Where can you find a healthcare professional who will come to your home? Where is a good independent living facility? Where is a good assisted living facility? Where is a good nursing home? How will we pay for the care? Who covers "what" for senior care? The lack of planning and not knowing their rights has landed senior citizens in the hands of hospitals, at home care, and senior facilities where abuses in the form of physical, psychological, sexual, and financial abuse, neglect, and abandonment is the order of business for the day.

1975

Certainly, senior citizens suffered abuse long before 1975, but, in that year, *someone noticed* that senior citizens were being abused, understood that this behavior was criminal, and the *British Medical Journal* issued first reports of senior abuse as "granny battering."

1996 - 551,000 REPORTS

By 1996, nearly 450,000 adults aged 60 and over were abused and/or neglected in domestic settings. Factor in self-neglect, the total number of incidents was approximately 551,000. (National Senior Abuse Incidence Study. 1998. Washington, DC: National Center on Senior Abuse at American Public Human Services Association.)

2000 - 472,813 REPORTS

In 2000, states were asked to indicate the number of senior/adult abuse reports received in the most recent year for which data were available. Based on figures from 50 states, the total number of reports was 472,813. (A Response to the Abuse of Vulnerable Adults: The 2000 Survey of State Adult Protective Services. 2003. Washington, DC: National Center on Senior Abuse.)

2014 - 5,900,000 REPORTS

The numbers alone in just 14 years are enough to cause anyone to turn pale. Presently, nursing homes, hospitals, independent living facilities, and assisted living facilities range from excellent, nurturing facilities to torture chambers where loved ones suffer, are drugged, injured, beaten, neglected, or worse, die a violent death. Would you say anyone is making progress to put a stop to the abuses?

There are alarming reports of high percentages of seniors who have been and are victims in their own homes, and in the homes of relatives.

Relatives abusing seniors in family homes are not unusual, and the stories are often kept hidden from public view or investigation.

TRUTH: ABUSES ARE OCCURRING EVERYWHERE, MAYBE NEXT DOOR

MYTH: ABUSE ONLY HAPPENS IN NURSING HOMES

TRUTH: THE VAST MAJORITY OF ABUSE OCCURS AT HOME AND IN SOCIETY

MYTH: MOST OF THESE ABUSES AT HOME OR IN SOCIETY ARE REPORTED

Cases of flagrant, willful abuse of nursing home residents are apt to capture public attention. That's understandable, but it's somewhat misleading. The fact is that willful abuse, like other forms of senior abuse and neglect, is far more apt to occur outside institutional settings, in seniors' own homes, or in the homes of their relatives.

The vast majority of vulnerable seniors live with relative caregivers and relatives of senior victims account for most cases of intentional abuse. When caregiver abuse occurs, it's likely to be persistent, rather than an isolated instance of "snapping" under the stress of providing constant care.

SENIOR CITIZENS ASHAMED AND AFRAID TO REPORT FAMILY

Do you know someone who says "I don't want to tell the police what is happening to me at home, because they might send me to a nursing home, besides, it might get my family in trouble if I tell how I am being treated."

You ask, "Why would any person that is being mistreated, disrespected, and demeaned, be silent about their situation?" Due to feelings of shame, fear, and misplaced loyalty, abused seniors are unlikely to report that they are being abused or neglected by their family members. They derive some sense of security from living in familiar surroundings, and their fear of the unknown may outweigh their desire to escape from a terrible situation. Do they know that a person who is in an environment where they are mistreated is 300% more likely to die early?

Reports of intentional abuse often come from neighbors who notice that something's amiss, or from home health providers or hospital workers who see clear signs of mistreatment. If APS workers substantiate intentional abuse, they notify law enforcement officials to get them involved. They also try to get the abused senior's consent to be moved to live elsewhere. If the victim is unable to give informed consent, workers can ask a court to order that he or she be moved to a safe setting.

The next hurdle after someone is removed or moved from a family residence is to find a living facility that is safe and free of abusive caretakers. Common reported violations against seniors in institutional settings include serious physical, sexual and verbal abuses. Dehydration, malnutrition, poor sanitation, preventable accidents and untreated bedsores are reoccurring problems in care facilities, and Senior Citizens are the victims.

Authorities, government agencies, and individual organizations say the only way the mistreatment can be stopped is through shining a light on the tragedies, and educating the public about what abuse is, what ageism is, and how to recognize and report it.

CHAPTER 7

NOT ANALYZING YOUR MEDICATIONS CAN CAUSE DANGEROUS CONSEQUENCES TO YOUR LIFE

America's coming crisis is overmedicating everyone, including seniors. The fact is, unnecessary medications create favorable conditions for the abuse of Senior Citizens.

For many people, prescriptions are beneficial, even lifesaving in many instances. But often, the wrong or unnecessary drugs are prescribed. In fact, this problem is so concerned that researchers have dubbed overmedication and overprescribing of drugs by doctors in the U.S. America's Next Epidemic.

Centers for Disease Control (CDC) urge doctors to use better practices with respect to how they treat pain, and issue prescriptions for painkillers. CDC cautions doctors about overmedicating, and the use of unnecessary antibiotics. Overmedication of children, of seniors, and of the general population poses risks including adverse affects, drug/drug interactions, drug/disease interactions and inappropriate dosing regimens that have taken center stage for research, concern and media coverage.

Healthcare on NBC News presented a focus on The Epidemic of Overmedication, especially in older adults where overmedication can potentially exacerbate ailments, and cause harm.

Because the senior population has a higher prevalence of chronic diseases, multiple drug use is very common (Jorgensen et al 2001). An increase in the number of medications pose a higher risk.

Paying attention to medication labels and warnings could change outcomes for seniors and boomers, and could help them become less vulnerable, and more aware, with improved cognitive function. There are very few medications on the market that don't cause side effects. Those side effects coupled with more side effects between multiple prescriptions could be the reason a senior is experiencing problems.

1. Read labeling information, warnings and interactions on medications that have been prescribed.
2. Cross-reference medications for interaction details.
3. Take serious note of side effects on labeling information. If it is apparent a senior is having a reaction or experiencing one of the listed side effects, act on it by reporting the reaction, and asking that this medication be changed.
4. Contact the doctor who prescribed the medications. Patients have the right to ask for something different. Do not allow a doctor to ignore a drug reaction or stated interaction with other drugs. The doctor most likely wouldn't ignore it if it were a child with the same symptoms.

YOU HAVE THE RIGHT TO FIRE THE DOCTOR:

Doctors who berate patients for bringing in Internet information

Doctors themselves use the Internet. While there is certainly accurate and valid information available, not every statement online is valid. Your request for a change in medication might be met with acceptance, and action on the part of the doctor. The same request might be met with resistant disapproval from another doctor. There are those who are *put off* by the patient who brings in information gathered online. Increasing numbers of patients report the latter indignant reaction from doctors, "I have practiced for thirty years, and I know what I'm doing, and don't appreciate you telling me how to treat your symptoms." If your doctor reacts this way and refuses to even consider your concerns, and your research is current, *fire the doctor*, and find one who understands that something can be learned from laymen.

Find a doctor who values the fact that you have the right to be involved in the care of your family member or yourself and understands that the doctor-patient relations should be a collaborative effort. No one should have to endure the wrath of a medical professional caught up in his or her own importance, especially in a time when the Federal Drug Administration (FDA), and medical journals are online for public consumption. The well-versed researcher, who most likely is not a doctor, can quickly obtain up to date information, and warnings for consumers. Medical professionals are not infallible regardless of how many years they have practiced medicine. Those who truly are in medicine for the right reasons would never ignore questions or concerns from a patient or family member. Nor would they rudely attack someone who takes the time to try to learn more about possible alternatives for a problem. One in four doctors is sued every year for malpractice for alleged mistakes that occur during the care for patients, and 20% of the patients suing doctors have won those cases. Many of those settled cases involve medication errors.

HOW SENIOR CITIZENS ARE TREATED: THE BIGGEST CIVIL RIGHTS STRUGGLE OF OUR TIME

According to Senior Justice Coordinating Council, senior abuse, neglect, and exploitation are significant and under-recognized public health and human rights issues in the United States. Research has demonstrated that it has significant consequences for the health, wellbeing, and independence of seniors. Available data suggests that each year at least 10 percent (or 5 million) older adults are subjected to abuse, neglect, and/or exploitation. (Beach SR, Schulz R, Castle NG, Rosen J; Financial Exploitation and Psychological Mistreatment Among Older Adults: Differences Between African Americans and Non-African Americans in a Population-Based Survey; Gerontologist 2010). Further, only 1 in approximately 25 cases is ever reported to social service agencies. (Lifespan of Greater Rochester, Inc., Weill Cornell Medical Center of Cornell University & New York City Department for the Aging; (2011) *Under the Radar: New York State Senior Abuse Prevalence Study*; New York; Author). The problem is further exacerbated by the lack of standardized practice, public awareness, and public policy guidelines at the national level.

Part of the problem with recognizing and understanding the abuses that occur, is that people often ignore the stories of abuse they are told by Senior Citizens. There are those who regularly target senior citizens and get away with it because often, little investigation follows the complaints.

Alice remembers the lady who lived down the street, a lady who let her play dress up with her jewelry, who always bought her crude paintings made with colored markers when she was only seven. Alice called her Opal. Opal had to move in with her daughter years later. Alice, then in her twenties, went to visit her 70 year-old-friend, but was told by Opal's daughter that it wasn't a good day. A bit sad, Alice left. A couple weeks later, she decided to go back and try again. This time Opal's daughter let Alice see her mother. Opal spent a lot of time telling Alice that her daughter kept her locked in a room, and she wasn't allowed to have visitors very often. When Alice started to leave, Opal's daughter asked, "What did Mama tell you?" Alice repeated the story Opal had shared about being locked in a room. The daughter just laughed, and said, "Oh, you know Mama's mind is not so good these days, and she makes things up." Alice didn't think about it. After all, Alice was like most people today, who just don't know about these things, and don't give them a second thought. Years later, long after Opal died, Alice began to learn the importance of taking Senior Citizens seriously, listening to their stories and believing what they say over believing someone who is covering up the fact that they are mistreating a beloved relative. Alice, to this day is so sorry that she didn't believe Opal and try to do something to help her out of the lonely, sad situation she was experiencing.

CHAPTER 8

NINE OUT OF TEN PEOPLE SURVEYED DID NOT KNOW THE TYPES OF ABUSE AND MISTREATMENT AGAINST SENIOR CITIZENS

Senior abuse is divided into specific categories with recognizable signs that can occur with each individual type of abuse. Senior abuse is any abuse or neglect of any person age 60 or older by a caregiver or another person in a relationship involving the expectation of trust. Caregivers from whom you expect trust, include: doctors, nurses, employees of healthcare providers and facilities, family members, and those appointed to assist with daily activities.

> Attorney, Steve Levin believes, "It is one thing for a person to suffer a decline in their medical condition as a result of aging. However families need to be concerned when the decline or injury is a result of a physician, nurse or aide failing to do his or her job."

Types of senior abuse include:

- Physical
- Sexual
- Emotional
- Psychological

- Neglect
- Abandonment
- Financial
- Dehydration

How many times have you seen a friend at the grocery store, or around town who was bruised? How many times have you asked, "What happened?" And how many times did your friend say, "I just ran into the edge of the kitchen cabinet, I tripped?" How many would give a straight answer if those bruises were actually caused by someone they knew? How many times have you comforted a friend who was crying uncontrollably, but you didn't know it was because your friend was silently being mistreated? Did you notice that your friend's eyes were set back deep in their sockets? Did you think immediately that your friend was suffering from dehydration? As you read the signs of mistreatment, you will be able to not only see your friend, but, perhaps have deeper knowledge to reach out and save your friend, or better yet, inform them so help can be achieved.

WHAT IS PHYSICAL ABUSE?	SIGNS OF PHYSICAL ABUSE	SIGNS OF PHYSICAL ABUSE
Senior is injured Scratched – cut–slashed Burned – cigarette burns Bitten – fingernail gouges Slapped – back handed Pushed–shoved Hit Spitting on senior Kicked Food withheld	Bruises–black eyes Marks on body – welts Cuts – open wounds Sprains – broken bones Unhealed injuries Rope burns hands & feet Broken eyeglasses	Sudden behavior change Does not want to be alone with caregiver Medicine not being taken Caregiver not allowing others to visit senior
WHAT IS SEXUAL ABUSE?	**SIGNS OF SEXUAL ABUSE**	**SIGNS OF SEXUAL ABUSE**
Intentional touching (either directly or through the clothing), of genitalia, anus, groin, breast, mouth, inner thigh, or buttocks Non-consensual sexual contact of any kind Sexual contact with any person incapable of giving consent Sexually explicit photographing	Bruises around breasts or genital area Unexplained venereal disease or infections Torn or stained Under clothing Bloody stained underclothing A senior person's report of being sexually assaulted or raped	Fear of being in a room with certain individuals while clutching clothes close Bruises on arms from being restrained Sudden behavior change Fear of being alone when specific individuals are on duty, especially at night

WHAT IS PSYCHOLOGICAL OR EMOTIONAL ABUSE?	SIGNS OF PSYCHOLOGICAL OR EMOTIONAL ABUSE	SIGNS OF PSYCHOLOGICAL OR EMOTIONAL ABUSE
When a senior experiences trauma after exposure to threatening acts or coercive tactics	Being emotionally upset or agitated	Self isolation
	Being withdrawn	Long-term sadness
	Non communicative	Feeling of being a burden
Humiliation Embarrassment	Non responsive	Looking for ways out to confide in a neighbor or friend and seek help
Controlling behavior	Unusual behavior usually attributed to dementia (sucking, biting, rocking)	
Limiting access to transportation, telephone, money, resources		Appears disturbed or frightened
	A senior's report of being verbally or emotionally mistreated	Avoids eye contact or does not talk openly to others
Social isolation		
Disregard or trivializing needs	Pulling back if a person raises a hand toward the senior	Feels anxious, shy, depressed, or withdrawn
Damaging or destroying senior's property	Crying uncontrollably	Hopelessness or low self-esteem
	Depression	
Infliction of anguish, pain, or distress through verbal or nonverbal acts	Feeling lonely when family or caregiver is present	Changes in eating habits at mealtime
Verbal assaults, insults, threats intimidation, harassment- Treating a senior like a child		

NEGLECT	SIGNS OF NEGLECT	SIGNS OF NEGLECT
Failure or refusal of a caregiver or other responsible person to provide for the senior's basic physical, emotional, or social needs, or failure to protect them from harm	Not receiving adequate nutrition – weight loss Poor hygiene, soiled clothing, inadequate shelter Bedsores	Deprived of access to medical care–medicine Unsafe environment and unsafe activities Soiled bedding – old plates of food left out
FINANCIAL ABUSE	**SIGNS OF FINANCIAL ABUSE**	**SIGNS OF FINANCIAL ABUSE**
The unauthorized or improper use of the resources of a senior for monetary or personal benefit profit or gain	Report of forgery Misused funds or possessions Inability to purchase medicine or needed items	Reports coercion Report from senior of deception used to enforce surrender of finances or property
DEHYDRATION	**SIGNS OF DEHYDRATION**	**SIGNS OF DEHYDRATION**
One of the most commonly reported abuses in the U.S. when healthcare facilities or homecare individuals fail to provide senior with adequate hydration	Dry or sticky mouth Lethargy or coma with severe hydration Low or no urine output	No tears Sunken eyes Urine looks dark yellow

ABANDONMENT	SIGNS OF ABANDONMENT	SIGNS OF ABANDONMENT
Deserting a dependent person with the intent to abandon them or leave them unattended at a place for such a time period as may be likely to endanger their health or welfare.	Wandering the streets Living outdoors Searching trash cans for food Trapped in the house, unable to walk to the door	Inability to groom or conduct hygiene tasks Weight loss when unable to cook or find food No activity at the home of a senior

CHAPTER 9

NURSING HOMES–THE DREADED LIFE SENTENCE

The age range of seniors in nursing homes might surprise you. There are sixty-year old residents who have suffered debilitating changes in their lives, just as there are ninety-year old residents who in some cases have no family or can no longer live at home, and find these homes as their last residence. The Medicare website offers a comprehensive view of nursing homes to allow a person to compare and evaluate every aspect of the homes across America. At a glance, it can be learned which homes fail to meet standards, and also provide important materials for the decision making process. To access the site, visit www.medicare.gov/NHCompare for more information.

Nursing Home Compare: Provides an interactive tool that allows Medicare beneficiaries and their caregivers to access comparison information about nursing homes. It contains information on every Medicare and Medicaid-certified nursing home in the country, including over 17,000 nationwide. Nursing Home Compare includes:

- Nursing home characteristics such as number of beds, type of ownership and whether or not the nursing home participates in Medicare, Medicaid or both.
- Resident characteristics including percent of residents with pressure sore, percent of residents with urinary incontinence and more.
- Summary information about nursing homes during their last State inspection.

- Information on the number of registered nurses, licensed practical or vocational nurses, and nursing assistants in each nursing home.

Nursing Home Checklist: Provides a detailed checklist for rating different nursing homes visited based upon, Quality of Life, Quality of Care, Nutrition and Hydration, and Safety.

About Nursing Home Inspections: Explains, in more detail, the nursing home inspection process and its goals.

Alternatives to Nursing Home Care: Describes the Medicare covered programs that are available to those in need of Nursing Home Care, but who would rather live in the comfort of their own home.

Paying for Care: Provides basic information about Medicare, Medicaid, and Long Term Care Insurance as they pertain to Nursing Home Care.

Nursing Home Resident Rights: Lists the rights, by law, that are given to all nursing home patients.

Nursing Home Awareness Campaigns: Provides information on important nursing home awareness campaigns, such as Nutrition and Hydration Awareness Nutrition Care Alerts.

Nursing Home Publications: Links you to the site's Publication Page. You will be taken directly to the section containing Nursing Home related publications.

Nursing Home Related Sites: Links you to the site's Helpful Contacts section. You will be taken directly to the page containing Nursing Home related websites.

THE NURSING HOME CHECKLIST

Use the Nursing Home Checklist when you visit a nursing home.

Take a copy of the Nursing Home Checklist when you visit to ask questions about resident life, nursing home living spaces, staff, residents' rooms, hallways, stairs, lounges, bathrooms, menus and food, activities, safety, and care.

Checklists are available at www.medicare.gov/NHCompare

JUST SEND US TO PRISON!

Neglect is cited by many nursing home residents as, "We get one bath a week, and linens are only changed once a week. If someone in the home urinates during the night in a bed, the person is forced to sleep on the sheets until the week ends."

This is one reason some believe senior citizens might be better off in prison where a daily bath is provided, there is immediate medical care, meals are decent portions, there is a gym, library, and, best of all, they say, "drugs are prohibited." Those who advocate that seniors should go to prison rather than long-care facilities, believe that prisoners should be sent to nursing homes instead of prisons to be punished for their crimes.

KNOW YOUR RIGHTS

Often, the rights of senior citizens are ignored in nursing homes. One in three nursing homes is reported annually for abuses of varied nature to seniors. In order to ensure that every person entering a home is protected, know, understand and enforce nursing home rights. Centers for Medicaid and Medicare explain those federal rights.

WHAT ARE MY RIGHTS IN A NURSING HOME?

As a nursing home resident, you have certain rights and protections under Federal and state law that help ensure you get the care and services you need.

- You have the right to be informed, make your own decisions, and have your personal information kept private.

The nursing home must tell you about these rights and explain them in writing in a language you understand. They must also explain in writing how you should act and what you're responsible for while you're in the nursing home. This must be done before or at the time you're admitted, as well as during your stay. You must acknowledge in writing that you received this information.

At a minimum, Federal law specifies that nursing homes must protect and promote the following rights of each resident.

- You have the right to be treated with respect: You have the right to be treated with dignity and respect, as well as make your own schedule and participate in the activities you choose. You have the right to decide when you go to bed, rise in the morning, and eat your meals.
- You have the right to participate in activities: You have the right to participate in an activities program designed to meet your needs and the needs of the other residents.
- You have the right to be free from discrimination: Nursing homes don't have to accept all applicants, but they must comply with Civil Rights laws that say they can't discriminate based on race, color, national origin, disability, age, or religion. The Department of Health and Human Services, Office for Civil Rights has more information. Visit http://www.hhs.gov/ocr.
- You have the right to be free from abuse and neglect: You have the right to be free from verbal, sexual, physical, and mental abuse. Nursing homes can't keep you apart from everyone else against your will. If you feel you have been mistreated (abused)

or the nursing home isn't meeting your needs (neglect), report this to the nursing home, your family, your local Long-Term Care Ombudsman, or State Survey Agency. The nursing home must investigate and report all suspected violations and any injuries of unknown origin within 5 working days of the incident to the proper authorities.
- You have the right to be free from restraints: Nursing homes can't use any physical restraints (like side rails) or chemical restraints (like drugs) to discipline you for the staff's own convenience.
- You have the right to make complaints: You have the right to make a complaint to the staff of the nursing home, or any other person, without fear of punishment. The nursing home must address the issue promptly.
- You have the right to get proper medical care.
- You have the right to be fully informed about your total health status in a language you understand.
- Regarding your healthcare, you have the right to take part in this process. Family members can also help with your care plan with your permission. You have the right:
- To be fully informed about your medical condition, prescription and over-the-counter drugs, vitamins, and supplements.
- To be involved in the choice of your doctor.
- To participate in the decisions that affects your care.
- To take part in developing your care plan. By law, nursing homes must develop a care plan for each resident.
- To access all your records and reports, including clinical records (medical records and reports) promptly (on weekdays). Your legal guardian has the right to look at all your medical records and make important decisions on your behalf.
- To express any complaints (sometimes called "grievances") you have about your care or treatment.
- To create advance directives (a health care proxy or power of attorney, a living will, after-death wishes) in accordance with State law.
- To refuse to participate in experimental treatment.

- To have Your Representative Notified.

The nursing home must notify your doctor and, if known, your legal representative or an interested family member when the following occurs:

- You're involved in an accident and are injured and/or need to see a doctor.
- Your physical, mental, or psychosocial status starts to get worse
- You have a life threatening condition
- You have medical complications
- Your treatment needs to change significantly
- The nursing home decides to transfer or discharge you from the nursing home.

Get Information on Services and Fees: You have the right to be told in writing about all nursing home services and fees (those that are charged and not charged to you) before you move into the nursing home and at any time when services and fees change.

YOUR MONEY

The nursing home can't require a minimum entrance fee if your care is paid for by Medicare or Medicaid.

For people seeking admission to the nursing home, the nursing home must tell you (both orally and in writing) and also display written information about how to apply for and use Medicare, and Medicaid benefits. The nursing home must also provide information on how to get a refund if you paid for an item or service, but because of Medicare and Medicaid eligibility rules, it's now considered covered.

You have the right to manage your own money or to choose someone you trust to do this for you. In addition: If you deposit your money with the nursing home or ask them to hold or account for your money, you must sign a written statement saying you want them to do this. The nursing home must allow you access to your bank accounts, cash, and other financial records.

The nursing home must have a system that ensures full accounting for your funds and can't combine your funds with the nursing home's funds. The nursing home must protect your funds from any loss by providing an acceptable protection, such as buying a surety bond.

If a resident with a fund dies, the nursing home must return the funds with a final accounting to the person or court handling the resident's estate within 30 days.

YOUR PRIVACY

You have the following rights:

- To keep and use your personal belongings and property as long as they don't interfere with the rights, health, or safety of others
- To have private visits
- To make and get private phone calls.
- To have privacy in sending and getting mail and email
- To have the nursing home protect your property from theft
- To share a room with your spouse if you both live in the same nursing home (if you both agree to do so). The nursing home has to notify you before your room or your roommate is changed and should take your preferences into account
- To review the nursing home's health and fire safety inspection results

VISITORS

You have the following rights:

- To spend private time with visitors
- To have visitors at any time, as long as you wish to see them, as long as the visit does not interfere with the provision of care and privacy rights of other residents

- To see any person who gives you help with your health, social, legal, or other services at any time. This includes your doctor, a representative from the health department, and your Long-Term Care Ombudsman, among others.

SOCIAL SERVICES

The nursing home must provide you with any needed social services, including the following:

- Counseling
- Help solving problems with other residents
- Help in contacting legal and financial professionals
- Discharge planning.

LEAVE THE NURSING HOME

If your health allows, and your doctor agrees, you can spend time away from the nursing home visiting family or friends during the day or overnight. It's called a "leave of absence." Talk to the nursing home staff a few days ahead of time so the staff has time to prepare your medicines and write your instructions.

Caution: If your nursing home care is covered by certain health insurance, you may not be able to leave for visits without losing your coverage.

MOVING OUT

Living in a nursing home is your choice. You can choose to move to another place. However, the nursing home may have a policy that requires you to tell them before you plan to leave. If you don't, you may have to pay an extra fee.

Have Protection Against Unfair Transfer or Discharge: You can't be sent to another nursing home, or made to leave the nursing home, unless any of the following are true:

It's necessary for the welfare, health, or safety of you or others or your health has improved to the point that nursing home care is no longer necessary. The nursing home hasn't been paid for services you received or the nursing home closes.

You have the following rights:

You have the right to appeal a transfer or discharge to the State. The nursing home can't make you leave if you're waiting to get Medicaid. Except in emergencies, nursing homes must give a 30-day written notice of their plan and reason to discharge or transfer you. The nursing home has to safely and orderly transfer or discharge you and give you proper notice of bed-hold and/or re-admission requirements.

You have a right to form or participate in a resident group to discuss issues and concerns about the nursing home's policies and operations. Most homes have such groups, often called "resident councils." The home must give you meeting space and must listen to and act upon grievances and recommendations of the group.

Family and friends can help make sure you get good quality care. They can visit and get to know the staff and the nursing home's rules. Family members and legal guardians may meet with the families of other residents and may participate in family councils, if one exists. Family members can help with your care plan with your permission. If a family member or friend is your legal guardian, he or she has the right to look at all medical records about you and make important decisions on your behalf.

YOUR RIGHTS INCLUDE

- The right of citizenship. Nursing home residents do not lose any of their rights of citizenship, including the right to vote, to religious freedom and to associate with whom they choose.

- The right to dignity. Residents of nursing homes are honored guests and have the right to be so treated.
- The right to privacy. Nursing home residents have the right to privacy whenever possible, including the right to privacy with their spouse, the right to have their medical and personal records treated in confidence, and the right to private, uncensored communication.
- The right to personal property. Nursing home residents have the right to possess and use personal property and to manage their financial affairs.
- The right to information. Nursing home residents have the right to information, including the regulations of the home and the costs for services rendered. They also have the right to participate in decisions about any treatment, including the right to refuse treatment.
- The right of freedom. Nursing home residents have the right to be free from mental or physical abuse and from physical or chemical restraint, unless ordered by their physician with patient or guardian consent.
- The right to care. Residents have the right to equal care, treatment and services provided by the facility without discrimination.
- The right of residence. Nursing home residents have the right to live at the home unless they violate publicized regulations. They may not be discharged without timely and proper notification to both the resident and the family or guardian.
- The right of expression. Nursing home residents have the right to exercise their rights, including the right to file complaints and grievances without fear or reprisal.

ABUSE OF POWER BY CARE STAFF

Today there are those working in hospitals, nursing homes, or in your home who are just not interested in helping senior patients. Not too many years down the road, 1 in 5 Americans will be elderly. Does this mean an entire generation is at risk unless the acceptance of abuse and substandard care is ended now? A body of evidence is surfacing which indicates that nurses are not receiving an appropriate amount of training or understanding of caring for older patients. Will the care provided compromise the quality of life for the ageing population of boomers and seniors?

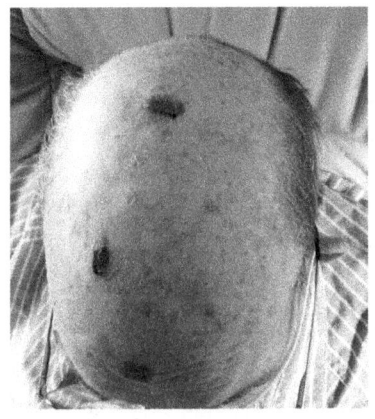

Can you even imagine how many senior patients are shoved or allowed to fall into sharp objects? Can you imagine a nurse or aide shoving someone into a van where there are boxes and other debris in their path, an invitation to trip and fall? It happens all the time. And, you wonder how these people who are rough or mean spirited with seniors, actually sleep at night.

Another example of this type of disrespect, contempt, and abuse was reported in a New Mexico nursing home. While at the nursing home the resident was left on a bedpan for approximately twenty-four hours. The bedpan became imbedded in the resident's skin and left a wound in the shape of the bedpan when removed. The injury was later assessed as a Stage II pressure ulcer. The State's Attorney General took a strong stand and secured a felony criminal conviction against the facility.

HOSPITAL THREATENS TO CALL ADULT PROTECTIVE SERVICES ON A DAUGHTER WHO QUESTIONED THEIR INEPT HANDLING OF HER MOTHER

A 65 year-old woman recently walked out of a care facility that was dangerously close to a highway. The facility contacted the daughter. She questioned personnel and management about how this could happen, saying, "My mother could have been hit by a car." She said her expectations were that her mother was in a safe environment. The home informed the daughter that her mother wandering off was not their responsibility. It was noted that the woman had deep scratches in her ankle area, as if a bracelet had been forcibly attached after the incident.

The same home, according to medication lists, drugged the woman into a semi-conscious state, and reportedly left her for the majority of a day lying in her urine in her bed. Hours later, the daughter said, "the home called an ambulance to transport my mom to the hospital where it was noted that she was unkempt, dehydrated and weak." The day prior, the resident was communicating, lucid and candid in her actions while visiting on the phone with her daughter. After the arrival of the 68 year-old-woman at the hospital, records indicated that she had a decreasing level of consciousness. Shortly after arrival in the emergency room, and before the daughter's arrival, the hospital noted that behavior was agitated and nervous. Based on that assessment, the hospital told the daughter they gave her mother Geodon to calm her. The hospital had information in their hands that this woman had been diagnosed with dementia and heart problems as well as diabetes. With no regard for the stated health diagnosis, and with disregard for the fact that Geodon's listed label states specifically, 'Not approved for use in patients with dementia related psychosis,' this patient who was reported to have arrived in a diminished state of consciousness, was given an antipsychotic drug used in cases of schizophrenia and bipolar disorders, neither of which the patient had. Later in the day, the hospital advised the daughter that they gave the woman Haldol, another drug that is not approved by the FDA for any patient with dementia.

Both Haldol and Geodon, FDA states, can double the risk of death in patients with dementia. The daughter was voicing her dissatisfaction and fears, so the hospital refused to let her enter her mother's room, and further threatened the daughter by telling her they would call Adult Protective Services, and have her put in jail for interfering. When the daughter asked that her mother be transported to another hospital, she said, "They flatly refused." A final blow came when the family was told that the patient's long-time doctor wasn't allowed to practice at this hospital, a hospital that utilizes transient hospitalists (rotating out of town doctors), and disallows doctors in the area to treat their patients there unless certain agreements are made with the hospital. The label for the medication Geodon that was given to the woman is noted below.

Geodon warning: Increased mortality in senior patients with Dementia-related psychosis

FDA is reminding physicians that antipsychotic drugs are not for patients with dementia, and advises healthcare professionals to consider other options to manage dementia related psychosis. The warning further states, senior patients with dementia-related psychosis treated with antipsychotic drugs are at an increased risk of death. Analyses of seventeen placebo-controlled trials (modal duration of 10 weeks), largely in patients taking atypical antipsychotic drugs, revealed a risk of death in drug-treated patients of between 1.6 to 1.7 times the risk of death in placebo-treated patients. Over the course of a typical 10-week controlled trial, the rate of death in drug-treated patients was about 4.5%, compared to a rate of about 2.6% in the placebo group. GEODON (ziprasidone) is not approved for the treatment of patients with Dementia-Related Psychosis.

PART II

ANGELS OF THE COURTS

CHAPTER 10

IF VIOLATORS OF YOUR RIGHTS WON'T LISTEN, THEN, HIT THEM IN THE POCKETBOOK

An Illinois Attorney has been making a difference for families and senior victims through fighting for their rights; preserving their dignity and taking a firm stand against those who abuse senior citizens.

Steven M. Levin, co-founder and senior partner of Levin & Perconti, is a nationally known trial lawyer with more than 30 years of personal injury litigation experience and success. In 1992, he and John Perconti founded Levin & Perconti, a firm that has achieved over $520 million for its clients, including over $140 million in nursing home abuse and neglect cases.

PIONEERING NURSING HOME LITIGATION

Levin was one of the first lawyers in the United States to handle nursing home cases, and has established a reputation as one of the country's top litigators in the area of nursing home abuse and neglect. He represented hundreds of nursing home residents who have been victimized by improper care and treatment, achieving record-setting verdicts and settlements in these cases.

More importantly, Levin's vigilance in representing victims in nursing home negligence lawsuits has brought national attention to this rampant and unacceptable problem, sending a message that mistreatment of one of society's most vulnerable groups will not go unnoticed.

He serves on the Leadership Council of the National Consumer Voice for Quality Long-Term Care (formerly known as the National Citizens' Coalition for Nursing Home Reform), an organization dedicated to protecting the rights of nursing home residents and their families. He is also the former chair of the AAJ's Nursing Home Litigation Group. Steve's comments on nursing home litigation have been quoted in national news publications including *The New York Times* and *The Wall Street Journal*.

He stands by the belief that lawsuits not only bring relief to injured victims, but also motivate healthcare providers, businesses and manufacturers to make systemic changes to provide better care, service, and safer products.

AN INTERVIEW WITH STEVEN M. LEVIN, ATTORNEY

Steve Levin sees a lack of community education about recognizing abuse as a factor in a high percentage of abuses that are never reported. Levin said, *"Yes, unfortunately many of the families and individuals I represent do not appreciate or understand what could be the signs and symptoms of abuse or neglect. Sometimes long-term care providers mislead families into believing that abuse and neglect is really the effects of aging."*

The question and answer interview:

Q. Did you find in your initial cases there were those who discounted the complaints because of societal attitudes that seniors "just have" medical issues because they are old?

A. *"Yes, many of the families I meet do not realize that bed sores, dehydration or falls can be prevented and should not occur when appropriate care is provided. Appropriate care includes an appropriate risk assessment; an appropriate plan of care, sufficient staffing and supplies to implement the plan of care, and evaluations and reevaluations as to whether the plan being implemented is working.*

Many times what long-term care providers call unavoidable injuries are really failures to follow this planning, implementation and evaluation model.

It is one thing for a person to suffer a decline in their medical condition as a result of aging. However families need to be concerned when the decline or injury is a result of a physician, nurse or aide failing to do his or her job."

Q. How have you been able to change perceptions and impress upon the masses that many medical problems are in fact, due to negligence?

A. *"As in many areas of human endeavors, the tort system acts as a de facto regulatory body of the nursing home industry. Lawsuits and the publicity lawsuits receive improve care. I believe the most effective way to raise awareness is to tell my clients' stories publicly. Most people will, at some point have a loved one in long-term care, so they can relate. People suspect negligence or abuse because they have heard stories of someone else facing similar issues, and this knowledge leads them to take action. My clients' cases often receive local media attention, and I find this is a great vehicle for raising awareness and bringing other families forward."*

Q. Do you see a difference between adequate staffing in for-profit and not-for-profit nursing homes, and the quality of care a resident receives?

A. *"Studies have found that not-for-profit and publicly owned homes provide better quality care for residents. In my experience, many facilities that are owned and managed by large nursing home corporations are more likely to operate at minimal staffing levels to save money. When staff is stretched too thin residents are more likely to suffer serious injuries."*

Q. What are the most common complaints you hear about nursing homes?

A. *"The most common complaints relate to insufficient staffing. Families tell us that their bed-ridden mother isn't turned or repositioned often enough to prevent bed sores; that their aunt was left to lay in urine and feces soaked sheets because there was not enough staff to change them; that their father fell while trying to walk to the washroom on his own because no one answered his call button, etc. Families may not understand the complex medical aspects of neglect, but they can identify dignity issues and pain and suffering."*

Q. Is there any current legislation proposed that would further protect nursing homes and allow them to continue unacceptable practices?

A. *"No, but there is a current legislation in the House and Senate to protect nursing home residents. Federal legislation banning the use of mandatory arbitration agreements in consumer contracts, including nursing home contracts, would protect consumers. When a nursing home resident signs a contract that contains a mandatory arbitration clause, they sign away their right to seek justice through the court system if they are injured or a loved one is killed as a result of nursing home negligence. This allows nursing homes to provide substandard care without the threat of being held liable for their actions. Banning mandatory arbitration agreements would protect a nursing home resident's right to sue."*

Q. How can Americans become involved and have a voice regarding legislation?

A. *"The best thing to do is educate friends and family and ask them to contact their Representatives and Senators to show their support for legislation that would prohibit the use of mandatory arbitration agreements in nursing home contracts."*

Q. As a watchdog, do you see better care in nursing homes in your area, which is directly due to your high profile efforts on behalf of the consumers, or does the cycle continue, despite the light being shone on the abuse?

A. *"I believe that the public is more aware of the epidemic of poor care in nursing homes than when I first began representing clients in nursing home cases twenty five years ago. I believe that the public has a better understanding of resident's rights as a result of media coverage of nursing home lawsuits.*

As a result of heightened public awareness, I believe nursing home owners are motivated to provide better care to avoid litigation or bad press. They are less likely to provide substandard care when they know they can be held accountable and suffer financial loss. "

Q. What is your greatest concern regarding senior care?

A. *"As our population ages, more and more people require long-term care. However, corporations also see the financial opportunities that stem from an aging population, and the industry has shifted from local ownership to investor-owned corporations focused on profits. An increase in nursing home populations coupled with the potential for substandard care at the hands of profit-driven corporations will only lead to more victims of abuse and negligence."*

Q. What criteria must be met in order for an individual to bring a case of abuse or neglect into the court system?

A. *"In order for a family to bring a personal injury or wrongful death action on behalf of their loved one, we look at whether the resident's risks were appropriately assessed, whether a care plan was developed to address these risks, whether that care plan was implemented and whether the plan was reevaluated when necessary. We also look at whether there was appropriate communication between the resident, his or her family, the nursing home staff and the resident's physicians. We first examine these factors. If we find that the nursing home did not follow this model, they cannot claim the injury or death was unavoidable."*

Q. What do you consider as the most effective methods for a family member, victim, or friend to document suspected abuse for presentation to an attorney?
A. *"Document everything. Take photos, keep a journal that include information on your loved one's condition (including changes), your conversations with providers, and observations that you make when visiting the nursing home. Keep a daily record of what you hear and observe."*

Q. What are the top ten signs of abuse committed against seniors, and what are red flags when a person enters a facility before deciding to become a resident?
A.

> *Unexplained cuts or bruises*
> *Broken bones*
> *Pressure sores*
> *Fall injuries*
> *Sudden weight loss*
> *Dehydration*
> *Over-medication*
> *Medication errors*

"When a family visits a facility, they should not only assess the facility itself (smells, cleanliness, etc.) But also observe the residents living at the facility. If the facility has a foul smell that is a red flag that staff may not attend to residents' hygienic needs. If residents seem to be withdrawn, lifeless or over-medicated, they may rely on chemical restraints to "control" the population. If they are not willing to show you different areas of the facility, they may be hiding poor conditions."

Q. What can a family member do if doping of residents (chemical restraints) is apparent with the majority of patient heads hanging as they sit in their wheelchairs?

A. *"Antipsychotics are often prescribed to treat younger residents who suffer from mental illnesses. When nursing homes administer antipsychotics to senior residents who suffer from dementia it is considered an off-label use. The use of these medications in senior residents commonly causes lethargy, which leads to other serious problems. If you suspect that your loved one is being harmed by antipsychotics, request a conference with the nursing home staff and any and all physicians involved in your loved ones' care."*

Q. What caused you to become passionate about being an advocate for the senior, and how has your exposure to the heinous acts against seniors affected you personally?

A. *"In the 1970's and 1980's, I visited family members in nursing homes and was appalled by the conditions. When a client of mine approached me in 1988 about representing her family in a wrongful death suit against a nursing home, I was eager to help.*

Unfortunately at that time, attorneys did not represent older people in personal injury and wrongful death actions against nursing homes. They argued that these types of cases were not worth the cost of litigation because older people living in nursing homes suffered from pre-existing conditions, were no longer wage earners, and "were going to die soon anyway."

Through my research I uncovered a little-known Illinois law, the Nursing Home Reform Act of 1979, which was sponsored by Sen. Richard M. Daley (who later became Chicago mayor). This law, along with OBRA '87 (the federal nursing home law) set forth nursing home standards in Illinois, but no one was holding nursing homes accountable legally to meet these standards. Armed with this knowledge, my practice grew, as did my knowledge of nursing home misconduct and my involvement in the fight to protect our most vulnerable population. I am motivated by my belief that everyone has the right to live their last years in comfort and die with dignity."

PART III

SECRETS THAT WILL HELP YOU MAKE GOOD CHOICES

CHAPTER 11

INDEPENDENT LIVING: NOT ALWAYS THE TICKET TO FREEDOM

It's time to go on a shopping trip. You and your family have the opportunity today to begin visiting facilities, and making conscious decisions about where you want to live when the time comes for you to relocate. Then, there will be no need for a rush in the decision making process in that unexpected moment. Senior Citizens are big business, and bring in big bucks to providers of living accommodations. Getting a new resident's name on the dotted line can be the beginning of a nightmare for the senior and for their families. There are some red flags to look for when choosing what appears to be the perfect place to live.

Senior independent living facilities "not always as stated in brochures"
Seniors having to fight for their rights after moving in

Dana, a concerned daughter writes, "My 69 year old mother is a perfect example. I do not consider 69 to be old; however, she had a stroke in April and she has supposedly fully recovered, but her mind/memory is just slightly slower than it was before the stroke. Also her sight and hearing is not nearly as good as it once was, so she is showing signs of aging. Her husband died in April, right after she had her stroke so her life has literally been turned upside down. She is incredibly vulnerable and sensitive right now and we just moved her to an independent living "cottage" on the grounds of an assisted living facility. I researched the best places for her to live and we felt like this would be the perfect answer, but I'm already having some serious doubts about our choice."

Based on Dana's experience, she shares tips to help others avoid some of the negative experiences families have had with selecting a facility.

A. Get everything in writing before you or a loved one move into a facility. My mother and I were verbally assured that she would be allowed to smoke in her cottage. Now, after several thousand dollars worth of moving costs we are being told that she cannot smoke in her cottage. Personally, I don't want her to smoke, but we were told that she could and I believe it was just a ploy to get us to move in and fill a vacancy.

B. A month to month lease is what is offered at most places we looked at and while that initially sounds good, the stories I'm hearing from other families is that this is another ploy to get you to move in and as soon as you move, then the rates start going up dramatically and often.

C. Know exactly what you are paying for because her meals/housekeeping/maintenance is included in her monthly rent. I'm already being told by other residents, that the meals are very small portions, housekeeping is minimal and maintenance is barely adequate.

D. Find out exactly how long "management" has been employed at the facility because another common experience is that there is massive turnover in staff at every level. We looked at several facilities and this was a common theme. My mom is already, after only two days, being "talked down to" "placated" and "condescended to" even in my presence. She will *NOT* let the staff get away with that, but other less outspoken residents *will* let themselves be brow-beaten.

As a result of what I have seen in only two days of living in what we thought would be the perfect place, I now know that I will need to remain very, very visible in the facility so that they understand we *do not* intend to put up with a bunch of nonsense. I am documenting everything in case we need the information in the future.

Other safeguards that can be used when you and your family are sitting in the office of a facility and considering living there.

RECORD CONVERSATION

- Take a tape recorder or use a cell phone recorder. Tell the prospective facility management you are taping the conversation so you can review what is offered at the many facilities you are assessing for your future home or the future home of a loved one. Their reaction to being taped will tell you a lot. If the staff is defensive and cuts your meeting short, this is a red flag. People who are genuinely honest about the answers involved with a possible lease situation won't mind you taping their conversation, because *they* have nothing to hide.

REVIEW COPY OF LEASE BEFORE SIGNING

- Secure a copy of the lease or entry agreement and ask if you can take it home and read it before committing. If staff says no, the staff may be afraid you will run it by a lawyer in order to understand the tricky fine print, or the fine print that states you can only have arbitration if there's a problem, and can't take them to court if they harm someone.

SPEAK WITH OTHER RESIDENTS FIRST

- Speak privately with other residents before you commit. They will be honest with you in most situations. Staff may not be forthright because they are expected to have their public relations face on, regardless of what they really know, and aren't going to share with you.

ASK FOR A TEST DRIVE OF THE FACILITY

- Before you move into a facility, ask if you can have a 3-day stay to see if you like the place. Consider it a vacation and learn everything you can. Listen to conversations around you, and make an informed decision. If you are told "no," or if the facility presses you with that statement, that "there are only a few apartments," it's probably another red flag. Above all, do not let management pressure you into an instant decision.

CHECK THE INTERNET FOR FACILITY REVIEWS

- Find Internet reviews of facilities that are written by consumers and reviewers.

CHECK STATE WEBSITES FOR FINDINGS

- Review state findings and citations on state websites; see whether there have been recurring problems with federal or state agencies.

REPORT FACILITIES THAT DON'T HONOR WHAT THEY OFFER

- Should you move in and find that the facility is far overrated and your rights are abused, report the facility to your state attorney general or respective reporting agency. Get everything in writing.

SEXUAL ABUSE, DRUGS, UNSAFE CONDITIONS AT SENIOR LIVING FACILITY

At one senior independent living facility, residents involved the media after feeling that their complaints had been ignored or disregarded by management. Family members said they "feared for the safety of their loved ones" who lived there. Residents reported to management that a teenaged family member of one of the residents was sexually abusing other residents at the elevator by grabbing them by the shoulders and "dry humping" them. There were reports of air conditioning and heating being out for extended periods of time leaving apartments too cold or too hot, something that is important to the well-being of the senior, or anyone for that matter. Residents complained that some of their mail was being withheld and was found stuffed behind filing cabinets.

At one point, a senior resident requested that someone look into the pungent smell of something cooking "like drugs" coming from one of the apartments, and the "seedy" visitors coming through their hallway to that apartment. Police later arrested a resident who lived in one of the senior apartments for possession of drugs. Residents believed the facility was more interested in renting the apartments, than conducting background checks on the people moving into the facility so those who lived there "could be safe and not live in fear." The manager of the facility was complacent when questioned by the media, actually stating, "They can move if they don't like it here." The problem with that thinking is that most seniors who move into independent living have sold their homes and belongings, and have spent most of their assets to move into what they believe will be their last residence. Most are alone, and seeking safety and peace, so "just moving" isn't an option for them, nor is it a compassionate response from someone who is managing a facility of this type. After the media article was released, the company that owned the facility sent officials to investigate the complaints.

Rather than removing the manager, the company let him stay. A few of the concerns were addressed and corrected, residents said, but for the most part, the management's general attitude toward them remains cold, indifferent, and dictatorial. Residents said, "After it was rumored that news media would be coming in to do a story, a sign on a wall promoting the facility as a safe facility disappeared."

CHAPTER 12

I HAVE A RIGHT TO BE INVOLVED IN MY HOSPITAL CARE.

HOSPITALS POSE RISKS TO SENIOR PATIENTS

Merck Manual states that about 75% of patients who are 75 or older and functionally independent at admission are not functionally independent when they are discharged; almost half of adults who occupy hospital beds are 65 or older. This proportion is expected to increase as the population ages. Hospital care costs Medicare over $100 billion/yr., representing 30% of health care expenditures for hospital care.

Hospitalization, Merck states, can magnify age-related physiologic changes and increase morbidity, and only seriously ill elderly patients who cannot be appropriately cared for elsewhere should be hospitalized. Hospitalization itself poses risks to elderly patients because it involves confinement, immobility, diagnostic testing, and treatments (particularly changes in drug regimens). When patients are transferred to or from a hospital, drugs are likely to be added or changed, leading to a higher risk of adverse effects. Hospitals can be dehumanizing and impersonal. Acute hospital care should last only long enough to allow successful transition to home care, a skilled nursing facility, or an out patient rehabilitation. (Merck Manual).

Hospitals are generally satisfied that many seniors aren't assuming that hospitals are the best places for them. In fact, there is new concern that senior patients are getting sicker when they're in hospitals and many die there, in part because they have not received even a minimal amount of care. Care for seniors in the medical field and in some institution or hospital settings has raised a few eyebrows over the years, but the abuses for those who are unfortunate enough to land in the wrong hospital continue.

A wise man once said, "Your mortality depends on the hospital or medical facility in which you land for medical assistance."

Here are some helpful and potentially life saving tips to use when it comes to taking an older person to the hospital:

1. After entry into the hospital, be alert to unusual sudden changes in behavior, cognition, and function of the senior person you accompany to the hospital.
2. Ask the person you accompany to inform the facility that you are a contact person, and that all records and information can be shared with you. It is a good idea to have your parent or loved one put in writing, that permission is provided so all records can be shared with you. Keep it handy, should you need it.
3. Your attention, your questions, your knowledge could save a life from being destroyed. Take notes.
4. Ask to see records, and research every medication being prescribed.
5. If you see any of the adverse effects occurring in the patient, report it to the doctor. If the doctor refuses to remove the patient from the medication, and allows the patient to continue to have negative reactions, report the facility to the hospital administrator. If administration does nothing, transfer the patient to another facility, and get another doctor. Report it to your state hotline for medical authority.
6. Listen to your loved one or friend. Listen with intent when a loved one or friend tries to tell you they are not being treated right. Listen, and *hear* the request when a senior patient in the hospital is pleading to go home. It's not an uncommon request, but in many instances, it may be warning to be heeded from

the patient. Delve into the reasons further with the patient. If the patient can't communicate, ask him/her to squeeze your hand, blink, or lift a finger if what you ask is correct.

7. If the patient begins to hallucinate, has a serious behavioral change, or appears to be confused, (and this is not the norm), it is imperative you act quickly. It is quite likely that the patient is being given antipsychotics or other types of medications that cause confusion. You can demand that antipsychotics or other confusion/hallucination type medications *not* be given to your senior family member or friend, especially if the patient has never been subjected to such drugs. Understand that in some situations, patient families have reported that they asked that these medications not be given to their loved ones. The hospital took the patient(s) off of the medications for a day, and violated the requests by placing the patient back on the same medications that had caused the initial confusion without permission. Report facilities that are not honoring your requests (if you are a representative of the patient), as this is just another flagrant violation of your rights.

8. Notice patient skin condition when you arrive. Notice when the skin changes, becomes bruised and torn. Pay attention if

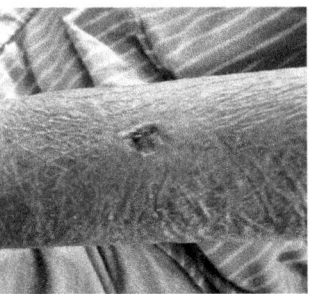

the patient reports a rub spot from lying in the same position. Most facilities probably will not self-report to you that this is happening. Be vigilant. Report to the doctor any sore that appears, and seek care for the wound. If no assistance to your request or demand is provided, report the facility to the state in which it is located. This is classified as negligence.

There have been thousands of successful lawsuits over infected bedsores or ulcers. Take pictures of any change you see happening. Take plenty of pictures. Keep them for future reference.

HOSPITAL PATIENT RIGHTS

When you enter a hospital, are you really going to read the patient rights sheets they give you? You wouldn't be there if everything was okay and you were in the right frame of mind at that moment. Certainly, your thoughts are about getting the medical help you need. The information below covers many important facts you need to know about your rights.

Not only do you or your appointed representative have the right to see your medical records, you have the right to request a copy of records.

All states provide valuable information for patients about obtaining copies of medical records.

Doctors and hospitals are required to keep medical records for a specific length of time as required by state law.

Any individual can request his or her own medical records. The law also permits access by other "qualified persons." This includes parents or guardians when they approved the care or when it was provided on an emergency basis. Attorneys representing patients may also request records, as can a committee appointed to represent the needs of an incompetent patient.

All requests for medical records must be made in writing to either the individual physician or the health care facility. The request should indicate that a qualified person is making the request and should be as precise as possible. The request should identify the provider from whom the information is requested and describe the information being sought. If the records are to be sent to a third party, such as another physician, provide the name and address of that individual. Requests must be signed. A practitioner or institution may request that the signature be notarized.

Once your request is received, a physician or health care facility generally has 10 days to provide you with an opportunity to inspect your records. The law does not provide a specific time period by which copies of medical records must be provided. However, many states consider 10 to 14 days to be a reasonable time in which a practitioner should respond to such a request.

In most states, the law allows physicians and institutions to charge 75 cents a page, plus postage, for paper copies of medical records. Physicians may charge the actual reproduction costs for radiographic materials, such as X-rays or MRI films. A provider may not impose a charge for original mammogram films, but may charge postage. However, an individual cannot be denied access to information solely because he or she is unable to pay.

A physician cannot refuse to let you or an authorized party see your records if you haven't paid your medical bill.

You do *not* have to tell the persons or institutions from which you request records – *why* you want the records.

Specify the dates for which you request the records, and specify what type of records you are seeking such as images and/or files of all treatment and medications.

One request, for instance, may be for photos taken by a hospital or care facility of torn skin. Make it clear that you want the actual digital image, not a photocopy. Allowing a patient in a hospital, nursing home or long-term care facility to develop a sore of this nature to the point of deadly infection is considered by law, in many cases, to be *abuse and neglect* by medical personnel. Because a person cannot reposition, the pressure rubs or tears from taping needles create open wounds that are prone to infection, and in some cases, have been stated as cause of death. You will find in most situations, it's not that the patient just took a turn for the worse for no known reason…but the facility or an individual may have caused the situation.

Many hospitals employ patient advocates, but in some cases, the advocate is no more than a façade to put on a public relations face for the facility. The best defense against negative or negligent treatment is to have family or friends who will serve as the advocate, and ask questions, challenge, concerns, and insist on proper treatment in the best interest of the patient.

REMEMBER

- You have the right to refuse medications or tests
- You have the right to ask to be transferred to another hospital
- You have the right to be involved in your treatment

CHAPTER 13

DANGEROUS ANTIPSYCHOTIC DRUGS

DOPING SENIORS TO DEATH

Patricia L. McGinnis, California Advocate tells U.S. Senate Committee, "Antipsychotics don't just hasten death, they often turn seniors into people their own families barely recognize by dulling their memories, sapping their personalities, and crushing their spirits."

Very often a nurse makes his or her own personal assessment and suggests to a doctor that a patient "should" have antipsychotic drugs. The nurse then asks the doctor to sign off on the suggested drugs. The common red flag subjective statements from nurses include:

- The patient was agitated
- Upset
- Nervous
- Aggressive
- Yelling
- Crying
- Freaked out during a test
- Spitting out pills
- Keeps getting out of bed

SOME NURSES SAY:

"Well, you have no idea what we deal with; some of them get physical with us, spit on us, spit out their pills, spit out their food, and push us to our limits."

SOME PATIENTS SAY:

"Did it ever occur to a nurse that we have trouble swallowing pills? "Did it ever occur to a nurse that the patient might have a known allergy, yet is being forced to eat the fruit of the day?" That fruit, the patient knows, almost killed her years earlier when she went into anaphylactic shock because of her intense allergic reactions to the fruit. For a patient that can't communicate well at the moment, the only recourse is to spit it out. "Did it ever occur to a nurse to double check to see if our medication side effects or allergies are causing us to be out of control, or does the nurse just slam us with something else to sedate us?"

WHAT YOU DON'T HEAR NURSES SAYING OPENLY:

- Drugs are cheaper than staff to take care of all of them
- We dope them up, their heads hang down
- We don't have to be running to their room all day to do all of the things they want us to do.
- We don't have to listen to them telling us how bad we are at our jobs
- Put a vest on her so she can't get up
- We are short handed, and this sure makes our shift easier.
- That old lady is threatening to sue us, shut her up

Fortunately, there are many nurses with a passion for taking care of older patients, and those nurses are more likely to find out what is causing the patient to be agitated, upset, nervous, or aggressive because they know medications, environment, and higher sensitivity to certain drugs can produce negative reactions. Even a side effect like twitching and involuntary movements can signal a medication side effect that can be dangerous.

BE CAREFUL HOW YOU ANSWER QUESTIONS IN A HOSPITAL

Would you like something to help you sleep?

When a hospital nurse or doctor asks if you need a little something to help you sleep, you have no idea what medication you are about to receive. If you are accustomed to taking an over the counter sleep-aid and it has worked fine for you for years, you may face a totally different outcome with what you are about to be given, or, like some have said, "You get knocked out for a day, and wake up groggy and headachy."

Are You In Pain?

Your back may hurt a little from being in the same position for too long, but it doesn't hurt any more than it would at home if you couldn't turn over. Perhaps asking for help to reposition will help you avoid medications you are not used to taking. You may have been taking a non-prescription pain pill at home or maybe you have used a muscle rub. Be specific as to what you want when you respond.

Senior Citizen drugged in hospital to shut her up.

An 84-year-old woman entered a hospital due to a collapse after learning she had a blood disease. She was communicative, pleasant, following instructions and hopeful for a full recovery. After the second day in the hospital, and after what she considered rough handling from a nurse, she was overheard telling the nurse before she drew blood, "If you don't do this right, I will sue you." She had never sued anyone, nor had she made a statement of that nature in her life. Within 24 hours after her statement to the nurse, she was unable to communicate, was hallucinating and confused. Her involved family asked what the hospital was giving her. Their response was, "Oh, nothing but potassium and nutrients." She just wanted her condition addressed. Instead, she was pumped full of Ativan, Risperdal, Haldol and Morphine, along with some Atropine, all of which can cause confusion, hallucinations, an almost comatose state and depression. Researchers have called this type of chemical cocktail a form of chemical restraint.

Hospital records document a patient's level of pain each day based on a scale of 1-10. Despite the fact that the patient's documented pain each day prior to drugging was non-existent, despite the fact that this patient had *no* Alzheimer's or dementia, and despite the fact that this patient was fully lucid the day before, you have to wonder if the chemical restraints were somehow tied to her statement to the nurse. The last thing bad hospitals want is a lawsuit, or public scrutiny.

After six weeks of prodding, tests, and a substantial list of medications, and after her clear skin on entry became torn, bruised, and bloodied, and organs began to shut down one by one, she was never able to return to her home. She died a medicated, haunting death. It was learnt after her death, and after obtaining her hospital records what medications she was given, and the individual and collective, negative impact on her health.

She had been extremely healthy for her age with no notable health problems in her past. At the age of 84, she was a golfer, lifted weights, sang in two choirs, lived home alone, and was focused on regular health screenings. She had a degree in Biology, had taught High School classes, and was an intelligent person. She asked a lot of questions regarding her healthcare – until she was rendered incapable of communicating because she was chemically restrained, while the family was lied to about why she could not communicate.

The sad reality of drugging a person is that a hospital or facility can take a sane, well-spoken person with no history of Alzheimer's or Dementia, and actually turn them into an insane, inaudible, mess rather quickly with certain off-label drugs. A nurse wrote a comment on a patient's record, "She looks so peaceful in her demented state." The patient to whom the nurse referred had been given Haldol,

Risperdal, Morphine, and Olanzapine all on that same day, so sure, there probably isn't anyone on earth who wouldn't look demented after that type of abuse of unwarranted medications.

Doctors and hospital staff are not always honest with patients or families.

A general life teaching is that "medical professionals *are* to be trusted, because they are experts in their profession," and that belief tends to stop many from looking deeper. While most doctors are honest, there is a segment of doctors and hospital staff who do not like to be questioned and are not up front about treatment, especially if they are dispensing drugs like antipsychotics for off-label purposes without clinical diagnosis and without patient consent.

Broken rib, hospital acquired MRSA, treated with antipsychotic drugs in hospital

A New Mexico resident summed up her feelings toward a New Mexico hospital's treatment of her mother, "As far as I'm concerned, they would rather kill you than take care of you. I saw how the nurses treated people. I saw how the techs treated people. You are treated like a piece of meat and NOT like a human being. No wonder so many people die when they trust their care to the hospital my mom entered."

Her 85-year-old mother entered a hospital with a broken rib. She was an active person who served as secretary for a service organization, was involved in a nationally known speaking group and had no history of previous health problems. She had been in the hospital for only a week before she began hallucinating and was confused. Prior to being doped, the woman was "kicked out of several areas of the hospital, including ICU because, her daughter said, "They needed her bed for someone else." Her communication level with her family members after landing in this medical center was "One on a scale of one to ten," they said. The family didn't understand why she was having these difficulties since only a week before; she was fine, living alone and involved in community.

She contracted MRSA in the hospital, adding another layer of problems. Many MRSA infections occur in hospitals and healthcare facilities. When infections occur in this manner it is known as healthcare acquired MRSA or HA-MRSA. These Rates of MRSA infection are also increased in hospitalized patients who are treated with quinolones. Healthcare provider-to-patient transfer is common, especially when healthcare providers move from patient to patient without performing necessary hand-washing techniques between patients.

Remember, the 85-year-old patient only entered the hospital for a broken rib. After being doped and catheterized, her organs began to malfunction. Her daughter recognized that the situation was not normal, and insisted on getting her mother released from that hospital into another. The daughter said it was a difficult process to get the hospital to release her. Upon release, she transferred her mother to another hospital. Within 48 hours, she said her mother was communicating and bodily functions began to work again. Bottom line was that the hospital she was transferred to took her off of the antipsychotic medications and unnecessary medications she was being given, and restored her ability to communicate and function. This is another example of placing chemical restraints on a patient, but more importantly, it is an example of a daughter who recognized that something was not right, questioned it, and took action instead of simply accepting what the hospital staff told her.

Most of the information regarding abuse is directed everywhere but at hospitals and doctors. Most fingers are pointed at nursing homes and staff, but most of those residents are under the care of outside doctors or doctors who practice in a hospital. Patients residing in homes are regularly taken to hospitals for urgent care where hospital doctors administer drugs and remedies for their conditions that often include some off label antipsychotics. Doctors hold the key to overmedication of Senior Citizens.

A family member of a Senior Citizen said he was doped in a hospital, and the daughter reports that the call button was intentionally left open to the nurse's station "So they could hear if the man told his family anything about them." The silence of this man, and possibly thousands of others may not be a coincidence in hospitals that are known to engage in this type of abuse. His records reflected heavy antipsychotic sedation without consent or clinical diagnosis of need for the medication.

Drugging of 86 year old man with mild dementia
Reprinted with permission, a media account from 10News I-Team, San Diego, California.

A woman told the 10News I-Team her father was improperly drugged in order to keep him restrained at a local care facility.

"He was a very hard working dentist," said Marian Hollingsworth.

Hollingsworth's father, Dr. Keith Blair, was an accomplished dentist and military veteran. He died last year at the age of 86, but Hollingsworth said the anti-psychotic drugs he was given without consent speeded up her father's death.

"He should've been allowed to go on his own time," she told the I-Team.

The drugs her father was given included Risperdal and Haldol, anti-psychotics that include a warning that says the drugs are "Associated with an increased risk of mortality in senior patients."

"It's a way of controlling them. It keeps him in bed," said Hollingsworth.

Hollingsworth said her father had mild dementia. His health rapidly declined after he went to two local hospitals for leg and back pain, and then was transferred to Arbor Hills Nursing Center in La Mesa.

"He was completely out of it. I shook him on the bed, I hollered his name. I asked the nurse what was going on. I couldn't wake him up. She said, 'Oh, he was sleepy last night.'"

After her father's death, his medical files revealed staff at both the hospitals and the nursing home gave him Risperdal and Haldol without consent. Hollingsworth filed a complaint with the California Department of Health.

"You shouldn't give these medications to people if you know it's going to cause death," said Hollingsworth.

Dr. David Graham, a Food and Drug Administration expert, testified before Congress about the practice of drugging the senior to control them.

"You've probably got 15,000 senior people in nursing homes dying each year from the off-label use of anti-psychotic medications," Graham said.

Experts said the practice is called chemical restraint.

"It's a public health issue and I believe it's a public health issue because the companies are laughing all the way to the bank," added Graham.

Longtime senior advocate Carole Herman is angered by the use of chemical restraints.

"We are actually paying for senior abuse in this country," Herman said.

Herman told the I-Team taxpayers foot the bill for anti-psychotic drugs given to senior people just to keep them quiet.

"You don't have to feed them, you don't have to take them to the bathroom," said Herman.

She blames what she calls the profit-driven nursing home industry and weak state regulations.

"Maybe if there was more enforcement, maybe they would clean up their act," said Herman.

Since 2006, the California Department of Public Health has issued 31 deficiencies, or written warnings, for the use of chemical restraint.

Most recently, in the Kern Valley Hospital District, a nursing home in Bakersfield got more than a warning. The home saw former and current employees indicted on criminal charges for doping up patients to keep them in bed.

Arbor Hills Nursing Center said their staff does not drug seniors. When asked about the case involving Blair, their legal staff issued the following statement that said, in part: "Arbor Hills Nursing Center met all applicable standards of care and did not in any way compromise his condition or cause him any harm."

The two hospitals where Blair first stayed and Arbor Hills all received deficiencies relating to how they administered anti-psychotic drugs, the I-Team learned.

"No one goes to jail, no one has anything on their records," said Hollingsworth.

Hollingsworth said the best advice she can give is for people to educate themselves about what assisted care facilities can and cannot do, and then serve as strong advocates for their senior relatives.

ABUSE: ANTIPSYCHOTIC DRUGGING OF SENIORS BY HOSPITALS AND NURSING HOMES

A U.S. Legislator once said, "If you walk into a nursing home and see seniors sitting in wheelchairs with their heads hanging down —- you should be mad as hell." The picture that statement leaves in one's mind is a picture of many facilities full of senior who have been drugged (chemically restrained), or who have been rolled to the main room in their wheel chairs because it is easier to control them and watch over them with limited staffing. More importantly, it is against the law, and, the good news is that some are headed to jail for overmedicating seniors.

A thirty-six year old was asked recently why senior citizens are so "Out of it in facilities," with heads hanging down, or lifeless heads thrown back with open mouths. Her response was, "I just thought that is what happens to all old people. I didn't know until this book was written and researched, that they were actually being doped. Now I will notice, and report facilities that do that to our senior citizens."

A seventy-five year old woman said, "I'm seventy-five, and I had no idea that rows of seniors in wheel chairs next to a nurses station represented highly tranquilized people who were actually being drugged so small staffs could keep an eye on them with no chance of them getting out of their chairs. Now, I know what signs to recognize. Why is no one warning us?"

THE FULL STORY

DIRECTOR OF NURSING FACES PRISON TIME FOR OVERMEDICATION

Not all nursing home neglect is a simple matter of unintended mistakes or oversights that cause harm to residents. At times there are far more organized, repeat efforts that place dozens (or even hundreds) of residents at risk of serious harm and death. In those more far-reaching cases, the consequences may be severe for those who engage in the conduct, including nursing home staff members, nurses, doctors, and administrators. While family members of those harmed can file civil lawsuits seeking accountability, criminal charges can also be filed (by the state) if criminal laws are violated.

Three Year Prison Sentence: That is what happened in a case that ended in a Director of Nursing at a long-term care facility being sentenced to three years in prison for conduct related to medication of facility residents. The defendant in the case pled no contest to state criminal charges alleging senior abuse, which led to the death of a resident. Interestingly, she also faced "assault with a deadly weapon" charges—with the weapon being the drug Risperdal.

Essentially, the charges stem from widespread use of chemical restraints. The legal documents in the matter argue that administrators "Allowed the staff to forcibly administer psychotropic medications to patients for their own convenience, rather than for their patients' therapeutic interests."

According to stories on the situation, the Director of Nursing grossly deviated from accepted practices in prescribing the dangerous medications. She would lead interdisciplinary meetings where she had a pharmacist write prescriptions for "troublesome" residents. Of course, she determined who was or was not considered "troublesome." The entire purpose of the prescriptions was to control the residents and make them easier to handle. It is a textbook example of blatant misuse of these antipsychotic drugs.

One obvious problem, of course, is that nurses are not allowed to order medication. Yet, notwithstanding the proper protocol, the pharmacist in question actually wrote out the orders and filled the prescription. A doctor eventually did sign off on the orders, but it was often months after the medications were actually given. Even then, the doctor rarely investigated the matter to determine if the drugs were necessary for the well being of the patient or simply for the comfort of the caregivers. Prescription protocols exist for a reason. When they are obviously violated—as was suggested in this case—then there must be consequences. Misuse of medications not only greatly reduces the quality of life for residents but it can lead to severe injury or even death.

Misuse of antipsychotic drugs in nursing homes remains a problem throughout the country. More and more attention is being drawn to the issue, but we still have a long way to go. If you suspect problematic use of medications for a loved one, please do not stay silent. Stand up, ask questions, and demand that you receive answers about how the drugs are necessary for therapeutic reasons. (Citation: Legal forum recapitulation)

CALIFORNIA TAKING ACTION

U.S. Senate Special Committee on Aging Forum, December 8, 2010; Testimony of Patricia L. McGinnis, California Advocates for Nursing Home Reform.

Mr. Chairman, members of the Committee, I thank you for this opportunity to participate in today's very important forum. I'd particularly like to thank the staff of the Senate Special Committee on Aging for organizing the forum. My name is Pat McGinnis and I am the Executive Director of California Advocates for Nursing Home Reform, a nonprofit organization in San Francisco that assists and advocates for people who need long-term care.

For more than 25 years, our organization has heard first-hand the confusion, distress, and loss that is associated with the misuse of antipsychotic drugs and other psychoactive medications to chemically restrain nursing home residents who have dementia. I want to start by reading a statement about nursing home drugging:

"Excessive use of tranquilizers can quickly reduce an ambulatory patient to a zombie, confining the patient to a chair or bed, causing the patient's muscles to atrophy from inaction and causing general health to deteriorate quickly...It appears many doctors give blanket instructions to nursing home staffs for the use of tranquilizer drugs on patients who do not need them."

This statement sounds as if it was made very recently, but it was actually made before Congress in 1970 and included in a 1975 report prepared by the Senate Special Committee on Aging titled "Drugs in Nursing Homes: Misuse, High Costs, and Kickbacks." Unbelievably, the problems have worsened in the 35 years since the Senate detailed them.

Today, the drugging problem has reached epidemic levels. Nationally, more than 350,000 nursing home residents – one of every four residents – are given antipsychotic drugs. The vast majority of these residents suffer from dementia and are receiving the drugs off-label, meaning the drugs are provided to control behavior, and not to treat a diagnosed mental illness.

The way antipsychotic drugs are used in nursing homes is a form of senior abuse. Instead of providing individualized care, many homes indiscriminately use these drugs to sedate and subdue residents. Antipsychotic drugs carry black box warnings indicating that their use nearly doubles a person with dementia's risk of death, but nursing home residents and their representatives are rarely informed about these warnings. Antipsychotics don't just hasten death; they often turn seniors into people their own families barely recognize by dulling their memories, sapping their personalities and crushing their spirits.

We would like to make it clear to the Committee that, while some psychoactive drugs may have positive benefits for the treatment of depression, anxiety, or even dementias, the drugs we are focusing on today are antipsychotics, such as Seroquel, Risperdal, Zyprexa and Haldol, which are designed for the treatment of those with schizophrenia.

There are many reasons that antipsychotic drugs have become the first alternative for intervention in nursing homes, particularly for residents who exhibit agitation or aggression. Drugs are cheaper than staff – at least on a short-term basis – as Medicare pays for most of these drugs. Additionally, many doctors who prescribe these drugs and the pharmacists who dispense them for those with dementia are ignorant of the risks and effects of the drugs prescribed and, in some cases, are intentionally misled by pharmaceutical companies. Just since 2009, over four billion dollars has been paid to the federal government by drug manufacturers to settle charges of fraudulent marketing, false claims, and kickback schemes. Finally, reimbursement for alternative therapies, particularly for therapists, psychologists and psychiatrists are limited under both Medicare and Medicaid.

It is a shameful situation, but there are some positives in this situation as well. The biggest problem with drugging, the pervasive culture that treats drugs as the first measure in behavioral control for people with dementia, is also a gateway to the inevitable solution. If we are able to shift this culture and de-emphasize drugging, we can dramatically reduce the misuse of antipsychotic drugs for people with dementia and, most importantly, improve their quality of life.

We already know what an effective campaign to shift this culture looks like. Over the last 25 years there has been a pronounced effort by consumers, advocates, the government, providers and others to stop the inappropriate use of physical restraints in nursing homes. The result has been startling. Physical restraint use has dropped from more than 25% of all residents to less than 3%. The key has been concentrated, sustained education, awareness, effort, oversight and enforcement.

CANHR has initiated a campaign to stop drugging in California and we are hoping that it will take root throughout the nation. Our campaign combines practical advice for residents, and their families, on how to stop misuse of the drugs, along with a broad movement to raise awareness, strengthen laws and enforcement, and target offenders. This past summer we launched a first-of-its-kind website on this campaign that includes a great deal of information to help consumers learn about their rights, the risks of the drugs, and most importantly, the effective alternatives such as those highlighted today. The site includes a well-received video series and a free advocacy guide, "Toxic Medicine" that we have distributed to the Committee.

We've also posted specific information on each California nursing home's use of antipsychotic drugs to help consumers avoid facilities that are using these drugs indiscriminately. The information shows that a resident's risk of being drugged varies tremendously by nursing home, with some facilities reporting no use of antipsychotic drugs while others drug all or nearly all of their residents.

The Campaign also has a political component, including a petition to the Governor and proposed legislation to strengthen informed consent requirements. I cannot emphasize enough the importance of informed consent in resolving this problem. It's not just about informing people about the risks and alternatives to these drugs, it's about treating people who suffer from dementia with dignity and respect by recognizing their right to make decisions about their medical treatment. A culture of respect for victims of this disease will go a long way toward curbing the drugging problem.

We believe our campaign is a good model for a national campaign on this issue. I urge the Committee and Congress to hold hearings on this problem and to embrace the recent national recommendations made by Consumer Voice to stop the chemical restraint of nursing home residents. I will discuss a couple of the key recommendations.

First, Congress should adopt laws protecting the rights of nursing home residents to give informed consent before they are drugged. American common law and various state statutes protect the right of informed consent, but it does not appear in federal nursing home law. Codifying informed consent requirements would give national priority to the concept that people with dementia, as any other health care recipients, deserve complete information about proposed treatments and the right to ultimately decide what medications they take.

Second, we propose an education campaign to elevate the issue of antipsychotic drugs for people with dementia into the national consciousness. The campaign would focus on people with dementia, their families and advocates, as well as health care providers. For people with dementia and their families and advocates, the campaign would offer information about antipsychotic drugs – from the types of medications that are most often abused, to side effects and Black Box warnings, to the supremacy of alternative approaches that we've heard about today. As part of the education campaign, CMS should post each nursing home's drugging rate on Nursing Home Compare so that consumers can locate nursing homes that don't use antipsychotic drugs as a substitute for basic dementia care.

For health care providers, the education campaign would offer best practices for doctors, pharmacists and facilities, stressing that, if antipsychotic drugs are to be used at all, they should only be used as a last resort after all non-pharmacological interventions have been attempted and failed. The essence of these practices should be the promotion of individualized care.

Individualized care fosters non-pharmacological interventions by placing a premium on relationships with people who have dementia, and dignified care approaches such as increased exercise, formal activities, and pain management. A recent study in Vermont was able to dramatically reduce the use of antipsychotics in nursing homes by focusing on relatively simple alternatives. One alternative was learning more about a resident's past, so as to better understand the resident's needs and personality. Another alternative was giving nursing home staff more consistent schedules so they work with the same residents and learn to pick up on early signs of trouble and circumvent bad behaviors.

What is especially helpful about non-pharmacological interventions is that they are less costly than drugging. Aside from the obvious high costs of the drugs themselves is the very expensive health outcomes they often precipitate – falls, infections, strokes, and hospitalizations that add to the escalating costs of Medicare and Medicaid. Using pills to substitute for one-on-one care, or for adequate staffing, turns out to be, not only bad medicine, but also a poor use of resources. Reimbursement for alternative psychotherapeutic interventions, particularly psychotherapy services, should be expanded.

Congress should investigate and the U.S. Government should continue to aggressively pursue drug companies' marketing of off-label uses of antipsychotic drugs for nursing home residents.

Heightened awareness and increased information can make a major difference in the quality of lives of people with dementia.

The massive reduction in physical restraint use in nursing homes is concrete evidence that federal leadership, coupled with an empowered consumer voice, can reach the far corners of the local nursing home, change the practices of health care providers and influence care in a way that dramatically improves the lives of our citizens with dementia.

Here is what we know:

1. The misuse and overuse of psychotropic drugs for people with dementia is at an all-time high;
2. There are many non-pharmacological alternatives to drugging that not only lead to better outcomes for people with dementia, but are also much less costly; and
3. A campaign to end over-drugging could improve the lives of perhaps millions of people with dementia.

Thirty-five years ago, the Senate Special Committee on Aging urged a "coordinated attack" on dangerous drug misuse in nursing homes, led by federal and state officials. With your help, we can finally begin that attack. Everyone here has demonstrated the sincerity of their concern for the plight of people with Alzheimer's disease and other dementia-related illnesses. We call upon our national leaders to not only join a campaign to end over-drugging, but to lead it.

PART IV

SECRETS ABOUT MEDICATIONS THAT LEAVE YOU VULNERABLE TO MISTREATMENT

CHAPTER 14

ARE SENIOR CITIZENS ERRONEOUSLY BEING DIAGNOSED WITH ALZHEIMER'S AND DEMENTIA WHEN IT MAY BE MEDICINES OR LACK OF VITAMIN B-12 CAUSING MEMORY PROBLEMS?

If you can't think clearly, someone will take advantage of you. If your memory is not up to par, it's easier for someone to take your car away from you or put you in a facility. It's easier for someone to take your money.

Due to the vulnerability caused by memory loss, be aware of ways you can protect yourself. Take extra care to be aware of what you are putting in your system, or what you should be taking that can affect your memory.

Recently, a woman was so forgetful that everyone was seriously worried about her. They just knew she had Alzheimer's or Dementia. Not true. A good, kind, caring doctor discovered that his patient had a vitamin deficiency. After a couple of weeks and replacing her needed vitamins, his patient was experiencing no forgetful episodes, and was back to her schedule, a busy, detail oriented life. Sometimes, it's easy to assume the worst. The happy endings do occur, however, it is always imperative to contact your doctor to discuss medication before discontinuing or adding any drug, or trying a remedy.

The mental state of many seniors, a laundry list of symptoms, and diagnosis that may or may not be accurate, could be the direct result of drug interactions, side effects, and unnecessary overmedication. Look into the medicine cabinet of a senior person living at home. You will probably find a pharmacy of sorts filled with prescriptions, many of which may or may not be needed, some which have stated interactions with other drugs in the cabinet, and most that carry serious side effects. Someone who cares about a senior loved one must check these interactions between medicines. Challenge medical providers, hospitals, doctors, dentists and facilities on behalf of the senior about any noticeable change in a loved one that very well could be medicine induced.

Do some research before jumping to a conclusion and assuming that your family member has Alzheimer's or Dementia. Check the medication being consumed first.

In a hospital, a senior woman was given three medications at the same time with stated side effects that could cause memory loss. Clearly, removing her from the medication would have been the appropriate thing to do, but instead, she was given a memory test after consumption of the three medications and it was then noted on her records that she was being diagnosed with Alzheimer's. Understand that ten days before she entered the hospital, she was of sound mind, lived alone, drove, and had never had memory problems. So in order to believe that it was the truth, one would have to believe that Alzheimer's just suddenly appeared over a span of ten days in the care of the hospital.

SOME MEDICINES THAT CAN CAUSE MEMORY LOSS

Memory loss increases your risk of mistreatment from others

AARP lists a short list of types of drugs that can cause memory loss. As a side effect, there is a chance that specific drugs within a drug type may be responsible for memory loss. Antianxiety drugs, Cholesterol drugs, Anti-seizure drugs, Antidepressant drugs, Narcotic painkillers, Parkinson's drugs, Hypertension drugs, Sleeping aids, Incontinence drugs, and Antihistamines.

MEMORY PROBLEMS THAT ARE NORMAL, NOT ALZHEIMER'S OR DEMENTIA

Don't be so quick to label a person. Just look at how quickly many people say, "I think she is getting Alzheimer's, she forgot where she put the milk and her glasses again." Think again. The following are considered to be normal. National Institute on Aging lists *normal changes* in memory that can have nothing to do with Alzheimer's.

AGE-RELATED CHANGES IN MEMORY

Forgetfulness can be a normal part of aging. As people get older, changes occur in all parts of the body, including the brain. As a result, some people may notice that it takes longer to learn new things, they don't remember information as well as they did, or they lose things like their glasses. These usually are signs of mild forgetfulness, not serious memory problems.

Some older adults also find that they don't do as well as younger people on complex memory or learning tests. Scientists have found, though, that given enough time, healthy older people can do as well as younger people do on these tests. In fact, as they age, healthy adults usually improve in areas of mental ability such as vocabulary.

OTHER CAUSES OF MEMORY LOSS

Some memory problems are related to health issues that may be treatable. Medication side effects, vitamin B12 deficiency, chronic alcoholism, tumors or infections in the brain, or blood clots in the brain can cause memory loss or possibly dementia. Some thyroid, kidney, or liver disorders also can lead to memory loss.

Emotional problems, such as stress, anxiety, or depression can make a person more forgetful and can be mistaken for dementia. For instance, someone who has recently retired or who is coping with the death of a spouse, relative, or friend may feel sad, lonely, worried, or bored. Trying to deal with these life changes leaves some people confused or forgetful.

The confusion and forgetfulness caused by emotions usually are temporary and go away when the feelings fade. Supportive friends and family can ease the emotional problems, but if these feelings last for a long time, it is important to get help from a doctor or counselor. Treatment may include counseling, medication, or both.

Worth repeating: National Institute on Aging advises that there are other conditions that may cause memory loss or dementia including:

- medication side effects
- chronic alcoholism
- tumors or infections in the brain
- blood clots in the brain
- vitamin B12 deficiency
- some thyroid, kidney, or liver disorders

Serious reasons for concern though may come with the following symptoms that can signal Alzheimer's or dementia:

- Asking the same question or repeating the same story over and over
- Becoming lost in familiar places
- Being unable to follow directions
- Getting disoriented about time, people, and places
- Neglecting personal safety, hygiene, and nutrition

If normal forgetfulness were a serious sign, there would be a lot of teenagers and adults being labeled with Alzheimer's. Count the times you mislaid your cell phone, glasses, house key, or forgot and locked the keys in the house. How many students forget their homework? How many non-senior individuals have to turn around and go back to the house because they forgot something? How many calls does a locksmith receive on any given day to retrieve keys that were locked in cars, because someone forgot to take them out of the car before locking it?

REPORTS OF MEMORY LOSS FROM STATIN MEDICATIONS

FDA has been investigating reports of cognitive impairment from statin use for several years. The agency has reviewed databases that record reports of bad reactions to drugs and statin clinical trials that included assessments of cognitive function.

The reports about memory loss, forgetfulness and confusion span all statin products and all age groups. Amy G. Egan, M.D., M.P.H., deputy director for safety in FDA's Division of Metabolism and Endocrinology Products (DMEP), says these experiences are rare but that those affected often report feeling "fuzzy" or unfocused in their thinking.

In general, the symptoms were not serious and were reversible within a few weeks after the patient stopped using the statin. Some people affected in this way had been taking the medicine for a day; others had been taking it for years.

What should patients do if they fear that statin use could be clouding their thinking? "Talk to your health care professional," Egan says. "Don't stop taking the medication; the consequences to your heart could be far greater."

This new information should not scare people off statins, says Amy G. Egan, "The value of statins in preventing heart disease has been clearly established," she says. "Their benefit is indisputable, but they need to be taken with care and knowledge of their side effects."

FDA will be changing the drug labels of popular statin products to reflect these new concerns. (These labels are not the sticker attached to a prescription drug bottle, but the package insert with details about a prescription medication, including side effects.)

WARNING: INCREASED CHANCE OF DEATH WITH HALDOL FOR SENIOR

FDA has included this warning on haloperidol (haldol): Studies have shown that older adults with dementia (a brain disorder that affects the ability to remember, think clearly, communicate, perform daily activities and may cause changes in mood and personality) who take antipsychotics (medications for mental illness) such as haloperidol have an increased chance of death during treatment.

The Food and Drug Administration (FDA) do not approve haloperidol for the treatment of behavior problems in older adults with dementia. Talk to the doctor who prescribed this medication if you, a family member, or someone you care for has dementia and is taking haloperidol. For more information, visit the FDA website: http://www.fda.gov/Drugs

PART V

ALL WE WANT IS YOUR MONEY

THE ABUSE OF SCAMS

CHAPTER 15

LEAVE US ALONE, WE WILL NO LONGER BE YOUR MEAL TICKET

Scams against Senior Citizens (National Council on Aging)

- Health Care/Medicare/Health Insurance Fraud

Since every U.S. citizen or permanent resident over age 65 qualifies for Medicare, there is rarely any need for a scam artist to research what private health insurance company older people have in order to scam them out of some money.

In these types of scams, perpetrators may pose as a Medicare representative to get older people to give them their personal information, or they will provide bogus services for senior people at makeshift mobile clinics, then use the personal information they have gotten from seniors to bill Medicare and pocket the money.

- Counterfeit Prescription Drugs

Most commonly, counterfeit drug scams operate on the Internet, where seniors increasingly go to find better prices on specialized medications.

This scam is growing in popularity—since 2000 the FDA has investigated an average of 20 such cases per year, up from five a year in the 1990s.

The danger is that besides paying money for something that will not help a person's medical condition, victims may purchase unsafe substances that can inflict even more harm. This scam can be as hard on the body as it is on the wallet.

- Funeral & Cemetery Scams

The FBI warns about two types of funeral and cemetery fraud perpetrated on seniors.

In one approach, scammers read obituaries and call or attend the funeral service of a complete stranger to take advantage of the grieving widow or widower. Claiming the deceased had an outstanding debt with the scammer, the criminal will try to extort money from relatives to settle the fake debts.

Another tactic of disreputable funeral homes is to capitalize on family members' unfamiliarity with the considerable cost of funeral services by adding unnecessary charges to the bill.

In one common scam of this type, funeral directors will insist that a casket, usually one of the most expensive parts of funeral services, is necessary even when performing a direct cremation, which can be accomplished with a cardboard casket rather than an expensive display or burial casket.

- Fraudulent Anti-Aging Products

In a society bombarded with images of the young and beautiful, it's not surprising that some older people feel the need to conceal their age in order to participate more fully in social circles and the workplace. After all, 60 is the new 40, right?

It is in this spirit that many senior citizens seek out new treatments and medications to maintain a youthful appearance, putting them at risk of scammers.

Whether it's fake Botox, like a variety in Arizona that netted its distributors (who were convicted and jailed in 2006) $1.5 million in barely a year, or completely bogus homeopathic remedies that do absolutely nothing, there is money in the anti-aging business.

Botox scams, with renegade labs creating versions of the real thing, may still be working with the root ingredient, botulism neurotoxin, which is one of the most toxic substances known to science. A bad batch can have health consequences far beyond wrinkles or drooping neck muscles.

- Telemarketing

Perhaps the most common scheme is when scammers use fake telemarketing calls to prey on older people, who as a group make twice as many purchases over the phone than the national average.

While the image of the lonely senior citizen with nobody to talk to may have something to do with this, it is far more likely that older people are more familiar with shopping over the phone, and therefore might not be fully aware of the risk.

With no face-to-face interaction, and no paper trail, these scams are incredibly hard to trace. Also, once a successful deal has been made, the buyer's name is then shared with similar schemers looking for easy targets, sometimes defrauding the same person repeatedly.

Examples of telemarketing fraud include:

"The Pigeon Drop"

The con artist tells the individual that he/she has found a large sum of money and is willing to split it if the person will make a "good faith" payment by withdrawing funds from his/her bank account. Often, a second con artist is involved, posing as a lawyer, banker, or some other trustworthy stranger.

"The Fake Accident Ploy"

The con artist gets the victim to wire or send money on the pretext that the person's child or another relative is in the hospital and needs the money.

"Charity Scams"

Money is solicited for fake charities. This often occurs after natural disasters.

- Internet Fraud

While using the Internet is a great skill at any age, the slower speed of adoption among some older people makes them easier targets for automated Internet scams that are ubiquitous on the web and email programs.

Pop-up browser windows simulating virus-scanning software will fool victims into either downloading a fake anti-virus program (at a substantial cost) or an actual virus that will open up whatever information is on the user's computer to scammers.

Their unfamiliarity with the less visible aspects of browsing the web (firewalls and built-in virus protection, for example) makes seniors especially susceptible to such traps. One example includes:

Email/Phishing Scams

A senior receives email messages that appear to be from a legitimate company or institution, asking the person to "update" or "verify" his or her personal information or a senior receives emails that appear to be from the IRS about a tax refund.

- Investment Schemes

Because many seniors find themselves planning for retirement and managing their savings once they finish working, a number of investment schemes have been targeted at seniors looking to safeguard their cash for their later years.

From pyramid schemes like Bernie Madoff's (which counted a number of senior citizens among its victims) to fables of a Nigerian prince looking for a partner to claim inheritance money, to complex financial products that many economists don't even understand, investment schemes have long been a successful way to take advantage of older people.

- Homeowner/Reverse Mortgage Scams

Scammers like to take advantage of the fact that many people above a certain age own their homes, a valuable asset that increases the potential dollar value of a certain scam.

A particularly elaborate property tax scam in San Diego saw fraudsters sending personalized letters to different property owners apparently on behalf of the County Assessor's Office. The letter, made to look official but displaying only public information, would identify the property's assessed value and offer the homeowner, for a fee of course, to arrange for a reassessment of the property's value and therefore the tax burden associated with it.

Closely related, the reverse mortgage scam has mushroomed in recent years. With legitimate reverse mortgages increasing in frequency more than 1,300% between 1999 and 2008, scammers are taking advantage of this new popularity.

Unlike legal refinancing unsecured reverse mortgages can lead property owners to lose their homes when the perpetrators offer money or a free house somewhere else in exchange for the title to the property.

- Sweepstakes & Lottery Scams

This simple scam is one that many are familiar with, and it capitalizes on the notion that "there's no such thing as a free lunch."

Here, scammers inform their mark that they have won a lottery or sweepstakes of some kind, and need to make some sort of payment to unlock the supposed prize. Often, seniors will be sent a check that they can deposit in their bank account, knowing that while it shows up in their account immediately, it will take a few days before the (fake) check is rejected.

During that time, the criminals will quickly collect money for supposed fees or taxes on the prize, which they pocket while the victim has the "prize money" removed from his or her account as soon as the check bounces.

- The Grandparent Scam

The Grandparent Scam is so simple and so devious because it uses one of the older adults' most reliable assets, their hearts.

Scammers will place a call to an older person and when the mark picks up, they will say something along the lines of: "Hi Grandma, do you know who this is?" When the unsuspecting grandparent guesses the name of the grandchild the scammer most sounds like, the scammer has established a fake identity without having done a lick of background research.

Once "in," the fake grandchild will usually ask for money to solve some unexpected financial problem (overdue rent, payment for car repairs, etc.), to be paid via Western Union or MoneyGram, which don't always require identification to collect.

At the same time, the scam artist begs the grandparent "Please don't tell my parents, they would kill me."

While the sums from such a scam are likely to be in the hundreds, the very fact that no research is needed makes this a scam that can be perpetrated over and over at very little cost to the scammer.

STRANGERS AND THOSE CLOSE TO YOU TO BE WATCHED

You should be aware that you are at risk from strangers—and from those closest to you. More than 90% of all reported senior abuse is committed by the older person's own family members, most often their adult children, followed by grandchildren, nieces and nephews, and others.

Common tactics include depleting a joint checking account, promising but not delivering care in exchange for money or property, outright theft, and other forms of abuse, including physical abuse, threats, intimidation, and neglect of basic care needs.

Everyone is at risk of financial abuse, even people without high incomes or assets. Understand the top 10 most common scams targeting seniors, so you can spot one before it's too late.

Don't isolate yourself—stay involved!

Isolation is a huge risk factor for senior abuse. Most family violence only occurs behind closed doors, and senior abuse is no exception.

Some older people self-isolate, by withdrawing from the larger community. Others are isolated because they lose the ability to drive, see, or walk about on their own. Some seniors' fear being victimized by purse snatchings, and muggings if they venture out.

Visit Seniorcare Locator to find services nearby that can help you stay active. Or contact your local senior center to get involved.

Always tell solicitors: "I never buy from (or give to) anyone who calls or visits me unannounced. Send me something in writing."

Don't buy from an unfamiliar company, and always ask for and wait until you receive written material about any offer or charity.

Neighborhood children you know who are selling Girl Scout cookies, or school fundraising items may be an exception, but a good rule of thumb is to never donate to anything if you are required to write your credit card information on any forms.

It's also good practice to obtain a salesperson's name, business identity, telephone number, street address, mailing address, and business license number before you transact business.

And always take your time in making a decision.

Shred all receipts that include your credit card number.

Identity theft is a huge business. To protect yourself, invest in—and use—a paper shredder.

Monitor your bank and credit card statements and never give out personal information over the phone to someone who initiates the contact with you.

Sign up for the "Do Not Call" list and ask to be removed from mailing lists.

Visit www.donotcall.gov to stop telemarketers from contacting you.

Be careful with your mail. Do not let incoming mail sit in your mailbox for a long time. When sending out sensitive mail, consider dropping it off at a secure collection box or directly at the post office.

To get more tips on protecting yourself from fraud, visit www.Onguardonline.gov. The site has interactive games to help you be a smarter consumer on issues related to spyware, lottery scams, and other swindles.

Use direct deposit for benefit checks to prevent checks from being stolen from the mailbox. Using direct deposit ensures that checks go right into your accounts and are protected. Clever scammers or even scrupulous loved ones have been known to steal benefit checks right out of mailboxes or from seniors' homes if the checks are lying around.

Never give your credit card, banking, Social Security, Medicare, or other personal information over the phone unless you initiated the call.

Misuse of Medicare dollars is one of the largest scams involving seniors. Common schemes include billing for services never delivered, and selling unneeded devices or services to beneficiaries.

Protect your Medicare number as you do your credit card, banking, and Social Security numbers, and do not allow anyone else to use it. Be wary of salespeople trying to sell you something they claim will be paid for by Medicare. Review your Medicare statements to be sure you have in fact received the services billed, and report suspicious activities to 1-800-MEDICARE.

Be skeptical of all unsolicited offers and thoroughly do your research.

Be an informed consumer. Take the time to call and shop around before making a purchase. Take a friend with you who may offer some perspective to help you make difficult decisions.

Also, carefully read all contracts and purchasing agreements before signing and make certain that all of your requirements have been put in writing.

Understand all contract cancellation and refund terms.

As a general rule governing all of your interactions as a consumer, do not allow yourself to be pressured into making purchases, signing contracts, or committing funds. These decisions are yours and yours alone.

PROTECT YOUR LOVED ONES: SIGNS TO LOOK FOR

If you know or care for an older adult, here are some additional warning signs that may indicate they are the victims of financial abuse:

There are unusual recent changes in the person's accounts, including atypical withdrawals, new person(s) added, or sudden use of a senior's ATM or credit card.

The senior suddenly appears confused, unkempt, and afraid.

Utility, rent, mortgage, medical, or other essential bills are unpaid, despite adequate income.

A caregiver will not allow others access to the senior.

There are piled up sweepstakes mailings, magazine subscriptions, or "free gifts," which means they may be on "sucker lists."

Every state operates an Adult Protect Services (APS) program, which is responsible for receiving and investigating reports of senior abuse, neglect, and exploitation, and in most states, the abuse of younger adults with severe disabilities.

APS is the "911" for senior abuse. Anyone who suspects senior abuse, neglect, or exploitation should make a report. The reporter's identity is protected. APS services are confidential, so the reporter may not be able to learn the outcome of the case.

APS respects the right of older persons to make their own decisions and to live their lives on their own terms. In cases of cognitive impairment, however, APS will take steps to protect the older person to the degree possible.

STEPS TO TAKE IF YOU'RE A VICTIM

If you think you've been scammed, don't be afraid or embarrassed to talk about it—waiting could only make it worse. Immediately:

- Call your bank and/or credit card issuer.
- Cancel any debit or credit cards linked to the stolen account.
- Reset your personal identification number(s).

- Contact legal services and Adult Protective Services if warranted. To find your local offices, visit Seniorcare Locator or call them toll-free at 1-800-677-1116 weekdays 9 a.m. to 8 p.m. ET.

Far too many older adults fall prey to scammers who are looking to make a quick buck. Here are 22 tips that can help you steer clear of them and stay safe.

HEALTH INSURANCE FRAUD

- Never sign blank insurance claim forms.
- Never give blanket permission to a medical provider to bill for services rendered.
- Ask your medical providers what they will charge and what you will be expected to pay out-of-pocket.
- Carefully review your insurer's explanation of the benefits statement. Call your insurer and provider if you have questions.
- Do not do business with door-to-door or telephone salespeople who tell you that services of medical equipment are free.
- Give your insurance/Medicare identification only to those who have provided you with medical services.
- Keep accurate records of all health care appointments.
- Know if your physician ordered equipment for you.

MEDICARE SCAMS

- Protect your Medicare number as you do your credit card numbers, and do not allow anyone else to use it.
- Be wary of salespeople trying to sell you something they claim will be paid for by Medicare.
- Review your Medicare statements to be sure you have in fact received the services billed.
- Report suspicious activities to 1-800-MEDICARE.

TELEMARKETING SCAMS

- Don't buy from an unfamiliar company.
- Always ask for and wait until you receive written material about any offer or charity.
- Obtain a salesperson's name, business identity, telephone number, street address, mailing address, and business license number before you transact business.
- Always take your time in making a decision.
- If you have information about a fraud, report it to state, local, or federal law enforcement agencies.

HOME REPAIR OR CONTRACTOR FRAUD

- Be an informed consumer. Take the time to call and shop around before making a purchase. Take a friend with you who may offer some perspective to help you make difficult decisions.
- Carefully read all contracts and purchasing agreements before signing and make certain that all of your requirements have been put in writing. Make sure you understand all contract cancellation and refund terms.
- As a general rule take control of all of your transactions as a consumer. Do not allow yourself to be pressured into making purchases, signing contracts, or committing funds. These decisions are yours and yours alone.

Learn more about scams and how to avoid them at www.ncoa.org/SavvySeniors

CHAPTER 16

FAMOUS ACTOR ABUSED

Testimony of Mickey Rooney U.S. Senate Special Committee on Aging

March 2, 2011

Chairman Kohl, Ranking Member Corker and Members of the Committee, my name is Mickey Rooney and I want to thank you for the opportunity to testify today. We are here today on a critical issue – preventing the abuse, neglect and financial exploitation of seniors. Unfortunately, I am testifying before the committee today, not just as a concerned citizen, but also as a victim of senior abuse myself.

Throughout my life, I have been blessed with the love and support of family, friends, and fans. I have worked almost my entire lifetime of ninety years to entertain and please other people. I've worked hard and diligently. But even with this success, someone close to me stole my money. I was unable to avoid becoming a victim of senior abuse.

Senior abuse comes in many different forms – physical abuse, emotional abuse, or financial abuse. Each one is devastating in its own right. Many times, sadly, as with my situation, the senior abuse involves a family member. When that happens, you feel scared, disappointed, angry, and you can't believe this is happening to you. You feel overwhelmed. The strength you need to fight it is complicated. You're afraid, but you're also thinking about your other family members. You're thinking about the potential criticism of your family and friends. They may not want to accept the dysfunction that you need to share. Because you love your family, and for other reasons, you might feel hesitant to come forward. You might not be able to make rational decisions. What other people see as generosity may, in reality, be the exploitation, manipulation, and sadly, emotional blackmail of older, more vulnerable members of the American public.

I know because it happened to me. My money was taken and misused. When I asked for information, I was told that I couldn't have any of my own information. I was told it was "for my own good" and that "it was none of my business." I was literally left powerless.

You can be in control of your life one minute, and in the next minute, you have absolutely no control. Sometimes this happens quickly, but other times it is very gradual. You wonder when it truly began. In my case, I was eventually and completely stripped of the ability to make even the most basic decisions in my own life.

Over the course of time, my daily life became unbearable. Worse, it seemed to happen out of nowhere. At first, it was something small, something I could control. But then it became something sinister that was completely out of control. I felt trapped, scared, used, and frustrated. But above all, I felt helpless. For years I suffered silently. I couldn't muster the courage to seek the help I knew I needed. Even when I tried to speak up, I was told to be quiet. It seemed like no one believed me.

But I never gave up. I continued to share my story with others. I told them about the abuse I have suffered. I am now taking steps to right all the wrongs that were committed against me. I am so thankful to my family, friends, and many fans all over the world that have expressed their love and support for me.

Ladies and Gentleman of the Committee, I didn't tell you my story so you would feel sympathy for me. I came here for you to think of the millions of us seniors. I am here today because it is so important that I share my story with others, especially those who may be watching at home, suffering silently as I was.

To those seniors and especially senior veterans like myself, I want to tell you this: You are not alone and you have nothing to be ashamed of. You deserve better. You have the right to control your own life, to be happy, and not live in fear. Please, for yourself, end the cycle of abuse, and do not allow yourself to be silenced any longer. Tell your story to anyone who will listen and above all, HAVE HOPE. Someone will hear you. If we all stand strong together and speak up, we can begin to take the necessary steps to end the cycle of senior abuse.

If senior abuse happened to me, Mickey Rooney, it can happen to anyone. Myself, who I am, what I hope to be, and what I was, was taken from me. And I'm asking you to stop this NOW.

PART VI

STATE BY STATE MONITORING OF LIVING ACCOMODATIONS

CHAPTER 17

HOW YOUR STATE MONITORS ASSISTED LIVING FACILITIES

This section was written by Robert L. Mollica, Ed.D., Senior Program Director National Academy for State Health Policy Washington, AHRQ Publication No. 06-M051-EF

SECTION 1. INTRODUCTION AND OVERVIEW INTRODUCTION

Assisted living has grown rapidly as an important source of services in residential settings for older people. Because of this rapid growth and differences among States in how assisted living is defined and licensed, and even what it is called, older people and families need information to understand what assisted living is, how it may meet their needs, and how to choose a facility. This report was commissioned by the Agency for Healthcare Quality and Research to describe the extent of information that is available to consumers and families from State agencies, and to describe State oversight policies and practices.

Assisted living has emerged as a popular choice for people who need supportive and health-related services and help with unscheduled activities of daily living. Simply understanding assisted living can be confusing, because there is no universal (or Federal) definition of the term, and there is no standard definition or term used by all States. The term assisted living is used in 41 States, but similar facilities may be licensed by States as personal care homes, residential care facilities, adult care homes, homes for the aged, and other types of facilities.

The services and level of care available also vary by State and within States. State regulations generally describe the parameters of the people who may be served and the services that may be offered, but facilities often set their threshold below what may be allowed by the regulations.

The supply of licensed units grew from about 612,000 in 1998 to 937,601 in 2004. However, the rate of growth slowed from 13 percent between 2000 and 2002 to 3 percent between 2002 and 2004. State licensing officials believe there is excess supply in many areas of their States, and that the growth rate has declined because of competition and pressure on occupancy rates. Because of its growth and the increasing needs of people who move to assisted living facilities, State oversight staff, policymakers, legislators, advocates, family members, consumers, and Federal agencies are interested in the oversight of facilities and the quality of care delivered to residents.

STATE UNITS ON AGING

All States operate programs and services for older adults under the Senior citizens Act. State agencies responsible for these activities may be an executive office, department, division, bureau, or commission and are generally referred to as State Units on Aging (SUAs). Some are cabinet level agencies; most are units within a larger umbrella agency or department. Some SUAs are also responsible for Medicaid home and community-based waiver services programs and State general revenue home care programs. Some aging agencies serve only older adults (ages 60 or 65 and older), while others also serve adults with physical disabilities and/or individuals with developmental disabilities.

SUAs are an important source of information for older adults and families about long-term care services, including assisted living options. SUAs have a broader mission than licensing agencies and are charged under the Senior citizens Act with a broad range of services to older adults, including services "designed to encourage and assist older individuals to use the facilities and services (including information and assistance services) available to them." Web sites typically include information about the services and resources available through SUAs, as well as general information about Medicare and resources available through Area Agencies on Aging. Thirty SUA Web sites contained information or links to information about assisted living. Eight of the SUAs are also responsible for licensing or certifying assisted living facilities.

COMPARING, RATING, AND PROFILING FACILITIES

Very few States are actively developing a system to rate or profile assisted living settings, although some States are interested in developing a rating system. Unlike nursing homes, most States do not require the reporting of assessment data that are needed to establish outcomes that can be tracked and compared with other facilities. Facility performance information can be obtained from survey reports and complaint investigations, but this information is not automated or published in most States. All licensing agencies will provide information about a specific facility to consumers who submit a written request to the licensing agency.

As a part of their Federal Medicare and Medicaid oversight responsibilities, the Centers for Medicare & Medicaid Services (CMS) manages a database that allows consumers to obtain information about nursing homes throughout the country. The Web sites of State agencies responsible for licensing and oversight of nursing homes also have information about nursing home quality or links to the CMS Web site. The Nursing Home Compare Web site contains information on quality measures, staffing and inspection results. Quality measures are based on Minimum Data Set (MDS) resident assessment information. Information about nurse staffing is collected by survey agencies prior to regular inspections. Inspection results present the citations issued by the survey agency following the regular inspection.

The quality measures allow consumers to compare facilities against State-wide and national averages on 15 outcome measures that include increased need for help with ADLs, residents with moderate to severe pain, pressure sores, percentage of residents receiving catheter care, weight loss, urinary tract infections, and others measured. The staffing results present the number of staff minutes per resident for registered nurses, licensed practical nurses, and certified nursing assistants. The inspection results describe the citation, the date the violation was corrected, the level of harm, and the scope of harm or potential harm. A summary table presents the number of deficiencies for the facility compared to the average for all nursing homes in the State and the Nation.

Comparable information is not available for licensed assisted living facilities. Data on outcomes generally are not collected by State licensing and oversight agencies and therefore are not available to compare facilities. In addition, unlike nursing home requirements, States set their own policies on the characteristics of residents who may be served, the services that may be provided, and staffing requirements; these State-to-State variations do not permit comparisons across States. Despite these limitations, a few States are interested in making better use of the survey information that is available.

Each facility receives a rating at the completion of the survey. The rating sheet lists the facility's name, the date of the inspection, address, name of the administrator, capacity, census, and the surveyor's name. The score and points deducted are listed above a scoring guide. The page has a "notice to the consumer" that states:

"The Department of Public Health periodically inspects assisted living facilities. This facility has earned a numeric score based on compliance with the assisted living regulations. The facility is required to post this score and its plan of correction in a conspicuous area available to the public. Please assist us in keeping standards high. If you believe that the facility has not corrected the problems cited in a reasonable time, please contact the Department of Public Health Assisted Living Unit."

A form is attached to the inspection report that lists the rule, a description of the deficiency, specifics about the deficiency, and the category of the deficiency.

The facility search function currently includes a description of deficiencies found during the survey process and the number of complaint investigations. Examples of deficiency citations include: The facility failed to establish and maintain an infection control policy and procedure; the facility failed to conduct criminal history checks of employees and applicants; and the facility failed to perform a comprehensive resident assessment that addressed all required physical, social, psychological and clinical issues. TDADS plans to devise a similar scoring system to rate and compare assisted living facilities. However, it is unclear whether this effort will be undertaken soon.

EXAMPLES OF STATE WEB SITES

Colorado is one of 10 States that post results from surveys and complaint investigations on their Web sites. One link leads consumers to basic information about residences, including name of the residence, location, and a contact person. A second link leads to more detailed residence profiles. Consumers select the city or county and the payment options (private pay only, Medicaid only, or both) that they want to search. The results list all residences meeting the search criteria. Clicking on a specific residence shows the administrator's name, the licensed capacity, the owner's name and type of ownership, the date of the current ownership, and the phone number for the ombudsman service.

The search results also include links to occurrence (incident) investigative reports and complaints. A dialogue box lists the date of any occurrences or complaints. Users can click on the date to access further details. Occurrence reports describe the date of the incident, a description of the incident, actions taken by the residence, the oversight authority's findings, and comments from the residence. The information is posted to the Web site within a few weeks of date of the occurrence.

The occurrence Web page links to an occurrence report manual, forms for providers to complete, and a note to consumers that states:

"Health facilities (such as long-term care facilities and acute-care hospitals) are required by statute to report certain types of occurrences to the Department of Public Health and Environment. When attempting to compare facilities in terms of quality-of-care and safety, consumers must keep in mind that the reporting of occurrences by a given facility does not necessarily mean that it has failed to act appropriately or is experiencing negative trends in delivery of healthcare. Instead, facilities that appear to have a higher number of reported occurrences may simply be doing a better job of meeting their obligation to report those occurrences as required.

OCCURRENCES ARE A SNAPSHOT. THEY ARE NOT THE ENTIRE STORY.

Examples of reportable occurrences include diverted drugs, physical abuse, and misappropriation of property, missing persons, and equipment misuse. The Department of Public Health and Environment reviews all occurrences for deficient practices and ensure appropriate action was taken by the reporting facility. Consumers are encouraged to review a facility's occurrence history in order to evaluate how it responds to certain types of events, keeping in mind that "the occurrence reports do not reflect such factors as facility size or the complexity of healthcare needs of its patients."

Many brochure and website guides in states provide information regarding; Activities/social/recreational. Questions in this area deal with the type, frequency and schedule of activities, the availability of transportation to participate in scheduled activities, whether residents are involved in deciding what activities will be planned, and whether religious and spiritual activities are available.

MEALS/DINING.

Most guides include questions about meal times, the appearance of the meals, and if snacks and special diets are available between meals. New Jersey's guide suggests asking whether dining room menus vary from day to day and meal to meal. Can residents request special foods? Are special diets accommodated? Are private dining areas available? Can residents eat meals in their units, and is there an additional charge? Can meals be provided at any time, or are there set times for meals? Can residents have alcoholic beverages?

RESIDENT AGREEMENT/CONTRACT.

Questions in this area vary widely. Some advise that consumers read the agreement closely and consult with others before signing. Kentucky has a list of issues that are required to be included in the agreement. Many of the questions dealing with the services available and their costs are found in the agreement.

COSTS AND FINANCING.

These questions often address information that is available in the resident agreement or contract. In addition to the basic rate, consumers should ask about changes in the rates, services available at an additional charge, and refund policies.

STAFFING.

Consumers are prompted to observe the staff's appearance and how they interact with residents. They should ask who will be providing which services and about staffing patterns and ratios, turnover, and credentials of managers and direct care staff. By observing residents, consumers may learn about the quality of care provided by the staff. Washington's guide asks how long the administrator has been in place at the facility.

States tend to require disclosure Statements for facilities that serve residents with dementia. Twenty-seven States have disclosure requirements for facilities that advertise themselves as operating special care facilities or units or providing care for people with Alzheimer's disease or other dementias. These facilities are required to describe in writing how they are different from other facilities. The regulations may require a description of the philosophy of care, admission/ discharge criteria, the process for arranging a discharge, services covered and the cost of care, special activities that are available, and differences in the environment.

OVERSIGHT PROCESS

Oversight and monitoring of assisted living facilities varies by State because each State is responsible for establishing its own licensing requirements. Much like nursing home inspections, surveyors follow protocols that track licensing requirements and standards. All States reported that they receive and investigate complaints. Complaints that involve resident care are investigated within specified time limits while complaints that do not involve direct care may be investigated by phone or during the next scheduled survey.

The typical survey process includes an annual, unannounced on-site inspection of the facility. The inspection includes a meeting with the administrator or manager; a tour of the facility; observations by the reviewer; resident and staff record reviews; interviews with a sample of residents, family members, and staff; and an exit interview.

Consumers need reliable sources of information to sort through as it relates to assisted living service options. The Internet has evolved into an excellent tool to help inform consumers about assisted living. Web sites help consumers make informed choices about the utility of assisted living as a viable option for them, and they help prospective residents choose from among the many facilities available to them. When touring a facility, informed consumers ask more questions about accommodations, staffing, services that are available or not available, findings from oversight agencies, and other factors. Better information support market forces and creates incentives for providers to improve the quality of their product. Information is readily available from company Web sites, assisted living associations, consumer organizations, and State agencies.

ALABAMA APPROACH

The Department of Health licenses assisted living facilities. Facilities are monitored through licensing review and periodic inspections by the Board of Health (depending on funding for inspectors). Incidents are reported through a hotline. Written reports may be requested to determine the cause of an incident or whether the facility acted appropriately. Currently, facilities are inspected every 18 months.

The Department has developed a scoring system based on survey findings that rates facilities as green, yellow, or red. The ratings must be posted by the facility for 18 months or until the next survey. Administrators from facilities receiving a red rating must attend a meeting with the licensing director and develop a consent agreement that describes the corrective actions that will be made and the timetable for making them.

Facilities that receive a yellow or red rating often request earlier reviews to consider corrections they have made that would raise their rating. However, the Department does not have sufficient staff to make return inspections and maintain the survey cycle for other facilities. The rating system was implemented in the fall of 2004. Each facility's survey report and rating will be posted on the Department's Web site when more ratings have been completed. The Department spokesperson felt that listing facilities on the Web site as they were rated would give an unfair advantage to those at the beginning of the cycle.

The survey staff members follow a protocol that focuses on admission and retention related criteria. The areas include weight loss, falls, medication administration, wandering, exiting behaviors, and other behaviors. Interviews with residents and staff follow a protocol but do not emphasize satisfaction measures because of their perceived limited use.

COMMUNICATING WITH CONSUMERS

The Department of Public Health Web site includes a list of facilities and regulations governing assisted living. The list includes the name of the facility, address, phone number, administrator, type of ownership (corporation, partnership, limited liability, non-profit), and license number.

ALASKA APPROACH

A new section on certification and licensing in the Department of Health and Social Services is responsible for screening applicants, issuing licenses, and investigating complaints. The reorganization was implemented to consolidate all licensing activities and the responsibility for licensing assisted living homes that had been spread among State agencies.

Licenses for assisted living homes are issued for 2 years. Regulations require an annual monitoring visit or self-monitoring report filed by the facility. Surveyors follow a checklist based on the regulatory requirements. Surveyors observe residents during a tour of the facility to determine the level of activity and whether they are dressed, groomed, and appear well nourished. Consumers may request information about complaints against a facility by telephone, and surveys findings may be requested in writing.

Staff members of the licensing agency describe its oversight and monitoring process as consultative. When a pattern of violations is identified, a more industry-wide—versus a one-on- one—training approach is implemented. The licensing agency holds orientation sessions quarterly for new assisted living homes.

COMMUNICATING WITH CONSUMERS

The Department of Health and Social Services, Division of Public Health Web site includes a guide to licensing for providers, regulations, and a list of licensed assisted living homes containing the name of the administrator and the name of the facility, address, phone number, and capacity. Forms related to the licensing requirements and process will be added to the Web site.

The Division of Senior and Disabilities Services has an extensive array of materials, including radio and television public service announcements, which are directed to providers interested in developing assisted living homes.

ARIZONA APPROACH

The Department of Health Services, Division of Licensing Services is responsible for licensing and inspecting assisted living facilities. The Division inspects facilities annually and upon receipt of a complaint. Licenses may be renewed for 2 years for facilities that do not have deficiencies.

Surveyors use a checklist based on the regulations to guide the on-site review. The review includes record reviews and interviews with residents, family members if available, and staff. The interviews are used to determine compliance with the regulations. Residents may be asked to comment on the food, activities, and who is at the facility at night. The surveyor may mention the name of the manager and ask if the resident knows the manager. Questions about making decisions and resident's rights are also asked.

Surveyors use the same format used for nursing homes to document deficiencies. Penalties for violations include civil money penalties, provisional licensing, and restricted admissions. Fines against unlicensed facilities have been increased. Once survey and complaint findings have been sent to the facility, they are available to the public.

COMMUNICATING WITH CONSUMERS

The Division's Web site contains a database of facilities and enforcement actions for all licensed entities (assisted living, day care, behavioral health, and nursing facilities). The enforcement action information includes the date of the action, the amount of the fine (if any), and a number to call for more information about the action.

The Division is preparing to post survey and complaint findings. Findings for childcare providers will be posted beginning in June 2005. Once completed, postings for nursing homes and assisted living homes will follow. Surveyors have been trained to write deficiencies without including confidential information so their reports can be posted without being redacted.

There is a one-page consumer's guide to choosing an assisted living facility. The guide includes sample questions and brief responses. For example, "Who regulates assisted living facilities?" "What is an assisted living facility?" "How can I find information about facilities?" "How do I file a complaint?" "How can I choose a facility?" and "Questions to ask."

ARKANSAS APPROACH

The Department of Human Services, Office of Long-Term Care is responsible for licensing residential care facilities. Facilities are inspected twice a year and upon receipt of a complaint. Licenses are renewed annually. Surveyors follow protocols based on regulatory requirements. A separate protocol is used for facilities that advertise that they provide dementia care. Surveyors use a form similar to Form 2567 used to prepare citations for nursing homes. Surveyors interview residents to ask about the quality of the food, administration of medications, and other services provided by the facility. Survey findings are available to the public through the Freedom of Information Act (FOIA).

It is a requirement that facilities maintain written policies, and procedures for monitoring quality of care.

The State believes that providing education to facilities has been successful. The State conducts mock surveys to educate the staff in newly licensed facilities about the process and expectations. The State offers staff in conjunction with the mock survey to teach facility staff about the regulations and how they are applied. In addition, the licensing agency provides educational seminars for all licensed facilities, usually in conjunction with trade associations. Survey nurses do not provide consultation and training. The agency assigns different staff to carry out the training and surveying functions.

COMMUNICATING WITH CONSUMERS

The licensing agency's Web site has links to the licensing regulations, a brief description of various settings, and a search function to find a facility. The database includes all licensed facilities by county, and it lists facilities by name rather than by licensing category. The search results include the name, address, and phone number; Web site and e-mail address (if any); the name of the administrator; the number of beds; payment sources accepted; and the type of facility (assisted living, nursing home). The provider section contains the application form, incident reporting form, and criminal background-check forms. The consumer section covers all licensed facilities, including assisted living, nursing homes, and intermediate care facilities for the mentally retarded (ICF-MRs).

The Division of Aging and Adult Services Web site provides information for developers interested in building affordable assisted living facilities. An "Assisted Living Choices" link contains the licensing regulations, a list of affordable facilities, and information about eligibility and how to apply for coverage.

CALIFORNIA APPROACH

The Department of Social Services, Office of Regulatory Development, and Community Care Licensing Division regulates residential care facilities for the senior (RCFEs). The licensing agency replaced the system of annual inspections and now randomly selects and inspects 20 percent of the licensed facilities each year. The selection is structured to ensure that every facility is inspected at least every 5 years. Surveyors use a manual that guides the inspection process. The inspection includes interviews with residents and staff and record reviews. The surveyor determines the number of interviews he or she conducts at each facility. Standard protocols are not used.

Surveyors use laptop computers to complete the inspections. Results are uploaded to a central server.

Legislation passed in 2003 requires unannounced inspections of facilities that are on probation, have pending complaints, operate under a plan for compliance, or must have an annual inspection because the facilities receive payment from Medicaid. Inspectors also verify that residents who were required to move from the facility by the department are no longer at the facility.

COMMUNICATING WITH CONSUMERS

The Division's Web site contains several documents to assist RCFE operators in complying with the licensing regulations. An online evaluation manual presents each regulation and related interpretive guidelines. A set of self-assessment guides is available; the guides are based on the regulations and serve as a checklist of the most common citations. Separate guides include a preadmission questionnaire, resident characteristics and admission criteria, administrative issues, operations issues (medications, units, and food service), resident records, and staff records. The Web site has basic descriptions of the different types of facilities licensed by the State— residential care facilities for the senior, residential care facilities for the chronically ill, adult day care, adult residential facilities, continuing care retirement communities, and social rehabilitation facilities—and a database to search for licensed facilities. The results include the name, contact person, address, phone number of the facility, and phone number of the regional office that has oversight responsibility. The Web site also has a section for posting information about new developments, regulatory changes, and other information of interest.

COLORADO APPROACH

The Department of Public Health and Environment, Health Facilities Licensing and Certification is responsible for regulating and licensing assisted living facilities. Facilities are licensed annually.

New facilities receive a health and life safety code inspection in each of the first 2 years. If there are no serious problems identified, future surveys are done on alternate years. Facilities with deficiencies receive both surveys annually. Health survey staff members are RNs or social workers who have a health care background.

The survey process was changed in 2004. Surveyors found that using a checklist meant they focused more on process and paper documentation with less observation and follow-up. Surveyors start with a tour of the facility and observe as many residents as possible to identify triggers for further follow-up. Some residents may be monitored to see if the services identified in the clinical record are delivered or to assess their participation in activities. Surveyors interview a minimum of five residents, plus one interview for every ten residents. Surveyors use a standard list of questions covering the care and services provided to them. In large facilities, surveyors organize a group meeting using open ended questions that address the quality of the meals, activities, treatment by the staff, access to help at night, how they spend their day, what kinds of care they receive, and issues or concerns that should be explored. Surveyors provide guidance during on-site reviews in a manner that cannot be construed as direction.

The Department implemented a Web-based deficiency reporting system. Facilities will receive a password to review the deficiencies, develop a plan of correction, and transmit the plan to the Department. Deficiencies and plans of correction will be posted on the Department's Web site. The system was developed and pilot tested with facilities. Web postings for facilities that do not use the Web-based process will include the list of deficiencies but not the plans of correction.

Surveyors and other staff provide technical assistance to providers. Providers are encouraged to contact the Department with questions rather than waiting until a problem is discovered.

COMMUNICATING WITH CONSUMERS

The Department's Web site has separate sections for consumers and providers. The consumer section contains links to licensing regulations, a list of licensed facilities, a profile of each facility, and the most frequently noted deficiencies. The facility profiles include information about reportable occurrences and complaints. Reportable occurrences include unexplained deaths, brain injuries, spinal cord injuries, life-threatening complications of anesthesia, life- threatening transfusion errors/reactions, severe burns, missing persons, physical abuse, verbal abuse, sexual abuse, neglect, misappropriation of property, diverted drugs, and malfunction/misuse of equipment. The occurrence report describes the incident, the action taken by the facility, and the Department's findings. Complaint information is presented for the number and type of complaints, a description of the allegation, and the Department's findings.

The provider section contains licensing information, summaries of advisory committee meetings, the informal dispute resolution policy, a policy and procedures checklist, administration training, and interpretive guidelines on resident agreements, keeping bedridden residents after admission, and hot water temperatures.

In addition to the consumer and provider sections, there is a section on brochures on the Web site. The brochure section has a guide to choosing a facility and materials on how to resolve complaints and protect personal property.

CONNECTICUT APPROACH

The Department of Health licenses assisted living service agencies (ALSAs) that serve residents in managed residential communities. Agencies are licensed and inspected biennially by RNs with experience in geriatrics. Surveys focus on resident reviews and interviews with a 10 percent sample of residents who receive ASLA services, staff records, and other regulatory requirements. Based on the clinical record reviews, surveyors talk with residents to determine whether they are receiving the care they need and whether the record correctly documents resident needs. Survey findings are available to residents and others upon request. They are not posted in each building.

ALSAs are required to establish a quality assurance committee that consists of a physician, a registered nurse, and a social worker. The committee meets every 4 months and reviews the ALSA policies on program evaluations, assessment and referral criteria, service records, evaluation of client satisfaction, standards of care, and professional issues relating to the delivery of services. The quality assurance committee also conducts program evaluations. They examine the extent to which the managed residential community's policies and resources are adequate to meet the needs of residents. The committee is also responsible for reviewing a sample of resident records to determine whether agency policies are being followed, whether services are being provided only to residents whose level of needs can be met by the ALSA, and whether care is being coordinated and appropriate referrals are being made when needed. The committee submits an annual report to the ALSA summarizing findings and recommendations. The report and actions taken to implement recommendations are made available to the State Department of Public Health.

COMMUNICATING WITH CONSUMERS

The Department of Health's Web site posts online applications for ALSAs and managed residential communities.

The Division of Senior Services' Web site presents a housing directory that includes listings of assisted living facilities with the name of the facility, a contact person and phone number.

DISTRICT OF COLUMBIA APPROACH

The District of Columbia licenses community residence facilities. The Assisted Living Residence Regulatory Act was passed in June 2000. The law includes a philosophy of care that emphasizes personal dignity, autonomy, independence, privacy, and freedom of choice. The philosophy is that services and physical environment should enhance a person's ability to age in a home-like setting by increasing or decreasing services as needed. The rule-making process has not been completed.

COMMUNICATING WITH CONSUMERS

The Department of Health Web site includes a list of community residence facilities with the name, address, phone number, and capacity. The site also contains a link to the licensing application and instruction packet.

DELAWARE APPROACH

The Department of Health and Social Services, Division of Long Term Care Residents Protection surveys facilities annually and upon receipt of a complaint. All surveyors are certified to conduct Federal surveys, and a few specialize in assisted living. Surveyors interview a sample of residents.

Facilities must develop and implement an ongoing quality assurance program that includes internal monitoring of performance and resident satisfaction. Satisfaction surveys of all residents must be conducted twice a year. Revisions to the regulations will require reporting of falls without injury and falls with injuries that do not require transfer to an acute care facility or do not require reassessment of the resident; errors or omissions in treatment or medication; injuries of unknown source; and lost items, in accordance with facility policy.

COMMUNICATING WITH CONSUMERS

The Division of Long Term Care Residents Protection Web site includes a list of facilities (name, address, phone, and capacity), a list of frequently asked questions, and information about the adult abuse registry and the criminal background check law.

The Division of Services for Aging and Adults with Physical Disabilities has a link on the home page that describes assisted living, a link to a list of facilities, and a link to information on coverage of services in assisted living settings for Medicaid beneficiaries and other low-income residents. The forms and publications button has a link to a four-page brochure that describes assisted living, the services available, and sources of further information.

FLORIDA APPROACH

The Florida Department of Senior Affairs is responsible for establishing regulations for assisted living facilities. The Agency for Health Care Administration (AHCA) is responsible for inspection, issuing licenses, and oversight. Licenses are issued for 2 years. Basic assisted living facilities are inspected twice each year by a registered nurse or appropriate designee. Facilities with an Extended Congregate Care or Limited Nursing Services license are visited twice a year. Survey guidelines are posted on the AHCA Web site. Abbreviated surveys may be conducted in facilities with a good compliance history.

Complaints are triaged into four levels. The most serious complaints are investigated within 24-hours. Survey findings are available at local libraries or by submitting a written request to AHCA. Surveyors follow protocols that track regulatory requirements including facility records, and staff and resident records. Surveyors talk with staff, residents and family members. They observe the residents, ask general questions (e.g., How do you like it here? Is the staff friendly? How is the food?) to assess whether the resident is receiving needed care and appropriate follow-up. For example, residents and/or their family members will be asked about their appetite if they seem to have lost weight. They will also be asked about when they began losing weight and how much weight they have lost. The surveyor will check with the staff to determine whether they are aware of the weight loss and how it is being addressed.

AHCA hired quality assurance nurses 5 years ago to provide consultation and assistance to nursing homes to improve compliance and quality of care. The program has been extended to assisted living facilities, and the nurses accompany surveyors on monitoring visits.

Rules adopted in 2001 allow facilities to voluntarily adopt an internal risk management and quality assurance program. Facilities are required to file preliminary and full adverse incident reports within 1 and 15 days, respectively. The reports are confidential as provided by law and cannot be used in civil or administrative actions, except in disciplinary proceedings by the Florida Agency for Health Care Administration or an appropriate regulatory board. Facilities must also report monthly liability claims filed. The quality assurance program is intended to assess care practices, incident reports, deficiencies, and resident grievances and develop plans of action in response to findings.

Since 2001, AHCA has prepared annual reports to the State legislature on adverse incidents in assisted living facilities and nursing facilities. Adverse incidents are those events over which facility staff or personnel could exercise control—rather than events that occur as a result of the resident's condition—which resulted in: Death, brain or spinal damage, permanent disfigurement, fracture or dislocation of bones or joints, limitation of neurological, physical, or sensory function, need for medical attention to which the resident has not given his or her informed consent, including failure to honor advanced directives, transfer of the resident, within or outside the facility, to a unit providing a more acute level of care, or any event (regardless of facility control) that resulted in:

- Abuse, neglect, or exploitation.
- Resident elopement.
- A report to law enforcement.

Assisted living facilities must notify the Agency within 1 business day of the occurrence of the incident. The agency is authorized to investigate any such incident as appropriate and may prescribe measures that must or may be taken in response to the incident. Assisted living facilities must submit a complete adverse incident report to the agency for each adverse incident within 15 days of the occurrence. The reporting facility also indicates if the incident was determined to be an adverse incident. The adverse incident report is confidential and is not discoverable or admissible in any civil or administrative action, except in disciplinary proceedings by the agency or the appropriate regulatory board.

The report noted that the content of reports from nursing homes has improved since 2001 and now clearly describe the incident and the action taken by the facility. On the other hand, reports from assisted living facilities do not clearly describe the incident and the actions taken to enhance resident safety and prevent recurrence of similar incidents.

COMMUNICATING WITH CONSUMERS

The Department of Senior Affairs maintains a Web site on assisted living that includes several resources for developers interested in building affordable facilities.

The Agency for Health Care Administration's Web site contains links to the statute and regulations, an application package, survey guidelines, background screening information, incident reporting forms, and a monthly liability claim form. The agency is reviewing privacy and other legal issues related to the posting of survey and complaint findings.

Adverse incidents may be reported online. The Web site explains how to determine if an incident is adverse and presents guidelines for completing the report and FAQs. Both sites have links to statutes, regulations, application forms, specialty licenses, survey guidelines, and approved trainers.

GEORGIA APPROACH

The Office of Regulatory Services (ORS) conducts initial, annual, and follow-up inspections and complaint investigations. Inspections are generally conducted on an unannounced basis. ORS has the authority to take the following actions against a licensee: impose fines, revoke a license, limit or restrict a license, prohibit individuals in management or control, suspend any license for a definite period or for an indefinite period, or administer a public reprimand. Fines and revocations are the most common actions. ORS has the authority to take the following actions against applicants for a permit: refuse to grant a license, prohibit individuals in management or control, or limit or restrict a license.

Surveyors interview six residents and staff members or 10 percent of the residents, whichever is greater, using open-ended questions that elicit information about their well being, length of stay, how they are treated, if they have had any problems and how they were resolved, and whether they know of problems that other residents have had.

COMMUNICATING WITH CONSUMERS

The ORS Web site includes links to the applicable rules and regulations, application for a permit, and a list of frequently asked questions about personal care homes and criminal background checks for employees. The Web site has a searchable database that also includes inspection reports. Each report includes a citation and description of the regulation and the evidence supporting the deficiency.

HAWAII APPROACH

The Department of Health licenses assisted living facilities. Facilities in good standing receive a 2-year license. A provisional license for a shorter period of time may be issued for facilities that have substantiated complaints. Facilities that receive a deficiency and submit an acceptable plan of correction are determined to be in "good standing."

Surveyors use a protocol that follows the regulatory requirements. Surveyors ask a standard set of questions during interviews with residents and staff. Resident questions probe for information about the person's needs, the service provided, food service, and other areas. Staff members are asked about their awareness of the resident's needs, the tasks they perform for specific residents, and the overall care plan. Reponses are compared to the resident's record.

The licensing agency holds quarterly meetings with providers to discuss general survey findings and other regulatory issues.

COMMUNICATING WITH CONSUMERS

The Department of Health Web site includes a list of residential care facilities and the number of reported vacancies. Data for assisted living facilities will be posted in the near future. Agency staff is examining options for developing a methodology to profile or rate facilities. The agency is also considering the posting of survey findings on their Web site, but they need additional staff support to do so. A comprehensive handbook is available to consumers. It describes different residential options and provides checklists to compare facilities. The handbook is not available on the Web site.

The Executive Office on Aging Web site has a series of links (information, useful links, and locating services) that lead to a search function: AssistGuide. This function allows consumers to search for available services, including assisted living facilities.

IDAHO APPROACH

The Department of Health and Welfare licenses residential and assisted living facilities. With the exception of the initial surveys for licensure, all inspections and investigations are unannounced. Inspections are conducted at least annually. Historically, the State used a consultative process that improved overall quality of care and compliance. Surveyors provided input and suggestions to address problems that were identified. Because of staff shortages, there is less time to provide consultation during the survey process. In October 2004, the department began surveying facilities every 3 years if there had been no deficiencies during two consecutive surveys and no complaints. To qualify, facilities must not have citations in the core survey areas—abuse, neglect, exploitation, providing adequate care to meet the needs of the resident, fire suppression/smoke detection system operable, allowing surveyors access to facility/staff/residents—and have a licensed administrator responsible for the day-to-day operation of the facility.

Surveyors interview residents about the care received, resident rights, the resident's perception of care, how they are treated by staff, what service needs they have and whether these needs are being met, whether they have a complaint, how the facility responds to complaints, and whether they are involved in care planning and other areas. The guidelines determine how many residents are interviewed based on the size of the facility; 3-10, three residents; 11-20, four residents; 21- 50, seven residents; and 51 or more, ten residents.

Inspections include reviews of the quality of care and service delivery, resident records, and other items relating to the operation of the facility. If deficiencies are found, the administrator submits a plan of correction, and follow-up surveys are conducted to determine if corrections have been made. Complaints against the facility are investigated by the licensing agency.

COMMUNICATING WITH CONSUMERS

The Bureau of Facility Standards' Web site will be expanded to include the 10 more frequently cited deficiencies, training programs, technical guidance, and links to best practices. Best practice information will include links to two State associations, the Centers for Disease Control and Prevention, the Agency for Healthcare Research and Quality, and national Web sites with links to best practices.

The Web site also includes a survey and technical assistance guide, policies and procedures, and survey checklists for residents' rights, the administrator, training, records, resident care, activity, nursing services and medications, food services, environment and fire/life safety, and behavior management.

The Commission on Aging is collaborating with the Idaho Legal Aid Services to prepare a consumer guide that will be posted on the Commission's Web site.

ILLINOIS APPROACH

The Department of Public Health licenses assisted living and shared housing establishments. Facilities are inspected annually. Visits are not announced and focus on compliance with the rules, solving resident issues and concerns, and the facility's quality improvement (QI) process.

The monitoring process is collaborative in nature, with an emphasis on meeting the needs of the residents. During this process, surveyors provide information on best practices and share concerns about the quality of care. They provide suggestions for how to improve services and/or offer the names of individuals the facility may contact for assistance. Oversight is not enforcement-driven but is based more on a social model promoting quality of care. Contract employees are being replaced with State employees for monitoring activities, particularly individuals who understand the social model and philosophy of assisted living.

Each facility must have a QI program that covers oversight and monitoring and resident satisfaction. A system is needed to detect and resolve problems. The existence, results, and process of the QI system cannot be used as evidence in any civil or criminal proceeding.

Facilities participating in the supportive living facilities (SLF) program are certified by Medicaid and are monitored at least annually by the Department of Public Aid. Monitoring includes contract requirements, resident autonomy, resident rights, adequacy of service provision, quality assurance process, safety of the environment, program policies and procedures, information provided to low-income residents, review of resident assessment and service plans, resident satisfaction surveys, check-in system, and food service.

Facilities must have a grievance process and a quality assurance process. Complaints may be heard informally. If not resolved or if the resident prefers, grievances may be submitted through the facility's formal process. Residents may use the Medicaid appeals process for denial or delay of service.

The rules require that facilities establish an internal quality assurance plan that covers resident satisfaction; an evaluation of the care and services provided; tracking improvements based on care outcomes; a system of quality indicators; procedures for preventing, detecting and reporting resident neglect and abuse; and ongoing quality improvement. A system with outcome indicators must be developed that measures: quality of services; residents' rating of services;

cleanliness and furnishings in common areas; service availability and adequacy of service provision and coordination; provision of a safe environment; socialization activities; and resident autonomy.

COMMUNICATING WITH CONSUMERS

The Department of Public Health's Web site contains the assisted living regulations, a list of facilities, and the application to obtain a license.

The Department of Public Aid Web site has a list of facilities and fact sheets for providers and residents that explain the program and certification requirements.

INDIANA APPROACH

The Department of Health regulates residential care facilities. The Department conducts annual surveys, follow-up surveys, and complaint investigations. Survey findings are posted at each facility and may be obtained from the Department of Health upon request. Most surveyors are registered nurses, and they use a protocol that tracks the regulations to guide their survey activities. During the on-site review, surveyors interview at least three residents, including the resident council president, if applicable. A standard set of questions based on the resident rights provisions of the regulations are asked, such as: Are you able to have privacy when you want it? Do staff and other residents respect your privacy? Do you have a private place to meet with visitors? Do you have privacy when you are on the telephone? Do you receive your mail unopened? Are you aware of the rights you have as a resident? Does staff treat you with respect? Does staff make an effort to resolve your problems? Has any resident or staff member ever physically harmed you? Has anyone ever taken anything belonging to you without permission? Has anyone ever yelled or swore at you? If so, did you report this to someone? How did they respond? Responses to the interviews are recorded on a form. Surveyors respond to questions from facility staff but do not provide consultation. Complaints are investigated based on their assigned priority level. Complaints alleging harm are investigated within 10 business days.

COMMUNICATING WITH CONSUMERS

The Department of Health's Web site includes a list of facilities (name, address, and telephone and fax numbers), a link to the regulations governing residential care facilities, and links to a training manual for special care facilities. The Family and Social Services Administration Web site includes a disclosure form that must be completed by special care facilities.

IOWA APPROACH

The Department of Senior Affairs is responsible for developing regulations for assisted living programs. Monitoring, inspections, and enforcement are the responsibility of the Department of Inspections and Appeals (DIA). Certificates are issued for 2 years. Monitoring visits are also done every 2 years by a registered nurse and masters' level sociologist. A protocol based on the certification requirements is used to guide the review. Monitors interview a sample (10-20 percent) of tenants, program staff, and family members using a protocol. Tenants are asked a series of questions about privacy, whether service schedules meet their preferences, whether their life is meaningful, and whether they recommend the facility to others. The regulations require that DIA make on-site visits to investigate complaints within 48 hours if there is immediate danger; however, the Department usually investigates within 24 hours.

During the monitoring process, staff members hold community meetings with tenants during their site reviews. The meetings often identify concerns about quality and practice for the monitors. A summary of the community meeting is included in the monitoring report, which is posted on the DIA Web site. During the review, rules may be clarified and explained to site managers and staff. Monitoring staff members often participate in training meetings organized by three associations representing assisted living programs.

COMMUNICATING WITH CONSUMERS

The DIA Adult Services Bureau Web site includes frequently asked questions, a list of standard facilities and dementia care facilities (name, address, phone, contact, number of units and beds, and the initial certification date), an application form and packet, and a form to request a waiver of a rule.

Inspection reports and complaint investigations were available for reviews that have been done since the regulations were changed in May 2004. After July 2005, reports were no longer posted due to staff reductions. Users must enter the name of the facility to access survey and complaint information. The information includes the date and type of the visit, number of deficiencies, percent quality, certification action, number of violations, class and description, fine amount, whether the violation is one time or daily, and the status of the violation.

The monitoring report includes the number of residents, tenant satisfaction, complaint history and observations from resident records, policy, and practice. The monitoring process includes interviews with residents and family members and a community meeting. The report includes a narrative summary of the interviews and meeting. The complaint report includes the date of the investigation, relevant definitions of terms, accreditation status, complaint history, a description of the complaint, and the findings.

Complaints may be submitted online through the Web site. The site also includes a registry for certified nurse aides.

The Department of Senior Affairs' Web site has links to the regulations governing certification of facilities, a brief description about assisted living, and a number to call to register complaints.

KANSAS APPROACH

Assisted living facilities are licensed by the Department of Aging. Surveyors inspect every facility annually. Consistent enforcement of the regulations has been credited with improved compliance and fewer complaints. Deficiencies are written more concisely with a focus on the consumer and outcomes. Under a new survey process, facility staff accompanies the surveyor during the review. Problem areas are identified and discussed with the staff. Educational efforts have been increased. The licensing agency conducts regular 1-day training courses for nurses, owners, and operators on the role of nursing in assisted living, how to conduct an assessment and develop a service plan, managing medications, and the nurse practice act. During the training, scenarios are presented, and participants prepare a care plan based on the information presented.

COMMUNICATING WITH CONSUMERS

The Department of Aging Web site contains a list of facilities (name, address, phone, name of the administrator, name of the building owner, the lessee, and licensed capacity), various forms for providers, licensing requirements, an interpretation manual, and complaint forms.

KENTUCKY APPROACH

The Cabinet for Health and Family Services, Division of Aging certifies assisted living facilities. The Division conducts a certification review upon application and an annual recertification review to ensure compliance with the certification requirements. Unless there is a formal complaint lodged against a facility, the Division does not monitor the quality of care in assisted living communities.

COMMUNICATING WITH CONSUMERS

The Division of Aging Web site includes a checklist for consumers to evaluate facilities, an application form, a link to the regulations, and a list of facilities (name, address, phone number, and the date that the certificate expires).

The consumer brochure includes a checklist of issues that cover certification, services offered, atmosphere, community features, the lease agreement, employee qualifications, food services, and social, recreational and spiritual activities. A section on frequently asked questions addresses assistance with medications, costs, third party coverage, and move-out issues.

LOUISIANA APPROACH

The Department of Social Services licenses adult residential care facilities. Licenses are issued for 1 year, and facilities are inspected annually or upon receipt of a complaint. Inspectors follow a protocol on laptop computers to complete surveys. Interviews with residents and family members are not required but may be done at the discretion of the surveyor. Inspectors clarify the regulations and explain how the requirements may be met when they meet with staff and administrators. The reports and citations are printed at the completion of the inspection. Licensing agency officials have an interest in profiling facilities but are not working on a method to do so at this time.

COMMUNICATING WITH CONSUMERS

The licensing agency's Web site includes a database of all types of licensed facilities and programs. Consumers may search by adult residential care facilities. The database lists recent inspection reports. Reports issued after July 2004 are generally available; reports prior to that time can be obtained from the Department.

MAINE APPROACH

The Bureau of Senior and Adult Services licenses residential care facilities. However, a new division of licensing and certification will consolidate licensing functions from multiple agencies. Licenses for residential care facilities are issued for 1 or 2 years based on the facility's previous history of compliance with health and safety requirements. The State uses the MDS- RAI (Minimum data Set – Resident Assessment Instrument) to establish case-mix payment rates and quality indicators to monitor quality of care. Information is shared with all facilities.

Surveyors use a standard set of questions to explore topics with residents and staff. Using assessment data, a sample of at least five residents, and up to ten percent of the residents in larger facilities that represent the facility's case-mix is selected prior to the survey. Residents may be asked if they like the food. If they respond negatively or express a complaint, they might be asked if they have spoken to the cook or other staff. Based on responses, follow-up questions are asked.

The Department is authorized to make regular and unannounced inspections of all facilities.

COMMUNICATING WITH CONSUMERS

The Bureau's State Unit on Aging Web site contains a searchable database that allows consumers to search by name, county, city, population served, accessibility, and type of facility. The results display the name, address, and phone number of all facilities meeting the search criteria. Entries can be made to search for facilities within specified distance within a zip code. Users can check facilities for which they would like further information, including licensing period, capacity, contact person, and directions to the facility.

The State created a Division of Licensing and Certification that consolidates licensing functions for multiple types of settings which had been spread across agencies. The new division will create its own Web site. Over time, the new site may include deficiency statements. Statements will have to be converted from a narrative format to a database platform. Deficiency statements are posted by each facility and are available from the licensing agency upon request.

MARYLAND APPROACH

The Department of Health and Mental Hygiene, Office of Health Care Quality regulates the State's assisted living programs. The law allows the Department to delegate monitoring and inspection of programs to the Office on Aging and the Department of Human Resources or to local health departments through an interagency agreement. Survey findings and plans of correction must be posted in the facility.

The Office of Health Care Quality created an Assisted Living Forum (ALF) in 2003 to review policy issues under consideration by the State legislature through a series of meetings for interested stakeholders "to advise the Department and assist in the evaluation of Maryland's Assisted Living Program." There is no set membership of the ALF, and its meetings are open to the public. All stakeholders, interested parties, consumers, and members of the public are encouraged to participate and comment on all stages of the evaluation.

The ALF forum held meetings in 2003 and 2004. The Web page lists the meeting dates and meeting summaries and draft reports on manager training topics, an assessment tool, scoring of the assessment tool, and reports and resources from other organizations. Topics considered in 2003 included: certification of assisted living managers, differences in small and large providers, and standards for specialty units.

Topics for 2004 included training requirements for assisted living managers in mid-to small programs, quality standards for mid-sized programs, and methods for improving the efficiency of the regulatory process.

COMMUNICATING WITH CONSUMERS

The Office of Health Care Quality Web site contains links to licensing regulations, material for providers, and information about the ALF. The site includes information on the use and scoring of the assisted living assessment tool that determines which level of care residents need, the form used by the manager to assess the resident's needs, and the health care practitioner's assessment form.

The Department on Aging Web site has a description of assisted living, links to subsidized programs for low-income residents, a 73-page consumer's guide to assisted living, and a link to the American Association of Homes and Services for the Aging.

MASSACHUSETTS APPROACH

The Executive Office of Senior Affairs (EOEA) is responsible for certifying assisted living facilities. EOEA conducts compliance reviews of assisted living residences every 2 years. The reviews include inspections of the common areas, living quarters (by consent of the resident), inspection of the service plans, and a review of the resident satisfaction survey. Additional reviews are conducted in response to complaints from residents or the ombudsman unit. When requested by a facility, the State provides consultation concerning compliance with the regulations. State policy is based on a social model of care. Survey reviews focus on supportive service plans and include health factors, since assisted living residences are not responsible for the health status of residents.

Survey staff follows a protocol that reflects the regulatory requirements. A sample of resident records is reviewed to document the presence of an assessment, a care plan, and resident agreement and that a disclosure form was provided. Informal conversations are held with residents and staff. Direct care workers are "shadowed" to observe how they perform their tasks. At the completion of the review, survey staff addresses issues of concern during a debriefing meeting with the administrator. A letter describing the findings from the review and a request for a corrective action plan is sent to the administrator. Most frequently, this relates to rewriting a policy or retraining staff. Medication issues are also common. The assisted living residence must submit documentation that corrective actions have occurred. If the State determines that the compliance review requires more intensive action (severity of the problem, number of residents affected, willingness of assisted living residence to address the problem), they will do a follow-up visit. Survey staff regularly find repeat violations on subsequent visits. Results of the survey are available to the public through a FOIA request.

COMMUNICATING WITH CONSUMERS

The EOEA Web site provides a brief overview of assisted living, the costs, and the role of the assisted living ombudsman program. A list of facilities is available by city/town with the name, phone number, and number of units for each facility. The site provides information about the Medicaid Group Adult Foster Care Program, which subsidizes services for Medicaid beneficiaries and the State housing agency.

MICHIGAN APPROACH

The Department of Human Services (DHS) licenses adult foster care homes and homes for the aged. Responsibilities for licensing and oversight were transferred from the Family Independence Agency. The Department of Labor and Economic Growth (or a local health department at the request of DHS) has responsibility for fire safety inspections. The DHS and the Department of Labor and Economic Growth inspect homes for the aged annually for fire safety. Licenses for homes for the aged are renewed annually, and adult foster home licenses are renewed every 2 years. "Licensing consultants schedule reviews of adult foster care facilities" and "licensing staff" does unannounced reviews of homes for the aged. Reviewers offer technical assistance to help licensees achieve minimum compliance with the regulations. Consultation may be available to help licensees achieve a higher level of compliance. Reviewers follow the licensing manual and use "review tools" for different aspects of the inspection (e.g., physical plant, quality, fire safety). All the tools are posted on the Department's Web site and may be used by operators to prepare for a review or for self- monitoring. Interviews of residents, staff, and resident representatives are one source of information but are not required. Interviews are more likely when reviewers are investigating complaints. Complaints alleging abuse, neglect, or financial exploitation are investigated within 24 hours.

COMMUNICATING WITH CONSUMERS

The DHS Web site provides an overview of adult foster care and homes for the aged. A searchable database includes several types of facilities: family homes; congregate homes; small, medium, and large group homes; and homes for the aged. The database contains information about the facility, the license number and expiration date, and capacity. It also includes inspection reports and investigation reports. Complaint forms can be completed online. Posting the information has reduced the volume of calls from consumers seeking recommendations or information about the quality of care provided by specific facilities.

Tools for facility administrators include an online licensing application request form and information about self-study and ongoing and scheduled training opportunities.

The Office of Services for the Aging Web site has a checklist, and an explanation of resident rights and protections.

MINNESOTA APPROACH

The Minnesota Department of Health licenses assisted living home care service agencies (community agencies licensed to provide services in group settings). Registered nurse reviewers are to evaluate and monitor the care provided, determine compliance with the licensing requirements and conduct surveys annually. Four types of surveys are conducted: focused surveys; expanded surveys when serious adverse outcomes or potential for adverse outcomes are identified through a focused survey, complaints, or as a result of the judgment of the reviewer; licensing follow-up surveys to verify correction of identified violations; and initial licensing surveys. The process includes consultation/technical assistance to educate providers and improve compliance.

Agencies that have been licensed for 2 consecutive years and do not have any serious violations may not be surveyed annually. The survey process includes an entrance conference; a tour; interviews with staff, residents or their representatives; observations; and a record review. Surveyors review the records of two current residents and one former resident. When current residents are interviewed, the sample may be expanded based on the findings. The survey guide lists potential questions that might be asked of residents, such as: Tell me about the care you receive. Do you have a contract or written service plan? Are you receiving the services you thought you would receive? Are you satisfied with the care? Does the staff treat you with respect? Are they kind to you? Does the registered nurse visit you? If so, what does she do?

The Office of Health Facility Complaints handles complaints. The Office's Web site allows complaints to be submitted electronically. A database includes information on all resolved complaints and a description of the issue, investigative findings, and conclusions.

COMMUNICATING WITH CONSUMERS

The Department of Health has a Web site with extensive information for providers. The site includes an application form, a general guide to home care services, a survey manual, survey guidelines, and a guide to the survey process. The guide lists the indicators of compliance, outcomes observed, and comments that include whether the indicator was met, a plan of correction was ordered, and education was provided. The comments section includes a description of the deficiency. Results of surveys are posted for surveys conducted after July 2004. The State is interested in developing a system to profile agencies. A 2-year process to profile nursing homes was ready for release to the public in 2005; however, a bill pending in the legislation would delay its use.

"MinnesotaHelpInfo" is a search tool developed for all Department of Human Service agencies and programs. The button on the Web site of the Board on Aging Web site allows consumers to enter a zip code or city and search for a range of service providers, including assisted living. The search provides the name, address, and phone number of the facility, as well as a button for more details (information about the features of the program, who is appropriate, how you enroll, the fees, the area served, and the provider's Web site and phone number).

MISSISSIPPI APPROACH

The Department of Health licenses personal care homes/assisted living facilities. Licenses are issued for 1 year, and facilities are inspected annually. Surveyors follow a handbook during the inspection process that parallels regulatory requirements. Informal interviews are conducted with residents, family members, and staff.

Operators are required to spend 2 concurrent days with the licensing agency for training and mentoring within 6 months of employment. The operator may be assigned within central offices or with a survey team. Surveyors who have passed the Surveyor Minimum Qualifications Test are also required to spend 2 concurrent days with a licensed facility for training and mentoring within 6 months of employment.

COMMUNICATING WITH CONSUMERS

Personal care home/assisted living regulations are posted on the Department's Website.

MISSOURI APPROACH

The Department of Health and Senior Services licenses two levels of residential care facilities annually. Facilities are inspected twice a year. The second inspection may be waived for facilities that are in good standing based on previous inspection reports, their history of compliance, and the number and severity of complaints, and whether there was a change in the ownership, operator, or director of nursing. Inspectors bring a copy of the regulations and policies with them during the review. Inspectors meet with the administrator and conduct a tour of the facility. Inspectors interview 10 percent of the residents or a minimum of 3 and a maximum of 25, depending on the licensed resident capacity. Interviews are open-ended, and inspectors will spend time talking with residents who are identified as having difficulty navigating a path to safety. They will also talk with residents observed to have bruises about problems they may have getting to the bathroom and into and out of bed, whether they have problems with other residents or are fearful or worried about other residents. Inspectors do not provide consultation or technical assistance but do refer staff to other organizations under contract with the State to assist nursing and residential care facilities.

Complaints are triaged based on the level of harm to residents. Complaints involving imminent risk are investigated on site within 24 hours. Lesser complaints are investigated within 30 days.

COMMUNICATING WITH CONSUMERS

Section 198.528 of the revised statutes, passed in 2003, requires posting on the Department's Web site of the most recent survey findings of deficiencies and the effect a deficiency would have on the facility; the facility's proposed plan of correction; and information on how to obtain a copy of a complete facility survey conducted during the last 3 years.

A searchable database includes links to each inspection report, including a description of the citation, the date corrected, the level of harm, and a plan of correction when required. The system uses the Automated Survey Process Environment (ASPEN) database used for handling nursing home licensing and survey information. Complaints may be added to the system in the future.

The database allows users to search by county, city, or zip code. The results show the name, address, city, phone number, licensure level, number of licensed beds, the administrator, and the operator of the facility.

MONTANA APPROACH

The Department of Health and Human Services licenses assisted living/personal care homes. Licenses may be issued for 1, 2, or 3 years. Registered nurses conduct unannounced on-site surveys within 120 days of the issue of a provisional license and annually, biannually, or triennially thereafter (depending on whether the facility has been granted an extended license) or upon receipt of a complaint. Surveyors provide guidance to operators during exit interviews or while discussing a plan of correction. During the inspection, surveyors interview a 10 percent sample of residents, staff, and family members using a structured questionnaire. Additional interviews may be conducted if the surveyors find a pattern that merits further review. Surveyors receive annual training. The content of the training is based on survey findings and trends. For example, if deficiencies in specific areas increase, training will be held on the regulations, how they are interpreted, and how facilities found in violation may comply with the requirements.

COMMUNICATING WITH CONSUMERS

The Department of Health and Human Services Web site contains the licensing regulations, an application packet, and other tools for operators. Other tools include the survey tool and guidelines, a complaint survey tool and guidelines, employee and resident file review checklists, Statement of deficiencies and plan of correction forms, menu and recipe options, links to training resources, staff screening and hiring resources, resources for infection control and skin care, and a list of optional forms that will assist facilities in complying with the regulations. A quarterly newsletter has recently been instituted. A list of facilities is available on the Web site.

The Montana Senior and Long Term Care Division Web site has an icon for housing resources that lists assisted living/personal care homes. The link leads to a description of the two types of assisted living arrangements licensed in the State and a link to search for a provider. The search button includes assisted living on the drop down menu. The results include the name, address, and phone number of each facility. A consumer guide is available in a question and answer format that describes the options (retirement home, adult foster care, personal care home A and B, assisted living, and residential hospice care), the services that can be expected, and the criteria for admission, payment issues, and the content of an admission agreement. A checklist is also included.

NEBRASKA APPROACH

The Department of Health and Human Services licenses and monitors assisted living facilities. The Department may conduct an on-site inspection at any time it deems necessary. Each year, a 25 percent random sample of the licensed facilities is selected for inspection; inspections may be conducted more often in the event of complaints, incidents involving death, imminent danger or serious harm, or lack of selection over 5 years. The Department is in the 5th year of the survey cycle and must ensure that facilities that have not been visited are surveyed. The initial licensing survey is announced. Renewal surveys are not announced.

The Department provides education on the regulations during on-site reviews and participates with State assisted living associations to provide education at conferences. Surveyors are able to share effective practices used by other facilities or refer staff to other facilities.

Survey protocols are shared with the facility. Surveyors meet with the administrator and staff, tour the facility, and interview a sample of residents. At least four residents are interviewed using a protocol. Additional residents are interviewed in larger facilities. Family members or representatives for people with dementia are interviewed.

When an inspection reveals violations that create an imminent danger of death or serious physical harm or have a direct or immediate adverse effect on the health, safety, or security of residents, the Department must impose disciplinary action. The Department conducts a follow-up inspection within 90 days. For violations that do not constitute imminent danger, the Department may request a statement of compliance from the facility. The statement of compliance must indicate any steps that have been or will be taken to correct each violation and the estimated time to correct each violation. If the statement of compliance fails to address the problem(s), the Department may initiate disciplinary action against the facility.

COMMUNICATING WITH CONSUMERS

The Department's Web site includes the list of facilities and licensing regulations, with links to specific sections that affect requirements for obtaining a license. A Web-based application for approval of administrator training is also available. The site includes a list of facilities (name, address, phone and fax, capacity, type of ownership, and whether the facility serves Medicaid waiver participants).

The Division on Aging Web site has links to the Medicaid HCBS waiver on the Department's Web site. Assisted living is highlighted as one of the services covered by the waiver. The link connects to a Web site developed by Answers4families.org, which is a project of the Center on Children, Families, and the Law at the University of Nebraska, and is supported by funding from the Aging and Disability Services, the Office of Protection and Safety, and the Office of Family Health; and the Nebraska Department of Education, Early Development Network.

NEVADA APPROACH

The Bureau of Licensure and Certification licenses residential facilities for groups. The Bureau conducts unannounced, annual, on-site inspections and investigates complaints. The annual inspection follows standard protocols for a focused survey that looks at primary health and safety regulations such as care needs, staff training, background checks, and medication needs. A full survey is conducted as needed, based on observation and the results of the focused review. Inspectors review resident records and interview a sample of residents that includes residents recently admitted from a hospital or community setting, those who have special care needs, and those who receive home health or hospice care. All residents in facilities of 10 or less are interviewed. In larger facilities, surveyors interview a sample of residents based on the facility size. Inspectors ask residents how long they have lived at the facility, what their interests are, what kind of care they are receiving, and questions about medications and food service. Surveyors use the ASPEN software to record information. Consultation is not provided, but inspectors explain the regulations and comment on how other facilities respond to problems as they are identified. Inspectors may be registered nurses, social workers, or generalists with a health or aging background. Nursing home inspectors do not typically inspect residential facilities for groups, but some are cross-trained to help if there is a backlog.

COMMUNICATING WITH CONSUMERS

The State posts its licensing regulations and an application for licensure on a Web site. The site also presents a list of facilities that includes the name, address, phone number, and the number of beds. The Bureau purchases pamphlets from a national organization that explain how to select a facility. The Bureau uses funds collected from fines levied against facilities to pay for the pamphlets.

The Division of Aging Services Web site has a "links" button to multiple topics of interest to seniors. The nursing home/assisted living topic leads to Web sites of national associations.

NEW HAMPSHIRE APPROACH

The Department of Health and Human Services, Bureau of Health Facility Administration conducts annual health inspections of facilities. Separate life safety code inspections are also completed annually. The Department has five surveyors, four RNs, a social worker, and a national certified life safety code inspector. Based on the survey results, the Department has the authority to impose a fine or suspend, revoke, or deny a license. By statute, the Department offers education in the regulatory requirements. New administrators and administrators in newly licensed facilities are invited to meet with the survey staff who explains the requirements. Facilities that receive deficiencies may be referred to another facility that has been successful dealing with a similar issue.

The survey process includes an entrance visit; tour; interviews with residents, family members, if present, and staff; record reviews; and an exit interview. Surveyors use standard protocols for entrance interviews, tours of the physical environment, and reviews of medication orders. Residents who will be interviewed may be identified during the tour of the facility based on observations about their activity, cleanliness, and care needs.

Surveyors focus on quality of life and quality of care. Observations and discussions with residents are used to pursue quality of care issues. For example, if a resident is in bed at 11 am, the surveyor determines the reason. If a person is recovering from pneumonia, the surveyor checks to see that they are getting sufficient fluids and are being turned appropriately. If they are in bed because no one has helped them get up, the surveyor looks for a staff member to explain why. Survey staff also completes some resident assessments and compare their findings with the resident's record.

In January 2003, the State implemented a two-page standard disclosure form that serves as a guide and allows consumers to compare facilities. The form provides information to residents and prospective residents of assisted living, residential care, and congregate housing programs. The form provides specific information about services offered by the housing entity in its base rate. The form also lists other services available and the additional rates for those services. An individual designated by the facility administrator completes the form. The form is not submitted to the State but is kept at the facility and attached as the cover sheet of the residential services agreement.

COMMUNICATING WITH CONSUMERS

The licensing agency plans to adapt the ASPEN database for assisted living survey information and post it on their Web site.

The Bureau of Senior and Adult Services Web site has a brief description of assisted living, residential care, and congregate housing.

NEW JERSEY APPROACH

The Department of Health and Senior Services, Division of Long Term Care Systems license assisted living residences. The licensing agency conducts an annual resident profile survey that records admission and discharge, sex, age, residential setting prior to admission and after discharge, reason for admission, and information about ADLs, medications, and cognitive status. New Jersey sponsors an annual "Assisted Living Quality Initiative Best Practices Program." In 2005, the program focused on the dining experience and the role of resident feedback in enhancing dining services. Three awards were made based on facility size: small (under 50 residents), medium (50-99 residents), and large (100 and over residents).

A request sought information about the goals that were established by the assisted living community related to dining services and how the staff enhanced socialization in dining services in the community. The dining experience was addressed by asking facilities to describe any specialty dining provided (e.g. private dining, ethnic foods, barbeques, elegant dining, etc.) and any additional techniques that were used (e.g. decorations, flowers, music, candles, aromas, etc.). Evaluation was also an important part of the competition. Facilities were asked to describe how their community evaluated the effectiveness of their dining services program and what criteria were used to measure success, such as resident and/or family satisfaction surveys. Applicants were asked to provide examples of how the community's approach to dining services made a difference in terms of quality of care and quality of life for the residents.

Winners received a plaque from the licensing agency at the State's annual fall conference for providers. Each winning facility presented their program and involved the chef in the presentation.

COMMUNICATING WITH CONSUMERS

The Department has extensive information on assisted living for consumers and providers. The information is easily accessed from several Web pages. The Department's Web site has a multipurpose program and services drop-down menu. A click on "long-term care" leads to the Division of Long Term Care Systems Web page. Following links to assisted living, there is a searchable database of all licensed facilities (including nursing homes, assisted living residences, comprehensive personal care homes, adult day care, alternate family care, and child day care). Facilities may be searched by county, source of payment (private pay, Medicaid, and Medicare), and also for specialized care (behavioral management program, hemodialysis, peritoneal dialysis, and ventilator beds). The facility's name, address, phone number, capacity, and funding (private pay, Medicaid) are reported. "Guide for Choosing" checklist includes a series of questions to help consumers. Regulations, regulatory requirements, and medication aide training requirements are accessed through the regulations link and the facility and personnel licensure/certification link.

Consumers can also access information about assisted living on the program and services drop-down menu that lists Aging and Community Services. This Web page offers information about assisted living through links to the Community Choices and the Office of Community Programs. The Community Choice button gives consumers a link to multiple housing alternatives: assisted living, adult family care, residential health care facilities, congregate housing services program, and other subsidized housing options. The assisted living link leads to a description of three types of assisted living settings: assisted living residence, comprehensive personal care homes, and assisted living programs, including the services provided, staffing, costs, and links to local organizations for lists of facilities. The housing alternatives page also has a link to a facility checklist page that has a series of useful questions that are similar to the checklist available on the Division of Long Term Care System Web page.

The Office of Community Programs site has a link to information about coverage of assisted living under the Medicaid waiver and lists of assisted living providers.

NEW MEXICO APPROACH

The Department of Health licenses adult residential care facilities. The survey staff performs on-site survey/monitoring visits at all adult residential care facilities to determine compliance with the regulations, investigate complaints, and investigate the appropriateness of licensure for any alleged unlicensed facility. When violations are found, the facility submits a plan that addresses how violations will be corrected, when they will be corrected, how the facility will identify other residents that potentially could be affected by the same deficient practice, and how the facility will monitor its corrective actions.

COMMUNICATING WITH CONSUMERS

The Department of Health Web site has links to the licensing regulations, caregiver criminal background check manual, and incident reporting forms.

The State's Aging and Long Term Services Department Web site contains a brief description of assisted living under the section on long-term care services. There is also a link to a list of facilities compiled by the New Mexico Health Care Association.

NEW YORK APPROACH

The Department of Health, Division of Home and Community Based Care licenses adult care facilities. Licenses are issued for 4 years. Facilities are inspected annually or more often as needed. Inspections include, but are not necessarily limited to, examination of the medical, dietary, and social services records of the facility, as well as the minimum standards of construction, life safety standards, quality and adequacy of care, rights of residents, payments, and all other areas of operation. Two inspections per year are conducted for private proprietary adult homes. There are other policies regarding the oversight of adult homes. These new policies include: reinforcement of mandatory death reporting by homes and immediate investigations of such reports; multi-agency created profile of deaths at the homes to identify patterns; and increased surveillance.

The Department distributes letters to administrators that address new developments or requirements such as: reporting of deaths, attempted suicides, and felony crimes; notice of regulation (failure in systemic practices and procedures); maintenance of safe and comfortable temperature levels within adult homes; influenza prevention and control; establishment of a complaint hotline; emergency preparedness guidelines; statistical reporting requirements; case management obligations; facility access by individuals who are not residents; sprinkler head recall; waiver request/equivalency notification; guidelines for dementia units; availability of free or low-cost resources to residents; and notice of law (e.g., Long-Term Care Resident and Employee Immunization Act).

COMMUNICATING WITH CONSUMERS

The Department of Health Web site has a description and definition of the various types of residential facilities: adult homes, enriched housing, and assisted living programs. The Department posted a list of facilities by county that includes the name, address, phone number, type of facility, and number of beds. A list of facilities surveyed is posted quarterly. The list includes the name of the facility, the report date, and areas in which violations were found (e.g., admission-retention, environmental, resident services, food service). Details about the content of the report are not posted. A "do not refer" list is also posted which identifies facilities that have closed, may not accept new admissions, or are not certified. The site also has links to relevant press releases.

The Office for the Aging Web site has two resource buttons on the home page. A click on "senior housing" leads to a page with links to the definitions of 13 types of housing including adult homes, enriched housing, enriched housing/adult homes with limited home care agency, and assisted living programs. It also leads to a list of questions consumers should ask, and a search function by county and type of housing. The search results display the name, address, and phone number of the facility, and a link to the facility's Web site. The "find help" button leads to a Senior Citizen Resource Guide that describes adult care homes, assisted living, congregate housing, supportive housing, and enriched housing.

NORTH CAROLINA APPROACH

The Department of Health and Human Services, Division of Facility Services (DFS) licenses adult care homes. County Departments of Social Services (DSS) monitor adult care homes at least every other month. State staff members provide consultation, technical assistance, and training to the county monitors. State staff members also provide monitoring oversight and perform selected surveys of homes based on compliance history or lack of previous county monitoring.

Legislation passed in 2005 (SB 622) requires that DFS inspect adult care homes at least annually. The new law also gives DFS new responsibilities for reviewing the performance of county DSS functions. DFS will conduct annual reviews of county oversight activities. DFS may apply a range of corrective actions for failure to appropriately monitor adult care homes, such as providing technical assistance, advising staff about policies and procedures, and establishing a plan of correction. The law sets minimum training requirements for county adult home specialists.

SB 622 directs the Division of Aging and Adult Services to develop a quality improvement consultation program. The Division will implement a pilot quality improvement program and file a report with the legislature that addresses principles and philosophies that are resident-centered and promote independence, dignity, and autonomy; approaches to developing a continuous quality improvement process; dissemination of best practices; the availability of standardized instruments to measure adult care home performance on quality of life indicators; the training needs of county DSS staff; clarification of the roles of the DFS and county DSS offices; and the staffing needed to carry out the program.

COMMUNICATING WITH CONSUMERS

The Department of Health Human Services, Division of Facility Services Web site has links to the statute and regulations, as well as a listing of all adult care homes, which includes the name of the facility, address, phone number, and numbers of beds. It also includes a step-by-step explanation of the process for obtaining a license, but notes that there is a moratorium on new licensed facilities. The site has links to requirements for administrators, an application, and a schedule for tests for administrators; a list of courses for continuing education credits; and information about exams for staff who assist with medication administration. A log of penalties assessed against adult care homes is posted.

To find information on the Division on Aging and Adult Services Web site, click on the long- term care options/ombudsman link or the housing link. The long-term care link leads to adult care homes. This page describes adult care homes, has a link a to a list of licensed facilities, contacts in county Department of Social Service offices, a description of residents rights, information about the ombudsman program, and answers to frequently asked questions about long-term care options. The housing link leads to a statutory definition of assisted living, and a description of multi-unit assisted housing, including independent housing units with services.

NORTH DAKOTA APPROACH

The Department of Health, Division of Health Facilities licenses basic care facilities annually. Facilities are inspected every 2 years. Complaints are investigated as they occur. The inspections cover quality of life, quality of care, dietary services, medications, the environment, social services, personal care, and nursing services and include a life safety code inspection. Inspectors talk to residents about resident rights and whether they are receiving the services they need. The number of residents interviewed varies with the size of the facility.

In 2005, legislation was passed directing the Department to conduct a pilot study to determine whether announced or unannounced inspections have an impact on the number of deficiencies found. A report was due to the legislature for consideration during the 2005-2006 interim sessions, including a recommendation as to whether the unannounced survey process should continue for all basic care facilities.

COMMUNICATING WITH CONSUMERS

The Department of Health Web site has links to the regulations and a file that lists the name, address, phone number, administrator's name, and number of beds for each basic care facility. The site also allows users to search a database by city to obtain this information.

The Adult and Aging Services Division use the Department's Web portal. The "Senior Information Line" includes a glossary with definitions of assisted living and adult residential care homes. The site includes provider information, as well as a list of facilities; the name, address, and phone number of each facility; links to facility Web sites; and other information.

OHIO APPROACH

The Department of Health licenses residential care facilities. Facilities are inspected at least once prior to the issuance of a license, at least once every 15 months, and as the Department considers necessary. The inspections may be announced or unannounced, except that one unannounced inspection is conducted at least every 15 months. The State fire marshal or a township, municipal, or other legally constituted fire department approved by the fire marshal also inspects a residential care facility prior to issuance of a license, at least once every 15 months thereafter, and at any other time requested by the director. Inspections are compliance-based and do not incorporate a consultative or collaborative component.

The Department formed a speaker's bureau that is available to address topics related to the regulations and requirements, including the survey process and rules or statistical review of care issues cited in Ohio.

COMMUNICATING WITH CONSUMERS

The licensing regulations are available on the Department of Health's Web site. The site also has a link to a searchable database of licensed facilities. The information listed includes the name, address, and phone number of the facility; the name of the administrator; an e-mail address; the license status, date of issue, and date of expiration; licensed capacity; the date the facility opened; and the special services that are available, such as "dementia," "adult day care," or "hospice."

A consumer guide to long-term care is available on the Department of Aging Web site. It has a section on housing and care options with a link to the Ohio Assisted Living Association's Web site. The State legislature directed the Department to expand the information available about assisted living.

OKLAHOMA APPROACH

The Department of Health (DOH) is responsible for licensing and inspection of assisted living centers and continuum of care facilities. DOH conducts an unannounced inspection of each facility at least once every 15 months. DOH provides written notice of all violations, and the facility has 10 business days to respond with a written plan of correction. After review, the State provides the facility with its response. If an assisted living center provides or arranges for skilled nursing care, the State must assess the quality of that care against applicable national standards of practice adopted by the American Nurses Association and specialty nursing organizations.

Each center must have a quality assurance committee that meets at least quarterly to monitor trends and customer satisfaction and document quality assurance efforts and outcomes. The committee must include an RN or physician, the administrator, a direct care staff member or person responsible for administering medications, and a pharmacist consultant if a medication problem is to be monitored or investigated. The Department may inspect centers whenever it deems it necessary.

COMMUNICATING WITH CONSUMERS

The Department of Health Web site has a listing of facilities, including the name of the facility, address, phone number, number or beds, number of Alzheimer's beds, and the facility's identification number.

The Aging Services Division home page has a link to housing information, which includes a brief description of assisted living, continuum of care facilities, and residential care. This page also includes a link to the list of facilities maintained by the Department of Health. A guide on long-term care options presents brief explanations of residential resources.

OREGON APPROACH

The Oregon Division of Seniors and People with Disabilities (SPD) licenses assisted living facilities and residential care facilities. The licensing agency conducts periodic monitoring visits at least every 2 years. The facility must develop and conduct an ongoing quality improvement program that evaluates services, resident outcomes, and resident satisfaction. Staff of the Department may visit, inspect, and monitor assisted living facilities at any time (but no less often than once every 2 years) to determine whether they are maintained and operated in accordance with these rules.

COMMUNICATING WITH CONSUMERS

The SPD Web site has a database that allows users to search by facility type, name, and county. The search generates the name, address, phone number, administrator's name, and original date of license, capacity, and whether the facility accepts Medicaid. The site also lists facilities that have received an endorsement for Alzheimer's Care Units. The Web site has several links to tools for consumers, including an overview, what it means to be licensed, the types of facilities that might be considered, what the different types of facilities have in common, and how to start a search for a facility. A consumer's guide and uniform disclosure form are also posted.

PENNSYLVANIA APPROACH

The Department of Public Welfare, Division of Personal Care Homes, licenses personal care homes. Licenses are issued for 1 year or less, and homes are inspected at least annually. The survey guidelines are being revised to reflect changes in the regulations. The draft guidelines, which are not final, describe the procedures to follow for record reviews, staff and resident interviews, recording techniques, and methods for determining compliance. The guidelines also include interpretations of the regulations, examples of best practices, and recommendations and information that may be helpful to the personal care home staff. Complaints are triaged and must be investigated according to timeframes that are based severity. Inspection reports are available to the public upon request. The results of complaint investigations are available after redacting. The Department plans to post survey findings on its Web site within 2 years.

New regulations effective in October 2005 require homes to establish a quality assessment and management plan that includes incident reports, complaint procedures, staff training, monitoring of licensing violations and plans for correction, and establishing resident and/or family councils. The quality management plan includes the development and implementation of measures to address the areas needing improvement that are identified during the periodic review and evaluation.

COMMUNICATING WITH CONSUMERS

The Department of Public Welfare maintains a Web site that has general information about personal care homes, a guide for choosing a personal care home, and information about filing complaints. The site allows users to search for personal care homes by county and find the name of the facility, address, phone number, capacity, and whether it is for profit or non-profit.

RHODE ISLAND APPROACH

The Department of Health licenses assisted living facilities and inspect and investigate facilities at least once a year or as needed. Representatives of the licensing agency have the right to enter facilities at any time without prior notice to inspect the premises and services. Facilities are given notice by the licensing agency of all deficiencies reported as a result of an inspection or investigation. A consultation/collaboration model may be implemented when additional staff members are available. The licensing agency noted the importance of having registered nurses and pharmacy consultants available to monitor the assessment process, appropriateness of admission, and medication issues.

Residences are required to develop, implement, and maintain a documented, ongoing quality assurance program to attain and maintain a high quality assisted living residence. This ongoing process for quality improvement includes monitoring, identifying areas to improve, developing methods to improve them, and evaluating the progress achieved. Areas subject to quality assurance review include at least personal assistance and resident services, resident satisfaction, and incidents (for example, resident complaints, medication errors, resident falls, and injuries of unknown origin).

The administrator must maintain a written plan that includes three areas for quality assurance/improvement review and describe the monitoring, identification, and evaluation processes; tracking methods; and the person responsible for it.

There are minimum statutory requirements for the information that must be disclosed to potential residents and their families: identification of the residence and its owner and operator; the level of license; admission and discharge criteria; the services available; financial terms including all fees and deposits and any first-month rental arrangements; the policy regarding notification to tenants of increases in fees, rates, services and deposits; and the terms of the residency agreement.

COMMUNICATING WITH CONSUMERS

Facility licensing regulations are posted on the Department of Health Web site. The Board of Assisted Living Residence Administrators maintains a Web site with links to disciplinary actions taken against administrators, members of the Board, meeting dates, and the regulations for licensing administrators.

The Department of Senior Affairs home page has a link to home care services that includes a brief description of assisted living. The *Pocket Manual for Seniors* has additional information, including telephone numbers for the Department of Health and the Rhode Island Assisted Living Association.

SOUTH CAROLINA APPROACH

The Department of Health and Environment licenses community residential care facilities. Facilities are licensed annually. General inspections and fire, life and safety inspections are done on alternate years. Facilities with a history of compliance and no complaints may have a general inspection every 3 years. Inspectors must have a college degree, and an RN is available to assist with clinical issues. Inspectors provide technical assistance during their site visits. Facilities may also request technical assistance independent of an inspection visit. Inspectors use a checklist during their reviews. The process includes interviews with residents based on the inspector's observations.

Facilities must submit a plan of correction to the State-licensing agency when issues of noncompliance are documented. Consultations are available as requested by facilities or as deemed appropriate by the State.

Facilities must have a written quality improvement program. The program must establish desired outcomes and the criteria by which effectiveness is accomplished; identify and evaluate the causes of deviation from desired outcomes; develop action plans to prevent future deviations; establish quality indicators; analyze appropriateness of care plans; review all incidents and accidents including resident deaths, infections, or other occurrences that threaten the health and safety of residents; and create a systematic method of obtaining feedback from residents and other interested parties on the level of satisfaction with care and services received.

COMMUNICATING WITH CONSUMERS

The Department's Web site includes licensing regulations, a list of licensed facilities (name, address, phone, contact person, license number and expiration date, and the licensed capacity), and information for providers. The provider documents include licensing procedures and requirements, information on criminal background checks, emergency evacuation requirements, level of care criteria, changes in medication administration training, a self-inspection guide that tracks the regulations, special care disclosure requirements, staff orientation and in-service checklist, a request for consultation form, and frequently asked questions.

The Office on Aging hosts a Web site with a searchable database of all the services available in the State. Selecting assisted living (community residential care facilities) from the drop down menu produces the list of facilities with descriptions of the services available. Each listing has a link to an array of information that sometimes varies from facility to facility. The information includes a description of services available, location, area served, intake requirements, client information (conditions, age group, sex, grievance process), fees and payment sources accepted, hours of operation (service availability), address and phone number, and additional information about eligibility and affiliated programs or agencies.

SOUTH DAKOTA APPROACH

The Department of Health licenses assisted living centers for 1 year. Facilities are inspected at least annually, with surveyors using a protocol based on the regulations. The protocol reviews observation of staff passing medications, four record reviews (including one closed record), and interviews with three residents using a list of questions that address resident rights, staffing, meals, activities, and medications. Surveys and deficiency reports are computerized.

The governing body of each facility must develop a process to evaluate the quality of services provided to residents. Quality assurance evaluations must include the establishment of facility standards, interdisciplinary review of resident services to identify deviations from the standards and plans of correction, resident satisfaction surveys, use of services provided, and documentation of the evaluation. The Department also implemented a quality assurance process. Staff members review completed surveys to determine if the regulations cited are correct, whether there is sufficient evidence to issue the citation, and whether the plan of correction will prevent further violations.

The Department provides education and support to facilities regarding quality of care and compliance with the regulations during monitoring visits. Licensing staff is invited regularly to present at the semiannual association meetings. The State licensing office distributes to facilities up-to-date information concerning quality and trends in assisted living. The Department holds an annual public hearing for providers to discuss current issues and concerns.

COMMUNICATING WITH CONSUMERS

The Department of Health Web site has links to the licensing regulations and a list of licensed facilities.

The Office of Adult Services and Aging Web site describes assisted living and links to the State licensing regulations, presents a consumer's guide to assisted living, and links to Medicaid eligibility information. The guide has sections on requirements for assisted living, considering assisted living, looking for the right facility, staffing and services, costs, extra costs to consider, admissions agreement, what to know before signing an agreement, complaints, notice of non- discrimination, and contact information. Several of the sections include questions to ask facility staff.

TENNESSEE APPROACH

The Department of Health, Division of Health and Environment licenses assisted living centers. Inspections are conducted annually (9-15 months). Revised rules in 2003 added language concerning the reporting of unusual events. A facility must report the abuse of a patient or unexpected occurrence or accident that results in death or a life-threatening or serious injury to a patient to the Department of Health within 7 business days. Circumstances that could result in an unusual event are outlined in the regulations. Specific incidents that may result in a disruption of the delivery of health care services at the facility must also be reported within 7 business days. The facility must file with the Department of Health a corrective action report within 40 days of the identification of the event.

Survey staff members have a regulatory focus but do provide education about the requirements. The State inspection and monitoring process serves as a regulatory function only. However, when the State develops policy or interpretive guidelines, they do request the input of industry providers. If through the oversight process a particular problem area is identified, the State will work with the assisted living association to provide training and education at association meetings, rather than provide one-on-one consultation and training to individual providers.

The Department of Health develops interpretive guidelines for regulations. Department policy was issued to all ALFs in January 2004, to provide criteria for hospice waivers in the facilities. Another policy bulletin was issued concerning T.C.A. 68-11-20(5)(A)(i), which prohibits residents with latter stages of Alzheimer's disease or related disorders from being admitted or retained in an ALF.

COMMUNICATING WITH CONSUMERS

The Department's Web site includes links to the licensing rules, a description of the process to apply for a license, and a list of facilities (name, address, phone, administrator, ownership information, the license number, the licensed capacity, the date of the last survey, the date of the original license, and the expiration date).

The Commission on Aging and Disability Web site has a link to the list of licensed facilities posted on the Department of Health's site.

TEXAS APPROACH

The Department of Aging and Disability Services (DADS) licenses assisted living facilities. Facilities are licensed annually and are inspected by a team consisting of a registered nurse, social workers, and a life safety code specialist. Each member of the team has assigned tasks. During the inspection, surveyors meet with the person in charge, review the process, and request lists of residents and staff, schedules, training records, incident reports, policies and procedures, the services provided, and the facility's disclosure form. During a tour, the surveyor observes the general operation of the facility and resident activities. General interviews are held with a sample of residents, family members, and staff. A sample of resident records is also reviewed. Residents are asked if they are satisfied with the facility, the services, and food. If they are not satisfied, they are asked for details that may be explored with the manager. The team reviews their findings and completes the survey report. Survey reports may be posted at the facility, or requested from the Department.

COMMUNICATING WITH CONSUMERS

The DADS home page has a "find services" button with a drop-down menu that has a link to "find and compare long-term care facilities." The searchable database has information on four types of assisted living facilities. Users can search by facility name, county, zip code, area code, or Statewide. Search results list the name of the facility, address, owner, and number of licensed beds, as well as the number of complaints investigated and substantiated in 2003, 2004, and 2005, a listing of deficiencies cited during recent inspections, and recent events such as a change in ownership.

The business link on the home page leads to the long-term care policy and a link to forms. This page has links to disclosure forms for assisted living facilities and Alzheimer's assisted living facilities. It also contains links for providers to a general checklist used by surveyors, a checklist for life safety code requirements for different types of facilities, a list of providers for courses for assisted living managers, and several monitoring forms.

UTAH APPROACH

The Department of Health, Bureau of Health Facility Licensing, Certification, and Resident Assessment surveys facilities annually and issues a license for a 2-year period. The Department's Web site includes a report card that lists the name of the facility and the number of class I and II violations in 2001, 2002, and 2003. Details about the violations are not posted. A database of facilities by county or city includes the name, address, phone, type of facility, the date the license was issued, and the number of beds. A monthly census summary is also posted. Forms available on the Web site include interpretive guidelines, general forms for service plans, incident reports, negotiated risk contracts, resident assessment, and criminal background checks. A summary of the levels of care is also available.

COMMUNICATING WITH CONSUMERS

The Health Facility Licensing Web site contains an alphabetical list of facilities by county and a comparison of the level of care criteria for assisted living, Nursing homes, home health agencies, hospice, and hospitals. Interpretive guidelines are posted that list the standard contained in the licensing regulations and guidelines used by surveyors to determine whether the facility complies with the standard. The licensing regulations are posted on the Department's Web site.

VERMONT APPROACH

The Department of Disabilities, Aging, and Independent Living licenses assisted living residences and residential care facilities and conducts annual surveys. Facilities that receive deficiencies must submit and implement corrective action plans.

The Department works with facilities to help them comply with the regulations. The State investigates complaints that merit investigation. Assisted living residences must have a quality improvement process that includes an internal committee comprising the director, an RN, a staff member, and a resident. The committee must meet at least quarterly. Resident satisfaction surveys must be conducted annually and be used by the committee.

COMMUNICATING WITH CONSUMERS

The Department's home page has a link to "Licensing and Protection." On the left side of the page there are links to State regulations for assisted living residences and residential care homes and a list of all residential care and assisted living facilities. The list includes the name of the facility, level of care, address, phone number, contact person, and capacity.

VIRGINIA APPROACH

The Department of Social Services may issue 1, 2, and 3-year licenses to assisted living facilities. New legislation requires that the Board of Long-Term Care Administrators license administrators of assisted living facilities.

Surveyors enter information on a personal computer that has the standards and the previous history of compliance for the facility being inspected. Survey findings and corrective action plans are printed during the exit interview. Surveys are posted on the Department's Web site. Licensing officials are working to expand the system's capacity to generate management reports that would allow them to compare facilities owned by one company, to compare compliance history with other companies, and examine citation patterns of individual surveyors or regional offices.

COMMUNICATING WITH CONSUMERS

The Department's Web site includes a database with the name of the facility, address, phone number, administrator, expiration date for the license, and information about inspections. The database includes inspection dates, whether the inspection was complaint related, and whether or not there were violations. Clicking the inspection date loads the areas reviewed, action from previous violation reports, technical assistance provided, and comments by the surveyor. The report also lists the standards violated, a description of the violation, and the corrective action that will be taken by the facility.

The Website also has tools for providers, including a level of care worksheet, uniform assessment instrument and care plan, application for licensing and renewal, medication administration record, record of on-site health care oversight, record of staff training, model resident agreement, and other forms.

To find information about assisted living on the Department's home page, click services, topics, and assisted living. The assisted living link describes what the term assisted living means in Virginia and suggests clicking the link to the ombudsman program for questions about specific facilities. Click on publications and long-term care for a provider directory and a consumer guide that has a section on assisted living. The section explains what assisted living is and is not in Virginia, levels of services, meals, social activities, amenities, the admission assessment, staffing, and resident rights and responsibilities.

WASHINGTON APPROACH

The Aging and Disability Services Administration (ADSA) license boarding homes. Inspections are conducted every 12-15 months. The process for inspecting nursing homes and boarding homes is similar. ADSA dropped "quality improvement consultation" because of budget reductions. The consultation service helped facilities understand regulatory requirements and share best practices. Funds to continue the program have not been approved.

Case managers are a primary source of monitoring for quality assurance for Medicaid beneficiaries. During regular visits, the case manager checks to see if the client is satisfied, the negotiated service plan is being carried out, and that the plan is appropriate for the resident.

Homes can maintain a quality assurance committee that includes a licensed registered nurse, the administrator, and three other staff members. When established, these committees meet at least quarterly to identify issues that may adversely affect quality of care and services to residents, and to develop and implement plans of action to correct identified quality concerns or deficiencies. To promote quality of care through self-review without fear of reprisal, and to enhance the objectivity of the review process, the department does not require (and the long-term care ombudsman program does not request) disclosure of any quality assurance committee records or reports. Exceptions are when the disclosure is related to the committee's compliance with regulations, the records or reports are not maintained pursuant to statutory or regulatory mandate, or the records or reports are created for and collected and maintained by the committee.

COMMUNICATING WITH CONSUMERS

The ADSA home page has a button for boarding homes that connects to a consumer guide and a database that searches for facilities by county or zip code. The results include the facility's name, address, phone, Medicaid contract status if any, and capacity.

Under the "professionals" button, click "residential care" for a section for providers that includes regulations, a licensing application, frequently asked questions about licensing, a required disclosure form, other documents related to licensing, enforcement principles and procedures, instructions about nurse delegation, and a schedule of training programs. It also includes an aggregate list of the most frequent citations.

WEST VIRGINIA APPROACH

The Department of Health and Human Resources, Office of Health Facility Licensure and Certification licenses assisted living residences annually. The Office conducts on-site, unannounced inspections annually and as needed to investigate complaints. Survey reports are completed on laptop computers and e-mailed to the State office. Facilities with Class I violations are re-inspected until they reach compliance. Survey teams include an RN, a social worker, and an environmental surveyor. Surveyors review a sample of staff and resident records based on the size of the facility. The process is described as outcome oriented. Surveyors examine the facility's policies and procedures to determine if there is a policy to prevent or address poor outcomes. For example, staff is required to weigh residents monthly and report changes greater than 5 pounds to the physician.

Under previous regulations, facilities were assigned a grade, but the process was replaced by a system that groups deficiencies by class. State officials believe this process will result in a fairer description of the quality of care.

Survey teams can provide technical assistance to facility managers and staff. Assistance is often provided when a surveyor identifies an issue that could become a future violation. The team may provide written information about the issue, the regulatory requirement, and recommendations for addressing the issue.

COMMUNICATING WITH CONSUMERS

The Office posts a list of licensed facilities that includes the name of the facility, address, phone number, and type of facility on the agency's Web site. The Web site also includes application and renewal forms, a form to request a waiver of the 90-day limit for providing health and nursing services, and program licensing, survey requirements, and a disclosure form for Alzheimer's special care units. The Office is considering posting survey findings and deficiency reports.

WISCONSIN APPROACH

The Department of Health and Family Services, Bureau of Quality Assurance conducts periodic inspections of certified residential care apartment complexes (RCACs) and has the authority (but is not required) to inspect registered RCACS to determine compliance with regulatory requirements.

The Department maintains a Web site on RCACs and community-based residential facilities. The site has two databases of facilities. One links to the Wisconsin Assisted Living Association site and is organized by county. It lists name, address, phone number, contact, capacity, and e-mail and Web site addresses. It also includes a map. The State site lists facilities in PDF and Excel spreadsheet formats. In addition to the information included on the association site, the State site contains the number of apartments/units, the lowest and highest rates charged, the initial certification/licensing date, and any specialized programs (Medicaid waiver, developmental disabilities, dementia, or alcohol/drugs abuse).

COMMUNICATING WITH CONSUMERS

The Department's Web site includes regulations and statutes, licensing/certification information, applications, regulations, a description of the survey process and a guide, background checks, incident reporting forms, guidance on medication errors based on common errors, and a copy of residents' rights. A consumer guide to selecting community-based residential facilities is also available. Descriptive information is available for both RCACs and community-based residential facilities. The site links to county agencies and lists of all facilities in the county.

The Web site includes survey findings by type of facility for the previous 3 years. Facilities are grouped alphabetically by type. The information includes the date and type of survey, the number of the deficiency cited, the subject matter and the date compliance was verified, and whether the deficiency was corrected.

The Bureau of Aging and Long Term Care Resources home page links to the Bureau of Quality Assurance Web site.

WYOMING APPROACH

The Department of Health licenses assisted living facilities. The State has a contract employee who surveys facilities at least once a year. The cost of the contract is borne by the assisted living facilities. The survey division is required to provide a list of deficiencies to the facility within 10 working days of the survey, and the facility has 10 calendar days to provide a plan of correction for each of the cited deficiencies. If the facility fails to provide a plan of correction, licensure revocation proceedings may ensue. Each facility must have an active quality improvement program that is re-evaluated at least annually to ensure effective use and delivery of services. The program must have a written description, problem areas identified, monitor identified, frequency of monitoring, and a provision requiring the facility to complete annually a self-assessment survey of compliance with regulations, as well as a satisfaction survey that must be provided to the resident,

resident's family, or resident's responsible party at least annually. The State is responsible for receiving and investigating complaints.

COMMUNICATING WITH CONSUMERS

Licensing regulations are posted on the Secretary of State's Web site. The State Aging Division of the Department of Health's Web site list assisted living facilities that participate in the Medicaid waiver program.

PART VII

SUCCESSFUL LAWSUITS ON BEHALF OF SENIOR CITIZENS

CHAPTER 18

LAWSUITS: YOUR VOICE, YOUR POWER

Successful court cases that define justice for abused individuals in nursing homes.

Many people have attempted to seek change through senior abuse hotlines by reporting crimes against a loved one, but have failed to receive assistance. Others have pursued legal recourse, particularly through attorneys who have established themselves as advocates for the senior. In this chapter, I will examine many cases that were successfully litigated on behalf of a family or the abused. I am describing these cases in hopes that by learning the details, consumers and caregivers will begin to understand the broad spectrum of types of abuses that occur.

Included here are examples of diverse cases settled in the United States. My hope is that you will recognize some type of abuse and take action.

Due to attorney/client privilege in some of the listed settlement cases, the names and locations are not disclosed. These cases/settlements include:

- $3 million record nursing home pressure sore settlement against a nursing home and physician for a 59-year-old resident who developed multiple painful and infected bedsores, which took four years to heal.
- $2.9 million jury verdict against a nursing home for the family of a deceased 57-year-old resident who was suffocated due to the home's negligent care of her tracheostomy tube.

- $2.3 million settlement for the family of an 88-year-old assisted living facility resident who developed severe and infected bed sores which ultimately brought about her death. Her doctor was criminally indicted for his conduct and charged with involuntary homicide.
- $1.5 million settlement against a nursing home for violating a Nursing Home Care Reform Act by failing to monitor a mentally impaired resident's cigarette smoking, leading to severe burns and death.
- $1.5 million settlement for an 87-year-old nursing home resident that suffered severe burns when seated in a steaming-hot sitz bath.
- $1.4 million verdict against a nursing home for failure to manage a nursing home resident's behavior which caused a shoving match, fall, hip fracture and death of a 79 year old fellow nursing home resident.
- $1.3 million settlement for a 74-year-old nursing home resident that died as a result of a beating he received when the nursing home placed a younger resident with violent tendencies in his room.
- $1.2 million settlement for an 82-year-old nursing home resident that developed bed sores so severe that they caused an infection in the bone; she died as a result of complications from these injuries.
- $1.1 million settlement against a nursing home for a 75-year-old resident who developed multiple painful and infected bedsores, or pressure ulcers, which caused her death.
- $1 million nursing home settlement for the family of an 80-year-old nursing home resident that developed multiple stage IV pressure sores that contributed to the cause of her death.
- $1 million settlement for an 83-year-old nursing home resident who fell several times while a resident at the nursing home, with the last fall contributing to her death. Despite her risk for falls, the nursing home neglected to implement changes in her care plan to prevent further falls from occurring.

- $1 million settlement against a facility on behalf of the family of an 82-year-old man who suffered a fatal brain injury in a fall at the nursing home.
- $1 million Jury Verdict for the family of a 54-year-old nursing home resident who exited a window on the fifth floor of the nursing home and died from fall-related injuries. The jury found that the nursing home was negligent in failing to prevent the resident from exiting the window.
- $1 million settlement against a nursing home for a 75-year-old resident who suffered malnutrition, dehydration and Stage IV pressure sores, resulting in death.
- $1 million verdict against assisted living facility that admitted liability for failing to give a proper mechanical soft diet due to understaffing and poorly trained staff resulting in choking and death of a 67 year old man.
- $1 million settlement on behalf of a quadriplegic that developed severe pressure sores that his nursing home claimed were unavoidable. After leaving the home, it took one year for the sores to heal and they have not returned.
- $1 million settlement for failure to properly care for and monitor a wheelchair bound resident's risk of strangulation resulting in death.
- $1 million settlement for the family of a 78-year-old nursing home resident against a nursing home and doctor for failure to prevent and treat seven Stage IV pressure ulcers, which caused the resident's death.
- $1 million settlement in a case filed by the family of an 88-year-old man who developed multiple infected bed sores that required surgery, prolonged hospitalization, and extensive wound care to treat. The bed sore lawsuit alleged that the nursing home failed to take the proper measures to prevent his pressure sores from forming, and failed to prevent existing pressure ulcers from worsening.
- $999,000 nursing home negligence settlement against a nursing home and physician for the family of a 34-year-old woman who bled to death when the staff failed to properly

monitor her condition or report changes in her condition to her physician.
- $995,000 settlement against a nursing home for the mother of a 45-year-old nursing home resident with schizophrenia and alcoholism who died as a result of a gastric ulcer which perforated a vein and caused a hemorrhage. Signs and symptoms of the gastric ulcer, present two weeks prior to the resident's death, were not reported to the resident's physician.
- $950,000 settlement against a nursing home for allowing an 85-year-old woman with dementia to wander outside the nursing home, where she froze to death.
- $950,000 settlement against a nursing that has subsequently been shut down, for a 91-year-old nursing home resident who over a three year period suffered from malnutrition and dehydration sustaining a body loss of 1/3 of her total weight within the last three months, causing hospitalization and death.
- $950,000 settlement for the family of an 81-year-old nursing home resident in a wheelchair who fell down a flight of stairs and suffered a subdural hematoma and died seven months later.
- $925,000 settlement on behalf of the family of an 86-year-old nursing home resident who was so badly neglected that she became malnourished and dehydrated, and developed severely infected bed sores that caused an infection in her bone and in her blood, and resulted in her death.
- $919,000 nursing home neglect settlement for the son of a 54-year-old resident who died as a result of the nursing home's failure to properly monitor his condition or transfer him to the hospital during a hypertensive crisis.
- $917,912 nursing home negligence settlement on behalf of the surviving family of a 63-year-old nursing home resident who died when nursing home staff failed to properly administer medication prescribed to him to treat his gastrointestinal cancer and failed to ensure that he made follow-up visits with

his oncologist. As a result of these failures, his cancer spread and caused his death.
- $914,000 nursing home lawsuit settlement for the family of a former resident who died after suffering a stroke as a result of the nursing home's failure to properly administer her blood-thinning medication.
- $900,000 settlement against a nursing home whose failure to monitor a 58-year-old wheelchair-bound resident's unauthorized smoking caused the resident to sustain severe burns, resulting in death.
- $900,000 settlement against a nursing home that failed to appropriately feed and hydrate a 76-year-old resident, leading to his malnutrition, dehydration and death.
- $900,000 settlement for the family of an 81-year-old nursing home resident against two nursing homes. One nursing home failed to prevent the resident from falling and sustaining a hip fracture. Another nursing home failed to prevent the formation of and worsening of multiple pressure ulcers, including multiple Stage IV pressure ulcers.
- $862,500 settlement for a nursing home resident who contracted MRSA as a result of staff negligence while living at the defendant facility, causing him to undergo additional surgeries and amputation.
- $861,788 policy limit settlement for a 61-year-old nursing home resident that suffocated to death because nursing home staff failed to properly place his tracheostomy tube.
- $850,000 settlement against a nursing home for a woman who fell from her bed, resulting in a subdural hematoma and death.
- $825,000 settlement for the daughter of a former nursing home resident that suffered at least six falls during her residency. The facility failed to create any care plan to address her risk for falls until after her last fall, in which her eye burst, requiring an eye enucleation surgery. Her conditioned declined significantly after this surgery and she died one month later.
- $825,000 settlement for a 75-year-old nursing home resident with dementia and a history of wandering who

died of hypothermia after exiting the facility in bitter cold temperatures resulting from the home's failure to verify if his tracking bracelet was functioning, properly supervise him, and promptly notify the police.
- $820,000 nursing home settlement for the family of an 86-year-old woman who fell in her bathroom at the nursing home and sustained a cervical spine fracture which contributed to her death nine days later.
- $800,000 settlement for the family of a 56-year-old nursing home resident that suffered a hip fracture in a fall at the facility. After his fall, he developed a number of bedsores, a chronic bone infection and became malnourished, all of which led to a deterioration in his condition.
- $800,000 settlement against a nursing home for failing to appropriately monitor an 88-year-old patient's hydration levels after a fall, causing severe pain, appetite loss, severe dehydration and death.
- $800,000 settlement against an intermediate care facility for failing to appropriately supervise a 32-year-old mentally disabled woman on a facility outing where she choked to death.
- $760,000 verdict against a nursing home doctor who failed to respond to signs and symptoms of a bowel obstruction, leading to the death of a 67-year-old resident with Alzheimer's disease.
- $750,000 nursing home neglect settlement for the daughter of an 82-year-old nursing home resident who developed a deep pressure wound that took over two years to heal. She also became malnourished and immobile during her brief stay at the nursing home.
- $750,000 settlement against a nursing home for the family of an 80 year old Parkinson's nursing home resident with dementia who developed Stage IV pressure sores, dehydration and malnutrition resulting in hospitalizations and death.
- $750,000 settlement against a nursing home for an 86-year-old who developed pressure sores resulting in an amputation.

- $750,000 settlement for a 77-year-old nursing home resident that fell, suffered a subdural hematoma, and died.
- $750,000 settlement against a nursing home for an 80-year-old who was malnourished and developed pressure sores, resulting in death.
- $750,000 nursing home fall settlement for the daughters of an 89-year-old woman who died from post-operative complications after falling in the facility. The woman was left alone in the bathroom, and she fell, suffering a left femur fracture that required surgery.
- $715,000 nursing home settlement for a 74-year-old woman who died from malnutrition, dehydration, pressure sores and infection after receiving substandard cares at three nursing homes.
- $700,000 record settlement against a nursing home for a 43-year-old man who developed a Stage IV pressure ulcer that led to deterioration in his overall condition and contributed to his death.
- $700,000 nursing home neglect settlement against a nursing home for the death of a 72-year-old woman who suffered pressure ulcers, malnutrition, dehydration and sepsis while residing at the facility.
- $700,000 settlement against a nursing home for a 63-year-old resident who suffered a fractured femur, malnourishment, dehydration and a Stage IV pressure ulcer.
- $700,000 verdict awarded when an 82-year-old resident with Alzheimer's disease wandered out of the nursing home and was struck by a car, sustained a leg fracture and ultimately died.
- $690,000 nursing home settlement on behalf of the family of an 87-year-old resident who suffered a right femur fracture, skin breakdown and a bone infection which led to her death.
- $675,000 nursing home burn injury settlement for a 67-year-old resident who died from severe burns after her clothing caught fire while she was trying to smoke in her bathroom. Staff failed to create a care plan to address her unsafe smoking

behaviors, and failed to provide adequate supervision to prevent accidents.
- $665,000 nursing home settlement for the surviving family of a man who suffered a serious brain injury in a fall. His injuries contributed to his death six days after his fall.
- $650,000 nursing home settlement on behalf of an 80-year-old woman who developed infected pressure sores as a result of negligence on the part of staff and her attending physicians.
- $650,000 settlement for a 64-year-old woman who developed infected pressure sores and a bone infection that required prolonged long-term care stay and surgery.
- $650,000 settlement for the family of a 76-year-old nursing home resident against a nursing home for failure to appropriately prevent and treat pressure ulcers resulting in gangrene, bilateral leg amputations and death.
- $645,000 verdict plus attorneys' fees for the family of an 81-year-old man who suffered a serious brain injury after falling out of his wheelchair at a nursing home. He later died from complications linked to his injuries.
- $600,000 settlement for a 75-year-old who suffered a deep tissue injury during an improper transfer at a facility. The wound went untreated and became infected, and eventually required our client to undergo an above-the-knee amputation.
- $600,000 settlement against a home health agency and nursing home for a 54-year-old man who required a below-the-knee amputation after his care providers failed to prevent pressure sores on his leg from deteriorating and failed to properly treat his injuries.
- $600,000 settlement against a nursing home and hospital for a 71-year-old man who developed Stage IV heel pressure sores, resulting in amputation.
- $600,000 settlement against a nursing home in the death of a 46-year-old disabled woman who developed multiple infected pressure sores, resulting in death.
- $575,000 negligence settlement against a nursing home for the family of an 88-year-old woman who developed multiple

bed sores at a facility. The sores worsened and her condition deteriorated, causing her death five months after she was first admitted to the facility.
- $570,000 settlement for the family of a 99-year-old woman who died from compressional asphyxia after her neck became entrapped between her bed rail and mattress at the nursing home.
- $510,000 settlement against a nursing home for the family of a 78-year-old resident, who repeatedly took off her personal alarm, fell on her way to the bathroom and fractured her hip and died four months later from heart problems.
- $500,000 pressure ulcer settlement for the family of a 93-year-old man who died after developing infected decubitus ulcers at a facility as a result of nursing home negligence. Staff failed to provide him with the appropriate pressure relieving devices to prevent pressure sores from forming, and failed to properly assess his skin condition or treat his pressure ulcers once they developed.
- $500,000 nursing home bed sore settlement on behalf of a former resident that developed a number of infected bedsores at a facility. These injuries caused her overall physical and mental condition to deteriorate.
- $500,000 nursing home neglect settlement for the family of a 69-year-old resident who died as a result of developing numerous pressure ulcers, a sepsis infection, and suffering dehydration while under the facility's care.
- $500,000 settlement against a nursing home for a nursing home's failure to treat corneal abrasion and dental problems of 74-year-old resident which resulted in the loss of eye and multiple tooth extractions.
- $500,000 settlement for the family of a 47-year-old nursing home resident who choked to death after the nursing home failed to provide him with a proper diet or supervise him during mealtime.
- $500,000 settlement against a nursing home for the family of an 89-year-old resident who died as a result of the nursing

home's failure to treat his sacral pressure sore or prevent it from worsening.
- $475,000 settlement against a nursing home for its failure to obtain final lab report for urine culture of 82-year-old resident and notify the doctor of sensitivity findings resulting in patient remaining on an antibiotic which was resistant to infection, urosepsis developed and the resident died.
- $400,000 nursing home neglect settlement against a nursing home for the family of a 50-year-old man who died as a result of the nursing home staff's failure to properly monitor his blood sugar levels or notify his physician when his condition changed.
- Confidential settlement amount for a nursing home resident who asphyxiated and died after becoming entrapped between her mattress and bed rail. Her bed alarm was found unplugged, and the required alarm mat was missing.

CHAPTER 19

MISTREATMENT OF SENIOR CITIZENS IS A CRIMINAL PROBLEM

It is not only vulnerable older adults facing high risks of financial, physical, and psychological abuse, even you who are active seniors can be thrust into vulnerable situations by someone you trust. Too often, these abuses go undetected or are disregarded after they are discovered. Frequently family members or caregivers are the perpetrators; thus the abuse can mistakenly be seen as a private, family matter.

Abuse includes intentional actions by a caregiver or other trusted individual that causes harm to an older adult. Senior abuse can also include the failure of a caregiver or other responsible party to provide for the basic needs of a senior. The comprehensive definition of senior abuse includes financial exploitation of older people, as well as physical abuse, neglect, emotional abuse, and sexual abuse.

BACKGROUND

Senior abuse and neglect is an understudied problem in the United States. Historically viewed as a social rather than a criminal problem, most states did not establish adult protective services units to address senior abuse until the mid-1980s. The extent of senior abuse is unknown, in part because of the lack of definitive and comprehensive research in the area.

Senior abuse is frequently perpetrated by a spouse, relative, or acquaintance, which increases the likelihood that crimes are being underreported. Low household income, unemployment or retirement, poor health, prior traumatic events, and low levels of social support all can indicate a higher likelihood that older people may experience mistreatment.

This problem is compounded by the fact that the medical and criminal justice communities lack comprehensive forensic guidelines for identifying senior abuse and mistreatment. Financial exploitation of older adults has also not been thoroughly studied because of problems with detection, conflicting definitions of the crime, and underreporting.

The National Institute of Justice (NIJ) has been working in cooperation with its grantees and partners to help close the gap in the current research and scholarship on senior abuse and mistreatment. One of NIJ's primary objectives is to identify emerging promising practices and evaluate their effectiveness in improving prevention, detection, and intervention efforts. NIJ's Senior Mistreatment Research Program has produced significant research in determining the extent of senior abuse, identifying and evaluating forensic markers of senior physical and sexual abuse and neglect, and developing tools for use by practitioners in the field. The *NIJ Journal* also includes an overview of studies on the prevalence and detection of senior abuse, which will help criminal justice professionals to identify the warning signs of violence against older people, including distinguishing between normal bruising patterns and those that result from abuse.

The Office for Victims of Crime (OVC) is involved in a variety of efforts to help combat senior abuse and assist those who have been abused, neglected, or exploited. OVC develops publications to help educate both victims and caregivers in methods of dealing with the trauma brought on by senior abuse and mistreatment. OVC has also created a series of three DVDs designed for specific audiences. Using firsthand accounts from older victims, these materials will help victim advocates, law enforcement officers, judges, and other professionals learn how to communicate effectively with victims and find them appropriate resources for intervention and support.

The Bureau of Justice Statistics (BJS) is developing a data collection instrument that will enable it to use existing information to analyze the crime of senior abuse. BJS is also pursuing a project that will assess the records of adult protective services offices and law enforcement offices to provide insight into which senior abuse cases are reported to law enforcement, which are not reported, and why.

The Bureau of Justice Discusses Senior Abuse as a Criminal Problem.

Senior abuse and neglect is an understudied problem in the United States. Historically viewed as a social rather than a criminal problem, most States did not establish adult protective services units until the mid-1980s. [1]

Full extent of senior abuse is uncertain. Criminal justice researchers have generally paid little attention to senior abuse until recently. No uniform reporting system exists, and the available national incidence and prevalence data from administrative records are unreliable due to varying State definitions and reporting mechanisms. A 2007 nationally representative study of over 7,000 community residing seniors estimated that approximately one in ten seniors reported at least one form of senior mistreatment in the past year. See Extent of Senior Abuse for more from this study.

Research is still needed to determine the prevalence senior abuse, neglect and exploitation among seniors with dementia and those residing in residential facilities, to identify risk factors for victimization, and to evaluate the efficacy of interventions.

No forensic guidelines. The lack of research on the forensic aspects of senior mistreatment is of particular concern to criminal justice practitioners. At present, the medical community cannot easily distinguish between those types of injuries that indicate abuse or neglect and those that are the natural effects of illness or aging. Few experts are available to testify in court and limited data exist to bolster cases brought into the system.

CHAPTER 20

DAYS AND MONTHS JUST FOR YOU

By the President of the United States of America

A Proclamation

Senior citizens teach us the timeless lessons of courage, sacrifice, and love. By sharing their wisdom and experience, they serve as role models for future generations. During Senior citizens Month, we pay tribute to our senior citizens and their contributions to our Nation.

Our seniors deserve our greatest respect. Their example shows us how to persevere in the face of hardship, care for others in need, and take pride in our communities. Their patriotism, service, and leadership inspire Americans and shape the character and future of our country.

Millions of Americans are now living longer, more productive lives, and many are choosing to stay active in the workforce. Senior citizens are also giving their time and talents by volunteering in many ways— from mentoring youth and participating in environmental stewardship projects to serving the homeless and assisting in emergency preparedness. More than 500,000 senior citizens volunteer through Senior Corps, a network of programs that enables senior citizens to meet the needs and challenges of their communities. Through the USA Freedom Corps and Senior Corps, senior citizens are dedicating their time and energy to strengthening our Nation and serving a cause greater than themselves.

This year marks the 40th anniversary of the Senior citizens Act of 1965, which was created to improve the welfare of our seniors. By treating senior citizens with the dignity and respect they deserve, we honor their legacy and contributions to our Nation. Their guidance and love enrich our country and make America a better place for all.

NOW, THEREFORE, I, GEORGE W. BUSH, President of the United States of America, by virtue of the authority vested in me by the Constitution and laws of the United States, do hereby proclaim May 2005 as Senior citizens Month. I commend our senior citizens for their many contributions to our society. I also commend the network of Federal, State, local, and tribal organizations, service and health care providers, caregivers, and dedicated volunteers who work on behalf of our senior citizens. I encourage all Americans to honor their seniors, to care for those in need, and to publicly reaffirm our Nation's commitment to senior citizens this month and throughout the year.

IN WITNESS WHEREOF, I have hereunto set my hand this third day of May, in the year of our Lord two thousand five, and of the Independence of the United States of America the two hundred and twenty-ninth.

SENIOR CITIZENS ACT

Congress passed the Senior citizens Act (OAA) in 1965 in response to concern by policymakers about a lack of community social services for older persons. The original legislation established authority for grants to States for community planning and social services, research and development projects, and personnel training in the field of aging. The law also established the Administration on Aging (AoA) to administer the newly created grant programs and to serve as the Federal focal point on matters concerning older persons.

Although older individuals may receive services under many other Federal programs, today the OAA is considered to be the major vehicle for the organization and delivery of social and nutrition services to this group and their caregivers. It authorizes a wide array of service programs through a national network of 56 State agencies on aging, 629 area agencies on aging, nearly 20,000 service providers,

244 Tribal organizations, and 2 Native Hawaiian organizations representing 400 Tribes. The OAA also includes community service employment for low-income senior citizens; training, research, and demonstration activities in the field of aging; and vulnerable senior rights protection activities.

> **Observances to remember**
>
> - World Senior Abuse Awareness Day is June 15th each year.
> - Older American's Month is observed during the month of May each year.
> - Senior Citizen's Day is observed August 21st each year.
> - Older Person's Day is observed October 1st each year.
> - Grandparent's Day is observed September 7th each year.

PART XII

LIVING HEALTHY – LIVING LONGER

NUTRITION RESOURCES

CHAPTER 21

YOUR AHA MOMENTS

SENIOR CITIZENS OFFER HOPE FOR THE FUTURE

Researchers all seem to agree that diet and nutrition play a critical role in the health and wellbeing of Senior Citizens. It makes perfect sense to partake of the nutritional offerings at the grocery store, and provide a body with nutriment that could go a long way toward keeping one out of institutional settings such as hospitals and retirement homes.

A prime example of healthy living is Kathryn Wilson (Pictured)Left. This 6059-year cancer survivor is enjoying her 90th birthday, mainly due to what she calls, "clean, healthy living." Back in the early 1950s, it was discovered that she had breast cancer. After mastectomy and treatments, she still lives to tell her miraculous story of life after cancer. She loves playing slots, cruising, working in the yard and exploring new horizons. Her belief is that "clean living" is the key to growing old gracefully and staying out of hospitals. She enjoys life, is an avid reader, and enjoys her dogs.

LEARN HOW TO STAY WELL AND AVOID PROBLEMS

This is the second at which you can have *"your AHA moment"* to show the world that healthy living and exercise will help keep you out of the failed system for seniors.

95 YEAR-OLD YOGA INSTRUCTOR IS INSPIRATION OF HOPE FOR SENIOR CITIZENS

Extraordinary leaders and teachers change the way we perceive the world. The very best lead by their example.

TAO PORCHON-LYNCH ™, Master Yoga teacher, 95 years young, synthesizes the most positive aspects of Indian, European and American thought. Tao is uniquely equipped to spread Yogic insights, originating in India, to Westerners seeking enlightenment. She has trained and certified hundreds of yoga instructors, since founding the Westchester Institute of Yoga in 1982. Tao has over 70 years of yoga practice and more than 45 years of teaching yoga to students in India, France and the U.S.

Tao believes that following the principles of yoga can heal individuals and by extension, help heal our planet. At ninety-five, she is the embodiment of many profound Yoga principles. She exemplifies the positive "can-do spirit" that can accomplish anything. Tao is a living advertisement for how to tap into our human potential. She is unique in her ability to overcome the effects of aging to control her body and mind in harmony with Yoga's principles. Tao's philosophy is "There is nothing we cannot do if we harness the power within us." Her yoga principles and practices will be appreciated by current and future generations. Her current passion, in addition to yoga, is ballroom dancing and she is an award winning world-class dancer.

SENIOR CITIZENS HELPING OTHERS

With a stern, "you better get me out of here face," 92-year-old Dorothy Runnels, wife of the late U.S. Congressman, Harold Runnels, always finds the time to participate in worthy causes such as "go to jail" to raise bail to benefit Muscular Dystrophy.

She is an avid traveler and continues to be involved in politics. She is a person from whom consistent advice is sought. Her community spirit and involvement is such that most say, "keeping up with her is a challenge."

DIRECTOR OF ASSISTED LIVING FACILITY JUICING HEALTHY DRINKS FOR RESIDENTS

Seniors have hope knowing that there are assisted living facilities where directors engage in juicing for the residents. At one such facility in New Mexico, the director said that those who were walking stooped over, after experiencing a regular offering of juices, smoothies and shakes created from fruits and vegetables began to walk standing straight, and others that had no energy, suddenly began to perk up and experience a more mobile side of life. The director of the facility believes that nutrition is a major key in the process of maintaining good health and welfare.

Senior citizens who are ready to take the challenge for nutritional excitement will find the Food and Nutrition Information Center a valuable resource when it comes to healthy living. The publication is packed with information and easily accessible locations to learn the "how's and why's" of providing yourself with the nutrition you need to create a new "super you." Today is the first day of the rest of your life.

This information is a collection of general nutrition resources for older adults.

Resource List is available from the Food and Nutrition Information Center's (FNIC)

Web site: www.nal.usda.gov/fnic/pubs/olderadults.pdf.

CONSUMER CORNER: SENIORS

United States Department of Agriculture (USDA), National Agricultural Library (NAL), Food and Nutrition Information Center

Description: Nutrition topics of interest to seniors such as healthy eating to reduce risk of disease and dealing with changes that affect eating (such as taste changes or having to cook for one).

Web site: http://fnic.nal.usda.gov/consumers/ages-stages/seniors

EATING WELL AS YOU GET OLDER ~ NIH SENIOR HEALTH

DHHS, NIH, National Institute on Aging; National Library of Medicine

Description: Online resource with information and videos for seniors about how to eat well, eat safely, shop wisely and more. Large text availability, contrast and speech toggle improve resource's accessibility for older adults.

Web site: http://nihseniorhealth.gov/eatingwellasyougetolder/benefitsofeatingwell/01.html

EATING WELL OVER 50: NUTRITION AND DIET TIPS FOR HEALTHY EATING AS YOU AGE

Helpguide.org

Description: Online fact sheet provides information for older adults on why nutrition is important, nutrient needs, tips for creating a well-balanced diet, overcoming obstacles, and handling physical and lifestyle changes.

Web site: http://www.helpguide.org/life/senior_nutrition.htm

EVALUATING HEALTH INFORMATION

DHHS, NIH, National Library of Medicine

Description: A web page with many resources for learning how to determine if health information is reliable. The page includes tutorials, articles (some in both English and Spanish), a section specifically for seniors and links to more information.

Web site: http://www.nlm.nih.gov/medlineplus/evaluatinghealthinformation.html

FIT AND FABULOUS AS YOU MATURE

DHHS, NIH, The National Institute of Diabetes and Digestive and Kidney Diseases (NIDDK), Weight-control Information Network

Description: This 23-page booklet provides tips for healthy eating and safe physical activity for older adults, specifically African American women. Resource includes information about label reading, serving sizes and eating out.

Web sites: http://win.niddk.nih.gov/publications/mature.htm http://win.niddk.nih.gov/publications/PDFs/FitandFabulous.pdf (PDF | 1.8 MB)

Ordering Information: Print copies may be ordered online or by phone or mail from the Weight-control Information Network. Ask for NIH Publication No. 03-4927. See Section III for contact information.

HEALTHY AGING

Academy of Nutrition and Dietetics (AND)

Description: Online resource separated into two sections – "Nutrition for Older Adults" and "Food Safety Risks for Older Adults." Links to several online fact sheets including: "Healthy Eating for Older Adults", "Special Nutrient Needs of Older Adults", "and How Many Calories Do Older Adults Need?"

MYPLATE

United States Department of Agriculture

Description: Provides nutrition information, sample menus and recipes, tips for eating on a budget, and more for all ages. Provides a link to the SuperTracker – a tool that can be used to plan, analyze, and track diet and physical activity.

Web site: http://www.choosemyplate.gov

WHAT'S ON YOUR PLATE? SMART FOOD CHOICES FOR HEALTHY AGING.

DHHS, NIH, National Institute on Aging

Description: Booklet describes the Dietary Guidelines for Americans, 2010 with a special emphasis on applications for adults aged 50 and older. Topics include USDA food patterns, portion sizes, nutrition labels, nutrients, lifestyle, shopping, food safety, sample menus and recipes.

Web site: http://www.nia.nih.gov/health/publication/whats-your-plate-smart-food- choices-healthy-aging

Ordering Information: Print copies may be ordered from the National Institute on Aging by phone or online at http://newcart.niapublications.org/order/order.aspx?id=BK030.

YOUNG AT HEART: TIPS FOR OLDER ADULTS

At the age of 94, Larry Milberger is young at heart, and drives to work every day to run his multi-million dollar business. He believes in a strong work ethic, dependability, honesty, coffee every morning, and quality of work from his employees. He doesn't miss a meal, and is seen as a regular at a local steak house. After work, he takes a breather to enjoy his dogs, and some down-home country living. He drives a hard bargain in business and thrives on a good debate.

WEBSITES FOR SENIOR CITIZENS WITH YOUR HEALTH IN MIND

DHHS, NIH, NIDDK, Weight-Control Information Network

Description: Young at Heart is a booklet that provides tips for healthy eating and safe physical activity for older adults. Defines a healthy weight and offers ideas for planning and preparing meals. Also available in Spanish.

Web sites: http://win.niddk.nih.gov/publications/young_heart.htm http://win.niddk.nih.gov/publications/PDFs/youngatheart.pdf (PDF | 2.9 MB)

Ordering Information: Print copies may be ordered online, by mail, or by phone from the Weight-control Information Network. Ask for NIH Publication No. 02–4993.

DISEASE PREVENTION AND COMMON CONDITIONS

ANSWERS BY HEART

American Heart Association

Description: This website links to dozen of downloadable information sheets on cardiovascular conditions, treatments and tests, and lifestyle and risk reduction. Many of the sheets are also available in Spanish, Traditional Chinese, Simplified Chinese and Vietnamese.

Website: http://www.heart.org/HEARTORG/Conditions/More/ToolsForYourHeartHealth/ Answers-by-Heart-Fact-Sheets_UCM_300330_Article.jsp

Ordering Information: Pamphlets may also be ordered on many of the same topics at: http://educationpackets.heart.org/ or by contacting the American Heart Association directly.

THE FACTS ABOUT FIBER

American Institute for Cancer Research

Description: This brochure provides an overview of fiber and the importance of a high fiber diet for cancer prevention and to help with other health concerns. It also lists the amount of dietary fiber found in common foods.

Web site: http://www.aicr.org/site/DocServer/FPC-E7B-FIW.pdf?docID=1547 (PDF | 595KB)

Order Information: Copies may be ordered online, by mail, or by phone from the American Institute of Cancer Research. See Section III for contact information.

Order online at: http://www.aicr.org/site/PageServer?pagename=pub_facts_fiber

IT'S NOT TOO LATE TO PREVENT DIABETES

DHHS, NIH, NIDDK, National Diabetes Education Program

Description: This 4-page booklet includes physical activity and nutrition tips and resources to help prevent or delay the onset of diabetes.

Web sites: http://ndep.nih.gov/publications/PublicationDetail.aspx?PubId=75 and http://ndep.nih.gov/media/nottoolate_tips.pdf (PDF | 3.1 MB)

Ordering Information: Up to 10 print copies may be ordered for free online, by mail, or by phone from the National Diabetes Education Program. Publication number is NDEP- 75.

NUTRITION AFTER FIFTY: TIPS AND RECIPES

American Institute for Cancer Research

Description: Written specifically for people over the age of 50, this 40-page brochure provides general information and practical strategies for maintaining a healthy diet appropriate for cancer prevention. It includes answers to common age-related nutrition questions and recipes that are healthy and easy to prepare.

Web site: http://preventcancer.aicr.org/site/DocServer/Nov2007_After_50_FINAL.pdf?docID=1571 (PDF | 2MB)

Ordering Information: Copies may be ordered for free online, by mail, or by phone from the American Institute for Cancer Research.

Order online at http://www.aicr.org/site/PageServer?pagename=pub_nutrition_af.

ORAL HEALTH: OLDER ADULTS

DHHS, NIH, National Institute of Dental and Craniofacial Research

Description: This site provides links to information about oral issues commonly experienced by older adults such as dry mouth, gum disease, oral cancer and finding dental care.

Website: http://www.nidcr.nih.gov/OralHealth/OralHealthInformation/OlderAdults/

OSTEOPOROSIS ~ NIH SENIOR HEALTH

DHHS, NIH, National Institute on Aging; National Library of Medicine

Description: Online resource with information and videos for seniors about osteoporosis, including risk factors and prevention, warning signs, treatment and research, frequently asked questions and more. Large text availability, contrast and speech toggle improve resource's accessibility for older adults.

Web site: http://nihseniorhealth.gov/osteoporosis/whatisosteoporosis/01.html

WHAT I NEED TO KNOW ABOUT CONSTIPATION

DHHS, NIH, National Institute of Diabetes and Digestive and Kidney Diseases (NIDDK)

Description: This is a Web site providing and overview of constipation. It provides information on the diet and lifestyle changes individuals can make to prevent constipation and stay regular. Includes other organizations to contact. Available in English, Spanish and PDF versions.

Web sites: http://digestive.niddk.nih.gov/ddiseases/pubs/constipation_ez/index.htm (English) http://digestive.niddk.nih.gov/spanish/pubs/constipation_ez/index.aspx (Spanish) http://digestive.niddk.nih.gov/ddiseases/pubs/constipation_ez/constipation_508.pdf (PDF | 912 KB)

Order information: Hard copies available to order from the NIDDK. Call, write or order online at: http://catalog.niddk.nih.gov/detail.cfm?ID=175. Ask for DD-168.

WHAT IS THE DASH (DIETARY APPROACHES TO STOP HYPERTENSION) EATING PLAN?

DHHS, NIH, National Heart Lung and Blood Institute

Description: This site explains and helps people get started with the DASH eating plan for preventing and lowering high blood pressure.

Web site: http://www.nhlbi.nih.gov/health/health-topics/topics/dash/

SPECIAL CONCERNS FOR OLDER ADULTS

Food Assistance and Food Resource Management (including Thrifty Food Shopping, Meal Planning and Cooking)

EAT RIGHT WHEN MONEY'S TIGHT

USDA, NAL, SNAP-Ed Connection

Description: A collection of Web-available, print-ready nutrition education materials focused on food resource management. Includes shopping tips, food budgeting handouts, thrifty cooking ideas and more.

Web site: http://snap.nal.usda.gov/resource-library/eat-right-when-moneys-tight

SENIORCARE LOCATOR

DHHS, Administration on Aging

Description: The Senior care Locator is a public service that helps older adults and caregivers locate aging services in communities throughout the United States. Support is available via the Internet or over the telephone in Spanish and English. Seniorcare Locator provides information on home delivered meals, home health services, transportation, and other related services.

Web site: http://www.seniorcare.gov Phone: 800-677-1116

FOOD BANK LOCATOR

Feeding America

Description: Find contact information on emergency food providers such as food banks and food rescue programs in all 50 states and Puerto Rico through their Internet database or telephone support.

Web site: http://feedingamerica.org/foodbank-results.aspx Phone: 800-771-2303

MAKING YOUR KITCHEN "USER FRIENDLY"

Ohio State University Extension and Ohio Department of Aging

Description: This fact sheet helps older adults adapt their kitchen to make it easier to cook and use appliances. Estimated costs for each suggestion are provided.

Web sites: http://ohioline.osu.edu/ss-fact/0179.html http://ohioline.osu.edu/ss-fact/pdf/0179.pdf (PDF 39 KB)

MEALS ON WHEELS LOCATOR

Meals on Wheels Association of America

Description: The Meals on Wheels Association of America represents those who provide meal services to homebound people in need.

You can enter your zip code on this Web site and get contact information for local Meals on Wheels locations.

Web site: www.mowaa.org/Page.aspx?pid=253 Phone: 888-998-6325

NUTRITION ASSISTANCE RESOURCE GUIDE

USDA, NAL, Food and Nutrition Information Center

Description: This publication contains resources for people in need of food assistance. It includes a list of federal nutrition assistance programs, eligibility guidelines for each program, and resources to access more information about the programs.

Web sites: http://www.nal.usda.gov/fnic/pubs/nutritionassistance.pdf (PDF | 173 KB) Supplement (designed for those without access to the Internet): http://www.nal.usda.gov/fnic/pubs/nutritionassistance-supplement.pdf (PDF | 541 KB)

Ordering Information: Contact Food and Nutrition Information Center.

STRETCHING YOUR FOOD DOLLARS

Oregon State University Extension, Eat Well for Less

Description: This is a Web-based learning module divided into two sections: Strategies at Home and Strategies at the Store. Each section provides tips and information on spending food dollars wisely in each environment. The self-paced module can be completed in approximately 20-30 minutes.

Web site: http://extension.oregonstate.edu/fcd/nutrition/ewfl/module3/dollars1.html

SUPPLEMENTAL NUTRITION ASSISTANCE PROGRAM SPECIAL RULES FOR THE SENIOR

USDA, Food and Nutrition Service (FNS), Supplemental Nutrition Assistance Program (SNAP)

Description: Online fact sheet that provides information on the application process for food stamps and reviews eligibility requirements specific to older adults.

Web site: http://www.fns.usda.gov/snap/applicant_recipients/eligibility.htm#Special

FOOD SAFETY FOR OLDER ADULTS

DHHS, FoodSafety.gov

Description: This Web site provides links to resources on food safety for older adults including two brochures and a podcast on food safety for older adults.

Web site: http://www.foodsafety.gov/poisoning/risk/olderadults/index.html

OLDER ADULTS AND FOOD SAFETY

USDA, Food Safety and Inspection Service

Description: Online fact sheet that gives an overview of foodborne illness, safe food handling, cooking temperatures, and more for older adults.

USDA MEAT AND POULTRY HOTLINE

USDA, Food Safety and Inspection Service

Description: This toll-free hotline is staffed by food safety specialists who can answer questions about the safe storage, handling, and preparation of meat, poultry and egg products. Recorded messages are also available. Questions can be answered in English and Spanish. Questions can also be emailed to the hotline, or you can ask questions virtually via a live chat through "Ask Karen." Phone: 888-MPHotline (888-674-6854) TTY: 800-256-7072

Email: mphotline.fsis@usda.gov Ask Karen

Web site: http://www.foodsafety.gov/experts/askkaren/index.html Chat services available weekdays, 10:00 a.m. – 4:00 p.m. Eastern Time.

III. DIETARY SUPPLEMENTS/ FOOD-DRUG INTERACTIONS

HEALTHY LIVING FOR SENIORS: FOOD CAN AFFECT YOUR MEDICINES

University of Florida, Department of Family, Youth and Community Sciences, Florida Cooperative Extension Service, Institute of Food and Agricultural Services.

Description: This easy-to-read fact sheet for older adults reviews certain foods and food groups that may need to be avoided when taking some medicines.

Web sites: http://edis.ifas.ufl.edu/fy676 http://edis.ifas.ufl.edu/pdffiles/FY/FY67600.pdf (PDF | 792KB)

MEDICINES AND YOU: A GUIDE FOR OLDER ADULTS

DHHS, Administration on Aging

Description: This educational booklet discusses information about prescription drugs, how to cut medication costs and how to use medications safely. May be downloaded online or hardcopies can be ordered online.

Website: http://acl.gov/NewsRoom/Publications/docs/ Medicines_and_You.pdf (PDF | 339 KB)

TIPS FOR OLDER DIETARY SUPPLEMENT USERS

DHHS, Food and Drug Administration

Description: This is an online resource with information and links relating to dietary supplements. Topics include "points to ponder" before buying a supplement, the safety of dietary supplements, and tips on how to read product claims critically. Available in English and Spanish.

Web site: http://www.fda.gov/Food/DietarySupplements/ UsingDietarySupplements/ucm110493.ht m

B. BOOKS AND COOKBOOKS

American Dietetic Association Complete Food and Nutrition Guide, 4th Edition Roberta Larson Duyff, MS, RD, FADA, CFCS Wily Publishing, Inc., 2012 ISBN: 0470912073 NAL Call Number: RA784 .D89 2012

Description: This book serves as a nutrition guide based on the latest healthy eating advice and the 2010 Dietary Guidelines for Americans. Practical tips and advice for every stage of life are offered. The book includes sections applicable to any age group on nutrition, managing weight, healthy eating, and food safety.

Community Resources for Older Adults: Programs and Services in an Era of Change, 4th Edition Robbyn R. Wacker and Karen A. Roberto SAGE Publications, 2013 ISBN: 978-1452202464

Description: Information for students, professionals and older adults on community resources available for older adults, as well as how programs exist through federal legislation, who they are for, and how they are funded and delivered.

THE DASH DIET ACTION PLAN

Marla Heller, MS, RD Grand Central Publishing 2011. ISBN: 9781455512805

Description: This book provides an overview of the DASH (Dietary Approaches to Stop Hypertension) diet. Studies have shown that following the DASH diet lowers blood pressure and improves other health factors. This book includes a month of meal plans, recipes and shopping lists, tips on nutrition and physical activity.

The New American Heart Association Cookbook, revised 8th Edition American Heart Association Clarkson & Potter, 2012 ISBN: 0307587576

Descriptions: This cookbook offers advice on simple, heart-healthy meals that everyone can enjoy. It contains over 600 recipes and can also be a resource for menu planning, shopping for healthful ingredients, and healthy holiday cooking. Balance, variety, and common sense are all emphasized.

ONE BOWL: SIMPLE HEALTHY RECIPES FOR ONE

Stephanie Bostic, MS Stephanie Bostic, 2011 ISBN: 978-1463690724

Description: This cookbook provides simple, easy-to-read recipes for one person. Both vegetarian and non-vegetarian recipes are included, but the focus is on healthy, plant- based meals. The author provides advice on meal planning, keeping track of what you eat and keeping your pantry stocked with healthy items. Many of the recipes can also be expanded to feed more than one person.

REVIEW: THE DEADLY SECRETS REVEALED

DEADLY SECRET #1:

Senior Citizens, you are often given antipsychotic drugs without your consent, medical diagnosis, and knowledge simply to silence you. These drugs can be deadly.

SOLUTION:

Have you informed your family and friends what to recognize if this happens to you? Do they know what you want them to do to save you?

DEADLY SECRET #2:

Senior Citizens are overmedicated on prescription drugs that can cause serious side effects, interactions, and dangerous outcomes.

SOLUTION:

Who is checking your medications for these drug/drug interactions and side effects? Are you demanding that your medications be changed when you discover side effects and interactions between drugs you are taking?

DEADLY SECRET #3:

Senior Citizens are given many prescription drugs that cause memory loss.

SOLUTION:

Did you learn in this book what some of those drugs are? With your new knowledge, will you take action to rid yourself of something that is causing your memory loss so you are not vulnerable?

DEADLY SECRET #4:

Senior Citizens may have been misdiagnosed with Alzheimer's who do not have Alzheimer's. Is it a B-12 deficiency or medications causing your memory loss, or is it really Alzheimer's

SOLUTION:

Will you take action to discover if you have Alzheimer's, or if you could be preventing memory loss?

DEADLY SECRET #5:

Senior Citizens are often abused in care facilities and hospitals, and violators are getting away with it.

SOLUTION:

Are you ready to take action against facilities and staff that are violating your Civil Rights in order to stop this practice?

DEADLY SECRET #6:

Senior Citizens may be receiving fraudulent charges to Medicare from care providers. This is a violation of your rights, and fraud by your provider.

SOLUTION:

Will you report these violations to Medicare to save yourself and all taxpayers millions of dollars?

DEADLY SECRET #7:

Senior Citizens are not always told the truth about what they are being given by mouth, by injection, in your food and drink, and in your IV.

SOLUTION:

Are you ready to stand up against this practice, demand your records, and challenge your caregivers?

DEADLY SECRET #8:

Senior Citizens rights are violated daily by family, friends, and caregivers.

SOLUTION:

Are you ready to stand up for your rights and avoid increasing your chances of early death by 300%?

DEADLY SECRET #9:

Senior Citizens are scammed daily.

SOLUTION:

Now that you know what the scams are, are you ready to tell scammers to take a hike instead of your money because you are on to their game?

DEADLY SECRET #10:

Senior Citizens are keeping it a secret that they are abused in their homes.

SOLUTION:

Will you stand up and tell your abusive relatives that it is against the law to be abusive verbally, mentally, and physically, and report them?

DEADLY SECRET #11:

Senior Citizens are enduring daily Ageism violations in the workplace and in public.

SOLUTION:

Are you ready to take your employer to task, and to stand up to those who are rude to you and marginalize you?

DEADLY SECRET #12

Senior Citizens have deep trust in those who provide medical services, the attitude and upbringing that medical professionals are to be trusted unconditionally.

SOLUTION:

Do you now understand that your trust can turn into tragedy in certain situations, and will you use your rights to make a good decision for yourself?

DEADLY SECRET #13

Senior Citizen's rights are violated in many institutions, hospitals, independent living facilities, and care facilities.

SOLUTION:

Now that you have read your rights, will you demand that those rights be honored?

DEADLY SECRET #14:

Now you know that 1 in 5 Senior Citizens are abused in one way or another.

SOLUTION:

Will you help others to avoid the many dangers, and will you help them find peace?

THE MORAL OF DEADLY SECRETS

If you exercise your rights, know when you are being mistreated, demand fair treatment, and have insight into making positive decisions, you could live years longer and could save others through your knowledge and ability to recognize a negative situation and take action.

A SENIOR CITIZEN'S PRAYER

Dear God,

I pray that you will watch over me, and others like me; that you will guide the hands of the nurses and doctors taking care of us. Please help them understand, if they ask if we are in pain, it may be that our backs hurt because my friends and I are old, and we can't be in the same position for a long time. Maybe all we need is for someone to help us turn over, or simply to understand the kind act of rubbing our backs would help, not a strong shot of morphine. Please let those who take care of us who ask if we need something to help us sleep, know, that we *don't* need something that will knock us out for twenty-four hours, but instead, a simple Tylenol PM or a cup of sleepy time tea. Please, God, I know they are short handed and it's easier to put us to sleep so we can't bother them, but don't let them medicate us with antipsychotic drugs, and medications that strip us of our spirit. Like my friends, I want to feel, I want to know what is going on around me, and I don't want to be someone who is cast into the dark depths of silence. We want to be able to communicate with our beloved family and friends. Please help those who seem to take pleasure in hurting us through physical and mental abuse, by teaching them the way of kindness and compassion. Dear God, please stop the abuses that are cast upon me, and others. All of us are special, and we deserve to live, or at least, die with dignity "when" it is our time to go. Please make all of those who send millions of us to an early grave, stop the abuse now. *Thank you, God, for hearing my prayer. Amen*

FASTEST GROWING POPULATION DEMOGRAPHIC IN AMERICA

Demographics of the senior population

- The older population (65+) numbers over 40.4 million in America today.
- 300,000 baby boomers become senior every month.
- 78 million baby boomers will enter the ranks of senior over the next 17 years.
- The number of Americans aged 45-64 – who will reach 65 over the next two decades – increased by 31% during this decade.
- Persons reaching age 65 have an average life expectancy of an additional 18.8 years (20.0 years for females and 17.3 years for males).
- Older women outnumber older men at 23.0 million older women to 17.5 million older men.
- Older men were much more likely to be married than older women—72% of men vs. 42% of women. 40% older women in 2010 were widows.
- About 29% (11.3 million) of non-institutionalized older persons live alone (8.1 million women, 3.2 million men).
- Almost half of older women (47%) age 75+ live alone.
- About 485,000 grandparents aged 65 or more had the primary responsibility for their grandchildren who lived with them.
- The population 65 and over is projected to increase to 55 million in 2020 (a 36% increase for that decade).
- The 85+ population is projected to increase to 6.6 million in 2020 (19%) for that decade.

Demographics: Income – Social Security–Poverty

- The median income of older persons in 2010 was $25,704 for males and $15,072 for females. Median money income (after adjusting for inflation) of all households headed by older people fell 1.5% (not statistically significant) from 2009 to 2010. Households containing families headed by persons 65+ reported a median income in 2010 of $45,763.
- The major sources of income as reported by older persons in 2009 were Social Security (reported by 87% of older persons), income from assets (reported by 53%), private pensions (reported by 28%), government employee pensions (reported by 14%), and earnings (reported by 26%).
- Social Security constituted 90% or more of the income received by 35% of beneficiaries in 2009 (22% of married couples and 43% of non-married beneficiaries).
- Almost 3.5 million senior persons (9.0%) were below the poverty level in 2010. During 2011, the U.S. Census Bureau also released a new Supplemental Poverty Measure (SPM) that takes into account regional variations in the livings costs, non-cash benefits received, and non-discretionary expenditures but does not replace the official poverty measure. The SPM shows a poverty level for older persons of 15.9%, an increase of over 75% over the official rate of 9.0% mainly due to medical out-of-pocket expenses.
- About 11% (3.7 million) of older Medicare enrollees received personal care from a paid or unpaid source in 1999.
- Principal sources of data for the Profile are the U.S. Census Bureau, the National Center for Health Statistics, and the Bureau of Labor Statistics. The Profile incorporates the latest data available but not all items are updated on an annual basis.

According to the Census Bureau's "middle series" projections, the senior population will more than double between now and the year 2050, to 80 million, and as many as one in five Americans will be senior. A large majority of this growth will occur between now and 2030, when the "baby boom" generation enters their senior years. The "baby boomers" (those born between 1946 and 1964) started turning 65 in 2011.

Between today and 2030 the number of seniors will grow by an average of 2.8 percent annually. By comparison, annual growth will average 1.3 percent during the preceding 20 years and 0.7 percent during the following 20 years. In total, it is estimated that there are around 7 million senior people in need of long-term care, and that, depending on mortality and morbidity, there will be between 10 million and 14 million in 2020, and between 14 million and 24 million in 2060 (U.S. General Accounting Office, 1994, p.8).

The average lifespan has increased, but conventionally, "senior" is defined as a chronological age of 65 years old or older, while those from 65 through 74 years old are referred to as "early senior" and those over 75 years old as "late senior."

According to the Census Bureau's middle-series projections, the senior population will more than double between now and the year 2030, to 80 million, and as Toossi's report on the labor force will make clear, a large majority of this growth will occur "between now and after 2010, when the baby boom generation begins a precipitous baby boomer retirement boom" (Toossi and Fisco quoted earlier in 2013).

Between today and 2030, the number of seniors will grow by an average of ... Between today, in comparison, would reach only 5.1 percent ...

SHOULD I BE AFRAID?

APPENDIX I

EXCERPTS FROM U.S. GOVERNMENT REPORT – SENIOR GIVEN ANTIPSYCHOTIC DRUGS FOR "COMPLAINING" (MAY 2011 OEI-07-08-00150)

Fourteen percent of senior nursing home residents had Medicare claims for atypical antipsychotic drugs. Of the 2.1 million senior nursing home residents, 304,983 had at least 1 Medicare claim for an atypical antipsychotic drug from January 1 through June 30, 2007. Claims for senior nursing home residents accounted for 20 percent of the total 8.5 million claims for atypical antipsychotic drugs for all Medicare beneficiaries during the review period. Claims for these residents amounted to $309 million.

Eighty-three percent of Medicare claims for atypical antipsychotic drugs for senior nursing home residents were associated with off-label conditions; 88 percent were associated with the condition specified in the FDA boxed warning. Using medical reviewers' responses, we determined that, during the review period, almost 1.4 million atypical antipsychotic drug claims were for senior nursing home residents diagnosed with conditions that were off-label and/or were specified in the boxed warning. Physicians are not prohibited from prescribing drugs for off-label conditions or in the presence of the condition(s) specified in the FDA boxed warning.

Fifty-one percent of Medicare atypical antipsychotic drug claims for senior nursing home residents were erroneous, amounting to $116 million. For the period of January 1 through June 30, 2007, we determined from medical record review that over 726,000 of the 1.4 million atypical antipsychotic drug claims for senior nursing home residents did not comply with Medicare reimbursement criteria. The claimed drugs were either not used for medically accepted indications as supported by the compendia or not documented as having been administered to the senior nursing home residents.

NURSING HOME RESIDENTS

Twenty-two percent of the atypical antipsychotic drugs claimed were not administered in accordance with CMS standards regarding unnecessary drug use in nursing homes. For the 6-month review period, we determined using medical record review that 317,971 Medicare claims ($63 million) were associated with atypical antipsychotic drugs that were not administered according to CMS standards for drug regimens in nursing homes. Nursing homes' noncompliance with these standards (e.g., providing drugs in excessive doses or for excessive durations) does not cause Medicare payments for these drugs to be erroneous because the payments are made on behalf of the residents, not the nursing homes. However, failure to comply with CMS standards may affect nursing homes' participation with Medicare.

BACKGROUND

Senator Charles Grassley requested that the Office of Inspector General (OIG) evaluate the extent to which senior nursing home residents receive atypical antipsychotic drugs. For this evaluation, we are using the term "atypical antipsychotic drugs" for second-generation antipsychotic drugs developed to treat psychoses and/or mood disorders. Senator Grassley was specifically concerned about atypical antipsychotic drugs prescribed for senior nursing home residents for off-label conditions (i.e., conditions other than schizophrenia and/or bipolar disorder) and/or for residents with the condition specified in the FDA boxed warning (i.e., dementia). Moreover, Senator Grassley was concerned about whether Medicare is paying for drugs that may not be in the best interest of senior nursing home residents.

Atypical antipsychotic drug use by senior nursing home residents has also been an issue in law enforcement activities. For example, in November 2009, the United States reached a $98 million settlement with Omnicare, Inc. (a long-term care (LTC) pharmacy), to resolve allegations that it received kickbacks to recommend drugs, including Risperdal (an atypical antipsychotic), for use in nursing homes. In January 2010, the Department of Justice filed suit against the manufacturer of Risperdal and two subsidiaries alleging that the companies paid kickbacks to Omnicare, Inc., to induce it to purchase and recommend Risperdal and other drugs for use in nursing homes. The United States has entered into settlements with the manufacturers of several other atypical antipsychotic drugs to resolve allegations that the manufacturers promoted their drugs for uses that were not approved by FDA and were not reimbursable under Federal health care programs. The marketing of atypical antipsychotic drugs was outside the scope of this evaluation.

FDA DRUG APPROVAL, INCLUDING ATYPICAL ANTIPSYCHOTIC DRUGS

FDA has approved eight atypical antipsychotic drugs: Aripiprazole, Clozapine, Olanzapine, Olanzapine/Fluoxetine, Paliperidone, Quetiapine, Risperidone, and Ziprasidone. At the time of our review, FDA had approved all of these drugs for use in the psychiatric treatment of schizophrenia and/or bipolar disorder.

All drugs have benefits and risks. Risks can range from less serious (e.g., an upset stomach) to permanent and potentially life threatening.

If FDA determines that a drug's health benefits for its intended use outweigh its known risks, then FDA approves the drug for marketing for that use.

Risks associated with the use of atypical antipsychotic drugs that apply to all persons and are included in product labeling include, but are not limited to: neuroleptic malignant syndrome, a life-threatening nervous system problem; tardive dyskinesia, a movement problem; high blood sugar and diabetes; and low blood pressure resulting in dizziness and possibly fainting.

OFF-LABEL DRUG USE

After FDA approves a drug, physicians are permitted to prescribe that drug for other uses. This is commonly referred to as off label use.

Off-label use is not uncommon. A 2006 study in the Archives of Internal Medicine found that off-label uses accounted for 21 percent of prescriptions written in 2001. Specific to atypical antipsychotic drugs, a 2007 Agency for Healthcare Research and Quality (AHRQ) report listed the most common off-label uses: the treatment of agitation in dementia, depression, obsessive-compulsive disorder, posttraumatic stress disorder, personality disorders, Tourette's syndrome, and autism. Additionally, a 2009 study examining antipsychotic drug use among patients in the Department of Veterans Affairs health care system found that 60.2 percent of the individuals who received an antipsychotic drug had no record of a diagnosis for which these drugs are FDA approved (i.e., the drug was used off-label).

FDA'S BOXED WARNING

If drug manufacturers and/or FDA determine during the approval process or after a drug has been approved for marketing that the drug may produce severe or life-threatening risks, FDA requires that drug manufacturers include a boxed warning (also referred to as a black-box warning) on the product's labeling to warn prescribers and consumers of these risks. Physicians are not prohibited from prescribing a drug in the presence of the condition(s) specified in the boxed warning.

In April 2005, FDA issued a public health advisory for atypical antipsychotic drugs. FDA required manufacturers of these drugs to include a boxed warning regarding the increased risk of mortality when these drugs are used for the treatment of behavioral disorders in senior patients with dementia.

FDA noted that mortality for senior demented patients with behavioral disorders treated with atypical antipsychotics increased 1.6–1.7 times compared to mortality for those treated with a placebo. FDA, Public Health Advisory: Deaths with Antipsychotics in Senior Patients with Behavioral Disturbances, April 2005.

FDA WARNING attached to each drug includes risks and potential side effects. Among the risks and potential side effects listed for all eight atypical antipsychotic drugs is the increased chance of death in senior persons.

CMS requires that nursing home residents who have not previously taken antipsychotic drugs, including atypical antipsychotic drugs, not be given these drugs unless the drug therapy is necessary to treat a specific condition as diagnosed and documented in the medical record. CMS also requires that nursing homes administering antipsychotic drugs ensure that the residents receive gradual dose reductions and behavioral interventions in an effort to discontinue these drugs unless such measures are clinically contraindicated.

An adverse consequence is an unpleasant symptom or event that is due to or associated with a medication, such as impairment or decline in an individual's mental or physical condition or functional or psychosocial status. (CMS, State Operations Manual (Internet-Only Manual), Pub. 100-07, Appendix PP: Guidance to Surveyors for Long Term Care Facilities.)

A January 2007 AHRQ report assessed the off-label use of atypical antipsychotic drugs. AHRQ found that all of these drugs increase the risk of death for senior persons with dementia.

FINDINGS

Fourteen percent of senior nursing home residents had Medicare claims for atypical antipsychotic drugs.

From January 1 through June 30, 2007, 304,983 (14 percent) of the 2.1 million senior nursing home residents had at least 1 Medicare claim for an atypical antipsychotic drug. Claims for senior nursing home residents accounted for 20 percent (1,678,874) of the 8.5 million atypical antipsychotic drug claims for all Medicare beneficiaries during the review period.

Medicare atypical antipsychotic drug claims for senior nursing home residents.

Eighty-three percent of Medicare claims for atypical antipsychotic drugs for senior nursing home residents were associated with off-label conditions; 88 percent were associated with the condition specified in the FDA boxed warning.

For the 6-month review period, we determined through medical record review that 83 percent (1,197,442) of atypical antipsychotic drug claims were for senior nursing home residents diagnosed with conditions for which the drugs' use was not approved by FDA (i.e., the drugs were used off-label). Eighty-eight percent (1,263,641) of the drug claims were for residents diagnosed with dementia (the condition specified in the FDA boxed warning).

Descriptions of each atypical antipsychotic drug listed below are drawn from the Food and Drug Administration's approved labels at the time of our review. The most common side effects listed are those that were considered to be reasonably associated with the use of the drug.

Aripiprazole (Abilify). Indicated for the treatment of schizophrenia and acute manic and mixed episodes associated with bipolar disorder. Side effects include, but are not limited to: increased chance of death in senior persons; neuroleptic malignant syndrome; tardive dyskinesia; high blood sugar and diabetes; strokes; low blood pressure seen as dizziness, cardiac irregularities, and possibly fainting; seizures; increased body temperature; and difficulty swallowing. The most common side effects (incidence ≥10%) in adult patients in clinical trials were nausea, vomiting, constipation, headache, dizziness, akathisia, anxiety, insomnia, and restlessness.

Clozapine (Clozaril). Indicated for the treatment of severely ill schizophrenic patients who fail to respond adequately to standard drug treatment for schizophrenia and for reducing the risk of recurrent suicidal behavior in patients with schizophrenia or schizoaffective disorder who are judged to be at chronic risk for experiencing suicidal behavior. Side effects include, but are not limited to: increased chance of death in senior persons, agranulocytosis, seizures, heart problems including myocarditis, lowering of blood pressure, neuroleptic malignant syndrome, tardive dyskinesia, high blood sugar and diabetes, fever, blood clots in the lung, increased blood sugar, and liver disease. The most common side effects (incidence ≥5%) in clinical trials were: central nervous system complaints, including drowsiness/sedation, dizziness/vertigo, headache, and tremor; autonomic nervous system complaints, including excessive salivation, sweating, dry mouth, and visual disturbances; cardiovascular findings, including tachycardia, hypotension, and syncope; gastrointestinal complaints, including constipation and nausea; and fever.

Olanzapine (Zyprexa). Indicated for the treatment of schizophrenia, acute mixed or manic episodes associated with bipolar I disorder, and agitation associated with schizophrenia and bipolar I mania. Side effects include, but are not limited to: increased chance of death in senior persons, neuroleptic malignant syndrome, tardive dyskinesia, high blood sugar and diabetes, strokes, low blood pressure seen as dizziness and possibly fainting, cardiac irregularities, seizures, liver problems, increased body temperature, and difficulty swallowing. The most common side effects (incidence ≥5% and at least twice that for placebo) include: weight gain, dizziness, postural hypotension, constipation, personality disorder, akathisia, dry mouth, dyspepsia, increased appetite, somnolence, and tremor.

Olanzapine/Fluoxetine (Symbyax). Indicated for the treatment of depressive episodes associated with bipolar disorder. Side effects include, but are not limited to: suicidal thoughts or actions; increased chance of death in senior persons; neuroleptic malignant syndrome; tardive dyskinesia; high blood sugar and diabetes; strokes; bleeding problems; sexual problems; mania;

weakness, confusion, or trouble thinking caused by low salt levels in the blood; low blood pressure seen as dizziness and possibly fainting; cardiac irregularities; seizures; liver problems; increased body temperature; and difficulty swallowing. The most common side effects (incidence ≥5% and at least twice that for placebo) include: disturbance in attention, dry mouth, fatigue, hypersomnia, increased appetite, peripheral edema, sedation, somnolence, tremor, blurred vision, and weight gain.

Paliperidone (Invega). Indicated for the acute and maintenance treatment of schizophrenia. Side effects include, but are not limited to: increased chance of death and strokes in senior patients with dementia; QT prolongation; neuroleptic malignant syndrome; tardive dyskinesia; high blood sugar and diabetes; dizziness and fainting caused by a drop in blood pressure; impaired judgment, thinking, or motor skills; overheating and dehydration; seizures; difficulty swallowing; suicidal thoughts or actions; persistent erection; fever; and bruising. The most common side effects (incidence ≥5% and at least twice that for placebo) include: extrapyramidal symptoms, tachycardia, akathisia, somnolence, dyspepsia, constipation, weight gain, and nasopharyngitis.

Quetiapine (Seroquel). Indicated for the treatment of schizophrenia and both depressive episodes associated with bipolar disorder and acute manic episodes associated with bipolar I disorder. Side effects include, but are not limited to: increased chance of death in senior persons; neuroleptic malignant syndrome; tardive dyskinesia; high blood sugar and diabetes; low blood pressure seen as dizziness, cardiac irregularities, and possibly fainting; cataracts; seizures; low thyroid; elevated cholesterol or triglycerides; liver problems; persistent erection; increase or decrease in body temperature; and difficulty swallowing. The most common side effects (incidence ≥5% and at least twice that for placebo) in adults include: somnolence, dizziness, dry mouth, constipation, and increase in alanine aminotransferase, weight gain, and dyspepsia.

Risperidone (Risperdal). Indicated for the treatment of schizophrenia and short-term treatment of acute manic or mixed episodes associated with bipolar I disorder. Side effects include but are not limited to: increased chance of death in senior persons; neuroleptic malignant syndrome; tardive dyskinesia; high blood sugar and diabetes; strokes; low blood pressure seen as dizziness, cardiac irregularities, and possibly fainting; seizures; persistent erection; thrombotic thrombocytopenic purpura; increase or decrease in body temperature; and difficulty swallowing. The most common side effects (incidence ≥10%) include: somnolence, increase in appetite, fatigue, rhinitis, upper respiratory tract infection, vomiting, coughing, urinary incontinence, excessive saliva, constipation, fever, Parkinsonism, dystonia, abdominal pain, anxiety, nausea, dizziness, dry mouth, tremor, rash, akathisia, and dyspepsia.

Ziprasidone (Geodon). Indicated for the treatment of schizophrenia and acute agitation in people with schizophrenia. Side effects include, but are not limited to: dangerous problems with heart rhythm; increased chance of death in senior persons; neuroleptic malignant syndrome; tardive dyskinesia; high blood sugar and diabetes; low blood pressure seen as dizziness, cardiac irregularities, and possibly fainting; seizures; persistent erection; increase or decrease in body temperature; and difficulty swallowing. The most common side effects (incidence ≥5% and at least twice that for placebo) include: somnolence, respiratory tract infection, extrapyramidal symptoms, dizziness, akathisia, abnormal vision, asthenia, and vomiting.

RESOURCES FOR SENIORS

NEWSLETTERS

Administration for Community Living, eNews
http://acl.gov/NewsRoom/eNewsletter/Index.aspx
Format: Weekly electronic newsletter

American Cancer Society, New Connections
http://www.cancer.org/treatment/supportprogramsservices/supportresources/index
Format: Bimonthly electronic newsletter

American Diabetes Association, eNewsletters
http://main.diabetes.org/site/PageServer?pagename=EM_signup
Format: Electronic newsletters (several to choose from)

American Heart Association, Heart-Health E-news
http://www.heart.org/HEARTORG/General/Sign-Up-for-Our-Heart-Health-E- newsletters_UCM_314643_Article.jsp Format: Monthly electronic newsletter

American Institute for Cancer Research, Newsletter
http://www.aicr.org/site/PageServer?pagename=aicr_publications_newsletter
Format: Quarterly print newsletter

American Institute for Cancer Research, eNews
http://www.aicr.org/enews/
Format: Monthly electronic newsletter

Johns Hopkins Medicine Health Alerts, Medical Letter: Health After 50

http://www.johnshopkinshealthalerts.com/health_after_50/index.html#current
Format: Monthly print newsletter or electronic Health Alerts

National Center on Health, Physical Activity and Disability, NCHPAD NEWS
http://www.ncpad.org/NewsletterIndex
Format: Monthly electronic newsletter

National Institutes of Health, News in Health
http://newsinhealth.nih.gov/
Format: Monthly print and electronic newsletter

Tufts University, Health & Nutrition Letter
http://www.tuftshealthletter.com/
Ordering Phone: 800-274-7581 Format: Monthly print newsletter and email updates

University of California, Berkeley Wellness Letter
http://alerts.berkeleywellness.com/register/
Format: Monthly print newsletter and email alerts

SECTION II: OLDER ADULTS AND NUTRITION – RESOURCES FOR PROFESSIONALS
A. WEB AVAILABLE RESOURCES

ADMINISTRATION ON AGING BIBLIOGRAPHIC DATABASE

DHHS, Administration on Aging

Description: The database contacts abstracts of materials that support demonstration, research, and training programs designed to promote best practices in programs and services for older adults.

Web site: http://www.aoa.gov/AoARoot/AoA_Programs/
Tools_Resources/AoA_Biographic.aspx

Contact Information for State Units on Aging Nutritionists and Administrators

DHHS, Administration on Aging

Description: Reference for contacting state nutritionists and administrators.

Web site: http://www.aoa.gov/AoA_programs/HCLTC/Nutrition_Services/docs/Contact_Informatio n_SUA.pdf (PDF | 61KB)

Dietary Reference Intakes (DRI) USDA, NAL, Food and Nutrition Information Center

Description: National Academy of Sciences, Institute of Medicine, Food and Nutrition Board DRI tables for individuals, vitamins, elements, macronutrients, estimated average requirements and electrolytes and water.

Web site: http://fnic.nal.usda.gov/dietary-guidance/dietary-reference-intakes/dri-tables

EAT SMART, LIVE STRONG: NUTRITION EDUCATION FOR OLDER ADULTS ACTIVITY KIT

USDA, Food and Nutrition Service

Description: This toolkit is designed to improve fruit and vegetable consumption and physical activity among 60-74 year olds participating in or eligible for FNS nutrition assistance programs. The USDA Food and Nutrition Service (FNS) developed the intervention to help program providers and communities improve the health of a growing number of low-income older adults.

Web site: http://snap.nal.usda.gov/resource-library/nutrition-education-materials- fns/eat-smart-live-strong

Food and Drug Administration Automated Information Line

DHHS, FDA, Center for Food Safety and Applied Nutrition (CFSAN) Outreach and Information Center

Description: The Food and Drug Administration (FDA) Hotline is available to answer questions about safe handling of foods, cosmetics and dietary supplements.

Phone: 888-SAFEFOOD (888-723-3366) TTY: 800-877-8339

Helping Older Adults Search for Health Information Online: A Toolkit for Trainers

DHHS, NIH, National Institute on Aging

Description: Materials provide a 9-session course specifically for seniors on how to access reliable, up-to-date online health information on their own. Two NIH websites are featured. The material is free to be downloaded from the website.

Web site: http://nihseniorhealth.gov/toolkit/toolkit.html

LIFECYCLE NUTRITION: AGING

USDA, NAL, Food and Nutrition Information Center

Description: This Web resource consists of links to credible information and resources on nutrition and older adults. Topics include healthy eating, nutrition challenges related to aging, food safety issues and food assistance programs.

Web site: http://fnic.nal.usda.gov/lifecycle-nutrition/aging

SENIOR CITIZENS ACT AND AGING NETWORK

DHHS, Administration on Aging

Description: Includes links to the Senior citizens Act (OAA), the Senior citizens Act Reauthorization and the National Aging Network.

Web site: http://www.aoa.gov/AOARoot/AoA_Programs/OAA/Introduction.aspx

TUFTS MYPLATE FOR OLDER ADULTS

Tufts University, Friedman School of Nutrition Science and Policy

Description: Researchers at Tufts University have developed a modified MyPlate that emphasizes the nutritional needs of older adults. Nutrient dense foods, fluid balance and regular physical activity are all highlighted.

Web site: http://www.nutrition.tufts.edu/research/myplate-older-adults

BOOKS

Food Medication Interactions, 17th Edition Zaneta M. Pronsky, MS, Rd, LDN, FADA, Sr Jeanne Patricia Crowe PharmD, RPH. 2012 ISBN: 0971089655

Description: Extensive resource of medications with food or nutrient interactions listed, including grapefruit-drug interactions, drug-alcohol interactions and many others. Reference tables such as lab values also included.

Handbook of Nutrition in the Aged, 4th Edition Ronald Ross Watson, Editor CRC Press, Taylor & Francis Group, 2009 ISBN: 978-1-4200-5971-7 NAL Call No: QP86. C7 2009

Description: This professional resource includes information on nutrition requirements for older adults, as well as information on health promotion, bioactive foods and nutrients, and fruits and vegetables to prevent illness.

NUTRITION FOR THE OLDER ADULT

Melissa Bernstein, PhD, RD, LD and Ann Schmidt Luggen, PhD, GNP Jones & Bartlett Publishers, 2009 ISBN: 0763736244 NAL Call No: TX361.A3 B47 2010

Description: This is a comprehensive resource for professionals and students on nutrition and health promotion for older adults. Topics covered include the physiological changes of aging, weight, and nutrition problems in older adults; nutritional assessment and support for the senior; diet and cultural diversity; and exercise for older adults.

NUTRITION AND HEALTH ORGANIZATIONS

The organizations listed below may be able to provide additional information and resources on a variety of health related topics. Listing below does not imply an endorsement or approval by the Food and Nutrition Information Center.

Administration for Community Living Homepage: http://www.acl.gov Contact Information:

> Administration for Community Living One Massachusetts Ave NW Washington, DC 20001 Phone: 202-619-0724 Email: aclinfo@acl.hhs.gov

Alzheimer's Disease Education and Referral (ADEAR) Center Homepage: http://www.nia.nih.gov/alzheimers Contact Information:

> ADEAR Center PO Box 8250 Silver Spring, MD 20907-8250 Phone: 800-438-4380 Email: adear@nia.nih.gov

American Diabetes Association Homepage: http://www.diabetes.org Contact Information:

> American Diabetes Association ATTN: Center for Information 1701 North Beauregard Street Alexandria, VA 22311 Phone: 800-DIABETES (800-342-2383) Email: askADA@diabetes.org

American Heart Association Homepage: http://www.heart.org Contact Information:

> American Heart Association National Center 7272 Greenville Avenue Dallas, TX 75231 Phone: 800-AHA-USA-1 (800-242-8721)

American Institute for Cancer Research Homepage: http://www.aicr.org Contact Information:

> American Institute for Cancer Research 1759 R Street NW Washington, DC 20009 Phone: 800-843-8114 (in DC: 202-328-7744) Email: aicrweb@aicr.org

Arthritis Foundation Homepage: http://www.arthritis.org/ Contact Information:

> Arthritis Foundation National Office 1330 W. Peachtree Street, Suite 100 Atlanta, GA 30309 Phone: 404-872-7100 or 800-283-7800

Feeding America (formerly America's Second Harvest) Homepage: http://feedingamerica.org/ Contact Information:

> Feeding America 35 E. Wacker Dr., Suite 2000 Chicago, IL 60601 Phone: 800-771-2303 or 312-263-2303

Food and Drug Administration Homepage: http://www.fda.gov Contact Information:

> Food and Drug Administration 10903 New Hampshire Ave Silver Spring, MD 20993-0002 Phone: 888-INFO-FDA (888-463-6332)

Food and Nutrition Information Center Homepage: http://fnic.nal.usda.gov Contact Information:

> Food and Nutrition Information Center National Agricultural Library 10301 Baltimore Ave, Room 108 Beltsville, MD 20705 Phone: 301-504-5414

Food Safety Information Center Homepage: http://foodsafety.nal.usda.gov Contact Information:

> Food Safety Information Center National Agricultural Library 10301 Baltimore Avenue, Room 109 Beltsville, MD 20705 Phone: 301-504-6835

International Food Information Council Foundation Homepage: http://www.foodinsight.org Contact Information:

> International Food Information Council Foundation 1100 Connecticut Avenue NW, Suite 430 Phone: 202-296-6540 Email: info@foodinsight.org

Iowa COMPASS Center for Disabilities and Development Homepage: http://www.iowacompass.org Contact Information:

> Iowa COMPASS Center for Disabilities & Development 100 Hawkins Dr. #S295 Iowa City, IA, 52242-1011 Phone: 800-779-2001 or TTY: 877-686-0032 Email: iowa-compass@uiowa.edu

Meals on Wheels Association of America Homepage: http://www.mowaa.org/ Contact Information:

> Meals on Wheels Association of America 413 N. Lee Street Alexandria, VA 22314 Phone: 888-998-6325 Email: mowaa@mowaa.org

National Cancer Institute: Cancer Information Service Homepage: http://www.cancer.gov/ Contact Information:

> National Cancer Institute BG 9609 MSC 9760 9609 Medical Center Drive Bethesda, MD 20892-9760 Phone: 800-4-CANCER (800-422-6237) Live Chat is available online

National Center on Health, Physical Activity, and Disability Homepage: http://www.ncpad.org/ Contact Information:

> National Center on Health, Physical Activity and Disability 4000 Ridgeway Drive Birmingham, AL 35209 Phone: 800-900-8086 Email: email@nchpad.org

National Diabetes Education Program Homepage: http://ndep.nih.gov Contact Information:

National Diabetes Education Program One Diabetes Way Bethesda, MD 20814-9692 Phone: 888-693-NDEP (6337) Link to email form: http://ndep.nih.gov/ContactUs.aspx

National Heart Lung and Blood Institute (NHLBI) Homepage: http://www.nhlbi.nih.gov/ Contact Information:

NHLBI Health Information Center, Attention: Web Site P.O. Box 30105 Bethesda, MD 20824-0105 Phone: 301-592-8573 Email: nhlbiinfo@nhlbi.nih.gov (please include a valid return e-mail address in the body of the message)

National Institute on Aging Homepage: http://www.nia.nih.gov Contact Information:

NIA Information Center Building 31, Room 5C27 31 Center Drive, MSC 2292 Bethesda, MD 20892 Phone: 800-222-2225 Email: niaic@nia.nih.gov

National Institute of Arthritis and Musculoskeletal and Skin Diseases Homepage: http://www.niams.nih.gov/ Contact Information:

National Institute of Arthritis and Musculoskeletal and Skin Diseases Information Clearinghouse, National Institutes of Health 1 AMS Circle, Bethesda, MD 20892-3675 Phone: 877-22-NIAMS (877-226-4267) Email: NIAMSInfo@mail.nih.gov

National Institute of Diabetes and Digestive and Kidney Diseases (NIDDK) Homepage: http://www2.niddk.nih.gov/ Contact Information:

Office of Communication & Public Liaison NIDDK, NIH Building 31, Room 9A06 31 Center Drive, MSC 2560

Bethesda, MD 20892-2560 Phone: 301-496-3583 Link to email form: http://www2.niddk.nih.gov/Footer/ContactNIDDK.htm

National Institutes of Health (NIH) Osteoporosis and Related Bone Diseases Homepage: http://www.niams.nih.gov/bone/ Contact Information:

NIH Osteoporosis and Related Bone Diseases –National Resource Center 2 AMS Circle Bethesda, MD 20892-3676 Phone: 800-624-BONE (800-624-2663) or TTY: 202-466-4315: E-mail: NIAMSBoneInfo@mail.nih.gov

National Osteoporosis Foundation Homepage: http://www.nof.org Contact Information:

National Osteoporosis Foundation 1150 17th Street NW, Ste 850, Washington, D.C. 20036 Phone: 202-223-2226 or 800-231-4222 Email: info@nof.org

National Parkinson Foundation Homepage: http://www.parkinson.org Contact Information:

1501 N.W. 9th Avenue / Bob Hope Road Miami, Florida 33136-1494 Phone: 800-4PD-INFO (473-4636) Email: contact@parkinson.org

Supplemental Nutrition Assistance Program (SNAP), formerly the Food Stamp Program Homepage: http://www.fns.usda.gov/snap/ Contact Information:

Phone: 800-221-5689 More contact info: http://www.fns.usda.gov/snap/contact_info/default.htm

United States Department of Agriculture, Food and Nutrition Service Homepage: http://www.fns.usda.gov/ Contact Information:

Food and Nutrition Service 3101 Park Center Drive Alexandria, VA 22302 Phone: 703-305-2286

United States Department of Agriculture, Food Safety and Inspection Service Homepage: http://www.fsis.usda.gov Contact Information:

Food Safety and Inspection Service US Department of Agriculture 1400 Independence Ave SW Washington, DC 20250-3700 Phone: 888-MPHotline (888-674-6854) or TTY: 800-256-7072 Email: MPHotline.fsis@usda.gov

Weight-control Information Network Homepage: http://www.win.niddk.nih.gov Contact Information:

Weight-control Information Network 1 WIN Way Bethesda, MD 20892-3665 Phone: 877-946-4627 Email: win@info.niddk.nih.gov

This resource list was updated and revised by: Jennifer M. Anderson, MSPH, RD, Nutrition Information Specialist

Acknowledgment is given to the following FNIC reviewers:

Rachel Tobin, MS, RD, Nutrition Information Specialist Shirley King Evans, MEd, RD, Budget Analyst.

Locate additional FNIC publications at http://fnic.nal.usda.gov/resourcelists Food and Nutrition Information Center Agricultural Research Service, USDA National Agricultural Library, Room 108 10301 Baltimore Avenue Beltsville, MD 20705-2351 Phone: 301-504-5414 Fax: 301-504-6409 TTY: 301-504-6856 Contact: http://fnic.nal.usda.gov/contact

Web site: http://fnic.nal.usda.gov

The National Agricultural Library (NAL) provides lending and photocopying services to U.S. Department of Agriculture (USDA) employees. Non-USDA users can obtain materials from NAL through the interlibrary lending services of their local, corporate, or university library. For further information on NAL's document delivery services visit their

Web site: http://www.nal.usda.gov/nal-services/request-library-materials.

For questions on document delivery services please call 301-504-5717 or submit a question at http://www.nal.usda.gov/ask-question-3.

The use of trade, firm, or corporation names in this publication (or page) is for the information and convenience of the reader. Such use does not constitute an official endorsement or approval by the USDA or the Agricultural Research Service (ARS) of any product or service to the exclusion of others that may be suitable.

USDA prohibits discrimination in all its programs and activities on the basis of race, color, national origin, age, disability, and where applicable, sex, marital status, familial status, parental status, religion, sexual orientation, genetic information, political beliefs, reprisal, or because all or a part of an individual's income is derived from any public assistance program. (Not all prohibited bases apply to all programs.)

Persons with disabilities who require alternative means for communication of program information (Braille, large print, audiotape, etc.) should contact USDA's TARGET Center at 202-720-2600 (voice and TDD).

HELP AT YOUR FINGERTIPS

Both federal and local government officials offer numerous resources that you should use.

U.S. Dept. of Housing and Urban Development (HUD) provides a range of information to help older adults make informed choices about housing options and financial assistance. Call (202) 708-1112.

LEGAL ASSISTANCE

American Bar Association (ABA) Commission on Law and Aging

The ABA Commission on Law and Aging provides a listing of statewide resources available to help older persons with law related issues. Call (202) 662-8690.

Office of Fair Housing and Equal Opportunity (FHEO)—U.S. Dept. of Housing and Urban Development (HUD). This office administers and enforces federal laws and establishes policies that ensure that all Americans have equal access to the housing of their choice. It provides information about housing rights for older adults. Call (202) 708-1112.

MORTGAGE FINANCING

AARP

AARP offers information on the range of issue and concerns regarding reversed mortgages, including a guide to compare options and a quick mortgage loan calculator. Call (888) 687-2277 or visit www.AARP.org

National Reverse Mortgage Leaders Association (NRMLA) provides information and materials to help consumers understand reverse mortgages, determine when they are a good option and find a local lender for assistance. www.reversemortgage.org

MEDICARE

Nursing Home Compare is a tool that provides detailed information about the past performance of every Medicare and Medicaid certified nursing home in the country. Call: (800)-633-2273.

The National Citizens' Coalition for Nursing Home Reform (NCCNHR) provides guidance in selecting a quality nursing home and protecting residents' rights. Call (202)-332-2275.

National Senior Citizens Law Center (NSCLC)

The guide, Baby Boomer's Guide to Nursing Home Care, explains the many laws protecting nursing home residents and gives practical advice on how residents and their families can obtain the best nursing home care possible. www.nsclc.org/publications/index_html

Seniorcare Locator 1-800-677-1116 *www.seniorcare.gov*

Long-Term Care Ombudsman Resource Center Washington, DC 20036 1-202-332-2275 *www.ltcombudsman.org*

National Adult Protective Services Association 920 South Spring Street Suite 1200 Springfield, IL 62704 1-217-523-4431 *www.apsnetwork.org*

National Center for Senior Abuse Center for Community Research and Services University of Delaware 297 Graham Hall Newark, DE 19716 1-302-831-3525 *www.ncea.aoa.gov*

National Domestic Violence Hotline 24 hour a day reporting 1-800-799-7233; (toll-free) 1-800-787-3224 (TTY/toll-free) *www.thehotline.org/get-help*

National Family Caregiver Support Program Administration on Aging Washington, DC 20201 1-202-619-0724 *www.aoa.gov/AoA_programs*

National Library of Medicine MedlinePlus *www.medlineplus.gov*

Office for Victims of Crime U.S. Department of Justice 810 Seventh Street, NW, Eighth Floor Washington, DC 20531 1-202-307-5983 *http://ovc.ncjrs.org/findvictimservices/*

For information on nursing homes, nutrition, exercise, and other resources on health and aging, contact: National Institute on Aging Information Center P.O. Box 8057 Gaithersburg, MD 20898-8057 1-800-222-2225 1-800222-4225 (TTY/toll-free). *www.nia.nih.gov www.nia.nih.gov/espanol*

To sign up for regular email alerts about new publications and other information from the NIA, go to *www.nia.nih.gov/health*.

Visit *www.nihseniorhealth.gov*, a senior-friendly website from the National Institute on Aging and the National Library of Medicine. This website has health and wellness information for older adults. Special features make it simple to use. For example, you can click on a button to have the text read out loud or to make the type larger.

National Institute on Aging National Institutes of Health U.S. Department of Health & Human Services.

APPENDIX II

REVIEW OF CONGRESSIONAL REPORTS

U.S. SENATE, SPECIAL COMMITTEE ON AGING:

While special committees have no legislative authority, they can study issues, conduct oversight of programs, and investigate reports of fraud and waste. Throughout its existence, the Special Committee on Aging has served as a focal point in the Senate for discussion and debate on matters relating to senior citizens. Often, the Committee will submit its findings and recommendations for legislation to the Senate. Here is a sampling of documents:

Justice for All: Ending Senior Abuse, Neglect and Financial Exploitation (112th Congress, 2011)

Overprescribed: The Human and Taxpayers' Costs of Antipsychotics in Nursing Homes (112th Congress, 2011)

LISTENING SESSION: The War on Drugs Meets the War on Pain: Nursing Home Patients Caught in the Crossfire (111th Congress, 2010)

S.2838, the Fairness in Nursing Home Arbitration Act (110th Congress, 2008)

Foreclosure Aftermath: Preying on Senior Homeowners (110th Congress, 2008)

Nursing Home Transparency and Improvement (110th Congress, 2007)

Abuse Of Our Seniors: How We Can Stop It (110th Congress, 2007)

The Nursing Home Reform Act Turns Twenty: What Has Been Accomplished, and What Challenges Remain (110th Congress, 2007)

Exploitation of Seniors: America's Ailing Guardianship System (109th Congress, 2006)

Not Born Yesterday: How Seniors Can Stop Investment Fraud (109th Congress, 2006)

Old Scams–New Victims: Breaking the Cycle of Victimization (109th Congress, 2005)

Forum: Protecting Senior citizens Under Guardianship: Who is watching the Guardian? (108th Congress, 2004)

Internet Fraud Hits Seniors: As Seniors Venture Into the Web, the Financial Predators Lurk and Take Aim (108th Congress, 2004)

Predatory Lending: Are Federal Agencies Protecting Senior Citizens from Financial Heartbreak? (108th Congress, 2004)

Shattering the Silence: Confronting the Perils of Family Senior Abuse (108th Congress, 2003)

Guardianships Over the Senior: Security Provided or Freedom Denied? (108th Congress, 2003)

Safeguarding Our Seniors: Protecting the Senior from Physical and Sexual Abuse in Nursing Homes (107th Congress, 2002)

U.S Senate, Committee on the Judiciary, Subcommittee on Crime, Corrections, and Victims' Rights:

Senior abuse, neglect, and exploitation: are we doing enough? (108th Congress, 2003).

U.S Senate, Committee on Health, Education, Labor, and Pensions, Subcommittee on Aging:

Senior justice and protection: stopping the financial abuse (108th Congress, 2003) Proclamation 7895 of May 3, 2005

Remember to embrace and honor Senior citizens every day, and celebrate the special month set aside for them by the U.S. Government

WHERE TO REPORT ABUSE IN YOUR STATE

State	Report Senior Abuse Domestic/Community
Alabama	• 1-800-458-7214 More Information Alabama Adult Protective Services
Alaska	• 1-800-478-9996 (Toll free in Alaska) • Outside of Alaska: 907-269-3666 More Information Alaska Adult Protective Services
Arizona	• 1-SOS-ADULT or 1-877-767-2385 • 602-674-4200 • TDD: 1-877-815-8390 More Information Arizona Adult Protective Services
Arkansas	• Phone: (602) 542-4446 Fax: (602) 542-6575 • 1-800-332-4443 (Toll free in Arkansas) • Outside of Arkansas: 1-800-482-8049 • E-mail: Carolyn.singleton@arkanas.gov • Arkansas Domestic Violence/ Battered Women • Hotline: 1-800-332-4443 More Information Arkansas Adult Protective Services

California	• 1-888-436-3600 (Toll free in California) • Outside of California: Call County Adult Protective Services More Information California Adult Protective Services
Colorado	• 1-800-773-13661-800-773-1366 or • 1-800-886-7689, Ext. 2800 • (303) 692-2800 • E-mail: health.facilities@state.co.us • Fax: (303) 753-6214
Connecticut	• 1-888-385-4225 or • 1-860-424-5241 • After Hours/Emergency: 2-1-1 (In-State only) • E-mail: lynn.noyes@po.state.ct.us More Information Connecticut Protective Services for the Senior
Delaware	• 1-800-223-9074 More Information Delaware Adult Protective Services
District of Columbia	• 202-541-3950 More Information DC Adult Protective Services
Florida	• 1-800-96-ABUSE or 1-800-962-2873 • TDD/TTY: 1-800-453-5145 • Fax: 1-800-914-0004 More Information • Florida Adult Protective Services • Florida Mandatory Reporter Fax Transmittal Form

Georgia
- 1-888-774-0152
- 404-657-5250 (Metro-Atlanta)

More Information
Georgia Adult Protective Services

Guam
- 671-475-0268
- After Hours: 671-646-4455 (evenings, weekends, holidays)

Hawaii
- 808-832-5115 (Oahu)
- 808-243-5151 (Maui, Molokai, and Lanai)
- 808-241-3432 (Kauai)
- 808-933-8820 (East Hawaii)
- 808-327-6280 (West Hawaii)

More Information
Hawaii Executive Office on Aging

Idaho
- 1-877-471-2777

More Information
Idaho Adult Protection; State Adult Protection contact: Deedra Hunt; 208-334-3833
deedra.hunt@aging.idaho.gov

Illinois
- 1-800-252-8966 (Toll free in Illinois–Voice & TTY)
- Outside of Illinois: 217-524-6911 or 1-800-677-1116 (Seniorcare Locator)
- After Hours Hotline: 1-800-279-0400
- E-mail: ilsenior@aging.state.il

More Information
- Illinois Protective Services for Seniors
- Illinois Local Senior Abuse Provider Agency Directory

Indiana	- 1-800-992-6978 (Toll free in Indiana)
- Outside of Indiana: 1-800-545-7763, Ext. 20135
More Information
Indiana Adult Protective Services
Iowa	- 1-800-362-2178
More Information
Iowa Department of Human Services
Call the Abuse Hotline at **1-800-362-2178**, available 24 hours a day, 7 days a week.
Kansas	- 1-800-922-5330 (Toll free in Kansas)
- Outside of Kansas: 785-296-0044
More Information
Kansas Adult Protective Services
Kentucky	- Senior Abuse Hotline: 1-800-752-6200
- Spouse Abuse Hotline: 1-800-544-2022
More Information
- Kentucky Cabinet for Health and Family Services
- Kentucky Adult Protective Services
Louisiana	- 1-800-259-4990 (Toll free in Louisiana)
- Outside of Louisiana: 225-342-9722
- Adults with Disabilities (Ages 18-59)
- 1-800-898-4910
More Information
Louisiana Senior Protective Services
Maine	- 1-800-624-8404 (Toll free in Maine)
- Outside of Maine: 207-532-5047 or 207-287-6083 (After Hours)

- TTY: 1-800-624-8404
- TTY After Hours (In-State) 1-800-963-9490
- TTY After Hours (Out-of-State) 207-287-3492

More Information
Maine Bureau of Senior and Adult Services

Maryland
- 1-800-917-7383 (Toll free in Maryland)
- Outside of Maryland: 1-800-677-1116 (Seniorcare Locator)

More Information
Maryland Adult Protective Services

Massachusetts
- 1-800-922-2275 (Toll free in Massachusetts
- Voice/TTY)
- Outside of Massachusetts: 1-800-AGE-INFO (1-800-243-4636)
- TDD/TTY: 1-800-872-0166

More Information
Massachusetts Senior Protection Services and Programs

Michigan
- 1-800-996-6228

More Information
Michigan Adult Protective Services

Minnesota
- 1-800-333-2433
- TDD/TYY: 1-800-627-3529

More Information
Minnesota Aging Protective Services Unit
Minnesota Adult Protective Services Report Abuse of Seniors or Adults with Disabilities as well as institutional abuse: County

	Directory PHONE: 800-333-2433 (for county numbers) TTY (in Minnesota): 711
Mississippi	• 1-800-222-8000 (Toll free in Mississippi) • Outside of Mississippi: (601) 359-4991 • E-Mail: webspinner@mdhs.state.ms.us More Information Mississippi Adult Protective Services
Missouri	• 1-800-392-0210 More Information Missouri Adult Protective Services
Montana	• 1-800-551-3191 (Toll free in Montana) • Outside of Montana: 406-444-4077 More Information Montana Adult Protective Services
Nebraska	• 1-800-652-1999 (Toll free in Nebraska) • Outside of Nebraska: 402-595-1324 More Information Nebraska Adult Protective Services
Nevada	• 1-800-992-5757 (Toll free in Nevada) • Outside of Nevada: Carson City area: 775-687-4210 Reno area: 775-688-2964 Elko area: 775-738-1966 Las Vegas area: 702-486-3545 More Information Nevada Senior Protective Services
New Hampshire	• 1-800-351-1888 or • 603-271-4680 • After Hours: 911 or local police after hours,

- weekends, or holidays

More Information
New Hampshire Adult Protection Program
Bureau of Elderly & Adult Services (BEAS).
Call (603) 271-7014 or toll Free from
within NH at (800) 949-0470

New Jersey	- 1-800-792-8820 (Toll free in New Jersey) - Outside of New Jersey: - 609-341-5567 More Information New Jersey Adult Protective Services
New Mexico	- 1-800-797-3260 - 505-841-6100 (In Albuquerque)
New York	- 1-800-342-3009 (Toll free in New York) – Press Option 6 More Information New York Protective Services for Adults
North Carolina	- 1-800-662-7030 More Information North Carolina Adult Protective Services
North Dakota	- 1-800-451-8693 More Information North Dakota Vulnerable Adult Protective Services Aging Services Division 1237 West Divide Avenue, Suite 6 Bismarck, ND 58501 **Phone:** (701) 328-4601 **ND Relay TTY:** (800) 366-6888 **Fax:** (701) 328-8744 dhsaging@nd.gov **ND Aging & Disability Resource-LINK** 1-855-GO2LINK (1-855-462-5465)

Ohio	- 866-635-3748 (Toll free in Ohio) - Outside of Ohio: 1-800-677-1116 (Seniorcare Locator) More Information Ohio Adult Protective Services
Oklahoma	- 1-800-522-3511 More Information Oklahoma Adult Protective Services
Oregon	- 1-800-232-3020 - TTY/Voice: 503-945-5811 More Information Oregon Adult Protective Services
Pennsylvania	- 1-800-490-8505 More Information Pennsylvania Protective Services for Adults
Rhode Island	- 787-725-9788 or - 787-721-8225 - 401-462-0550 - Fax: 401-462-0545 More Information Rhode Island Department of Senior Affairs Protective Services Unit
South Carolina	- 803-898-7318 More Information South Carolina Adult Protective Services
South Dakota	- 605-773-3656 More Information South Dakota Adult Protective Services Online Referral/Request South Dakota local adult protection offices

Tennessee	• 1-888-APS-TENN or 1-888-277-8366 • Knoxville: (865) 594-5685 • Chattanooga: (423) 634-6624 • Nashville: (615) 532-3492 • Memphis: (901) 320-7220 More Information Tennessee Adult Protective Services
Texas	• 1-800-252-5400 (Toll free in Texas) • Outside of Texas: 512-834-3784 More Information • Texas Adult Protective Services Online Abuse/Neglect/ Exploitation Reporting Form
Utah	• 1-800-371-7897 • www.hsdaas.utah.gov More Information Utah Adult Protective Services
Vermont	• 1-800-564-1612 • 802-241-2345 • Fax: 802-241-2358 More Information Vermont Adult Protective Services APS Online Report Form
Virginia	• 1-888-83-ADULT or 1-888-832-3858 • Richmond Area: 804-371-0896 More Information Virginia Adult Protective Services
Washington	• 1-866-EndHarm or 1-866-363-4276 More Information • Washington Aging and Disability Services

- Administration Adult Protective Services (APS) Regional Reporting Numbers

West Virginia
- 1-800-352-6513

More Information
West Virginia Adult Protective Services

Wisconsin
- 608-266-2536
- E-mail: StopAbuse@dhfs.state.wi.us

More Information
- Wisconsin Department of Health and Human Services
- Wisconsin County Senior Abuse Agencies & Help Lines

Wyoming
- 1-800-457-3659 (Toll free in Wyoming)
- Outside of Wyoming: 307-777-3602

REFERENCES

1. U.S. Census Bureau, the National Center for Health Statistics, and the Bureau of Labor Statistics: A Profile of Senior citizens, 2012, Administration on Aging Administration for Community Living, U.S. Department of Health and Human Services.
2. Hartman et al. 2013: *Motivating the senior to exercise*: What prohibits senior people from exercising and how can they be motivated to partake in exercise? Background, section 1.
3. Pfuntner A., Wier L.M., Elixhauser, Agency for Healthcare Research and Quality, Rockville, MD.): Healthcare Cost and Utilization Project (HCUP) Statistical Briefs [Internet]. Rockville (MD): Agency for Health Care Policy and Research (US); 2006-.2013 Nov.
4. World Health Organization (WHO), The Commonwealth Fund, Medicare/Medicaid: A federal government website managed by the Centers for Medicare & Medicaid Services, 7500 Security Boulevard, Baltimore, MD 21244.
5. Burston, G. R. "Granny battering'" British Medical Journal, 1975, vol 3, p. 592: (National Senior Abuse Incidence Study. 1998. Washington, DC: National Center on Senior Abuse at American Public Human Services Association.)
6. Jogerst, Gerald J., et al. 2003. "Domestic Senior Abuse and the Law," American Journal of Public Health, Vol. 93, No. 12: 2131-2136.
7. National Center on Senior Abuse: *A Response to the Abuse of Vulnerable Adults*: The 2000 Survey of State Adult Protective Services. 2003. Washington, DC: National Center on Senior Abuse.) (National Ombudsman Reporting System Data Tables. 2003. Washington, DC: U.S. Administration on Aging.)
8. National Center on Senior Abuse, Bureau of Justice Statistics Centers for Disease Control (CDC.)

9. U.S. General Accounting Office, 1994, p.8.
10. National Senior Abuse Incidence Study. 1998. Washington, DC: National Center on Senior Abuse at American Public Human Services Association.
11. Jogerst, Gerald J., et al. 2003. "Domestic Senior Abuse and the Law," American Journal of Public Health, Vol. 93, No. 12: 2131-2136.
12. National Center on Senior Abuse: A Response to the Abuse of Vulnerable Adults: The 2000 Survey of State Adult Protective Services. 2003. Washington, DC.
13. U.S. Administration on Aging: National Ombudsman Reporting System Data Tables. 2003. Washington, DC: U.S. Administration on Aging.
14. Jorgensen et al 2001. Beach SR, Schulz R, Castle NG, Rosen J; Financial Exploitation and Psychological Mistreatment Among Older Adults: Differences Between African Americans and Non-African Americans in a Population-Based Survey; Gerontologist 2010).
15. Lifespan of Greater Rochester, Inc., Weill Cornell Medical Center of Cornell University & New York City Department for the Aging; (2011) *Under the Radar: New York State Senior Abuse Prevalence Study*; New York; Author.
16. Federal Food and Drug Administration: Geodon warning: Increased mortality in senior patients with Dementia-related psychosis.
17. Daniel R. Levinson, Inspector General (May 2011 OEI-07-08-00150) (CMS, State Operations Manual (Internet-Only Manual), Pub. 100-07, Appendix PP: Guidance to Surveyors for Long Term Care Facilities.)
18. FDA website: http://www.fda.gov/Drugs Testimony of Mickey Rooney U.S. Senate Special Committee on Aging March 2, 2011
19. Robert L. Mollica, Ed.D. Senior Program Director National Academy for State Health Policy Washington, AHRQ Publication No. 06-M051-EF September 2006.

20. GEORGE W. BUSH39194PT3: 119 STAT. 3744 PROCLAMATION 7896—MAY 3, 2005.
21. National Agricultural Library, USDA: Food and Nutrition Information Center, 10301 Baltimore Ave, room 105, Beltsville, MD, 20705-2351.

"Should I Be Afraid?"

AVAILABLE AT

Barnes and Noble, (barnesandnoble.com) Amazon, (amazon.com) in paperback, Nook and Kindle, and other booksellers and libraries through Ingram

Would you like to help other senior citizens? Consider ordering extra books to donate to a senior citizen organization, domestic abuse shelter, or senior library near you. Your generosity will help seniors help themselves through the power of information!

Need a speaker/trainer for your senior center, caregiving organization, nursing program, care facility, or senior related event?

**Contact Judy Hanna
for fee schedule and bookings:
eventcentral@valornet.com**

Note from the Publisher

Are you a first time author?

Not sure how to proceed to get your book published?
Want to keep all your rights and all your royalties?
Want it to look as good as a Top 10 publisher?
Need help with editing, layout, cover design?
Want it out there selling in 90 days or less?

Visit our website for some exciting new options!

www.chalfant-eckert-publishing.com

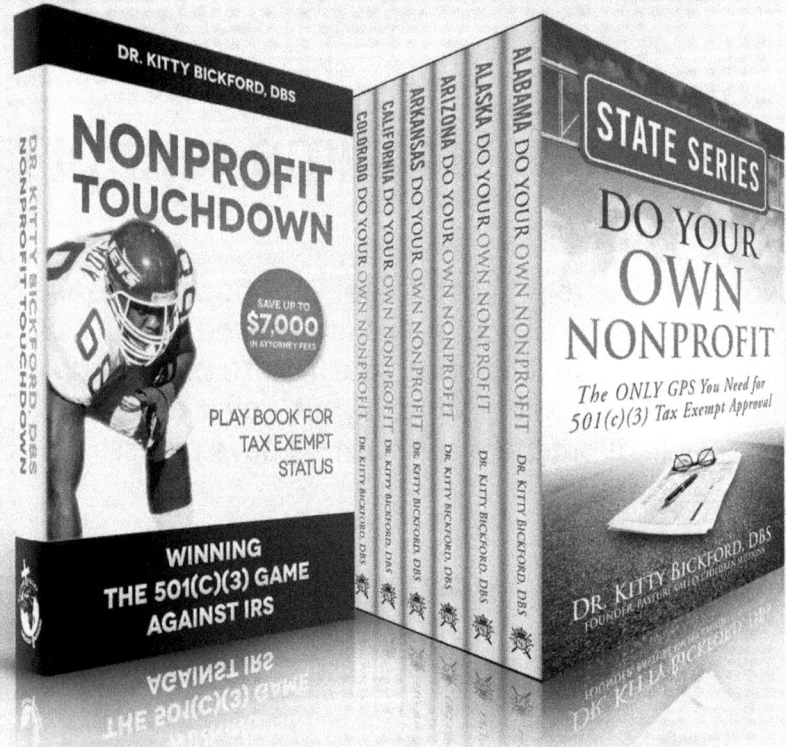

www.ingramcontent.com/pod-product-compliance
Lightning Source LLC
Chambersburg PA
CBHW061423040426
42450CB00007B/879